SURGEON
on HORSEBACK

DR. CHAS BRACKETT.

SURGEON
on HORSEBACK

The Missouri and Arkansas Journal and Letters

of Dr. Charles Brackett of Rochester, Indiana

1861 – 1863

★ ★ ★

FIRST INDIANA CAVALRY

NINTH ILLINOIS CAVALRY

Best Wishes—
James W. Wheaton

★ ★ ★

Compiled by James W. Wheaton

with annotations and introductions by Ed Gleeson

GUILD PRESS OF INDIANA, INC.

For information, contact

GUILD PRESS OF INDIANA, INC.
435 Gradle Drive
Carmel, Indiana 46032
TELEPHONE: 317-848-6421 FAX: 317-848-6810
WWW.GUILDPRESS.COM

Library of Congress
Catalog Card Number
98-72780

ISBN 1-57860-065-0

Printed and bound in the United States of America

Text designed by Sheila G. Samson
Cover designed by Steven D. Armour

Ed Gleeson, whose annotations appear in this book, is a Civil War
historian and the author of the following Civil War books (also
available from Guild Press of Indiana, Inc.):

Rebel Sons of Erin

*Illinois Rebels: A Civil War Unit History of G Company, Fifteenth
Tennessee Regiment Volunteer Infantry*

Erin Go Gray! A Trilogy of Irish Rebels

. . . My sons so far behave very satisfactorily; and if they should ever deviate greatly from the right course, I hope Heaven in mercy will spare me the mortification of witnessing their dishonor. I believe that they will all have true American principles & feelings; and if they are governed by them, there is no danger . . .

James Brackett
Cherry Valley, New York
July 23, 1843

CONTENTS

★ ★ ★

★ ★ ★

INTRODUCTION
AND ACKNOWLEDGMENTS

I would give all I have in this world except wife, & children to have peace once again, & I fear that Peace we will not have for some years. We are bound to succeed finally but it will be a long struggle . . .

. . . I am now in my own tent sitting on my little camp bed, with my little camp stove right hot, while Mondzoleski, & a young Englishman by name Bowdoin are preparing a hot Punch with Tea, & Whiskey . . . that Mondzoleski calls "Tchai". He & Bowdoin are quarreling about the orthography of the word, & from that to maccarone; they are fond of many words, & whiskey limbers up their tongues . . .

. . . I have been to bed, & now about 2 AM I am up again built a good fire, smoked a pipe, & am writing again to my dear one, with whom my thoughts continually associate. Our Officers were telling how much they had done for their wives before leaving home in the way of making wills, Deeds, &c for their benefit. I could think of nothing I had done especially for mine . . . But I hope we may long live to enjoy our property, & children together of course Yet death may come, & it is well to keep it in mind, not with gloomy feelings, but with a well grounded hope of a better life beyond, where wars, & separations are not known . . .

From the letters of Dr. Charles Brackett to his wife, Margaret

Dr. Charles Brackett of Rochester, Indiana, found himself in a very strange war in 1861 and 1862. While the Seven Days' Battles, Second Manassas, and

Fredericksburg were being fought in the East, he was part of an invading and occupying Union army west of the Mississippi that fought only minor actions, generally against bands of guerrillas or semi-organized partisans, and only rarely against Confederate regulars. Through Dr. Brackett's letters and journal, we follow the progress of this army from St. Louis to Pilot Knob, Missouri, and down along the Black River to Pocahontas, Powhatan, and Jacksonport, Arkansas, and finally to Helena on the Mississippi River. Through sheer numbers and power, the Union army inexorably deprived the Confederacy of this immediate Trans-Mississippi area—and with it the hope of two strong Confederate states. Brackett lived this story.

The diaries and letters of this cavalry surgeon from Indiana to his family allow us to track what he was doing—and thinking—as assistant surgeon with the First Indiana Cavalry Regiment, and then with the Ninth Illinois Cavalry Regiment almost daily over a period of about seventeen months. Only part of his existing 170 letters and 355 diary entries from this period have been published here, and those that appear have been abbreviated and annotated to concentrate on the military aspects because so little first-hand information is available about this part of the war. Much local and family information remains, however, that provides a clear picture of Dr. Brackett's character and home life, reaction to the military environment, and provision of medical services.

Charles Brackett, born on June 18, 1825, was one of eight children—seven sons and one daughter—of James and Eliza Brackett of Cherry Valley, New York. Of the sons, remarkably, four served together in the Ninth Illinois Cavalry: Albert, James, Charles, and Joseph. The youngest, Albert, was a professional soldier and was colonel of the regiment; James and Charles were physicians and served as surgeon and assistant surgeon, respectively; and Joseph was quartermaster. John and Lyman had both died before the war, and William chose not to participate. Their sister, Elizabeth Cary, was living in the East with her husband and family. Dr. Brackett's immediate family, his wife, Margaret, and four young children, Louise, Lyman, Rose Anna, and Mary, stayed behind, with Margaret trying to manage the ninety-acre farm, supervise the hired man, pay debts (and collect past-due medical bills), give birth to a new baby (Charles W.), and tend to the needs of her children. The family was together for the last time in November 1862.

It is not strange that the Brackett family wrote so many letters—after all, there was no other means of communication. What is strange, and wonderful, is that the letters have been preserved and are available to us today. The Brackett archives go back to the late 18th century in New Hampshire, and allow us to follow this family and its participation in the growth of the new nation throughout the entire nineteenth century. The wonder is not so much that these letters were passed down to the next generation by their recipients; rather, that at every later opportunity to throw away old things, they were saved.

This particular part of the Brackett archives was made available to me beginning in the late 1960s by a number of distant cousins whom I can't ever thank sufficiently. In particular, the late sisters Helen Brackett Knapp and Elizabeth Gearn of Damariscotta, Maine, preserved the letters sent by James Brackett to his brother Adino Nye Brackett of Lancaster, New Hampshire. At Margaret Brackett's death in 1908, Charles's letters to her and his diaries were given to their eldest daughter, Louise Holman. From her they went to her children Lucille Leonard, Hugh Brackett Holman, and Grace Beach. Lucille's son George Holman Leonard and his daughter Polly Keener provided copies and transcriptions of letters, as did Hugh's son, Hugh Bankson Holman. Some of the diaries were in the possession of Grace Beach's daughter, Margaret Beach Anderson, and she graciously permitted me to have them. Others had been given to my grandfather, Fred C. Williams. With the help of my former wife, Nancy Wheaton, I began transcribing the letters and diaries in the early 1970s by typewriter, and finished in 1979. The typed manuscript has lain untouched until now. Thanks to computers and optical character recognition (OCR) software, it was not necessary to retype all of this material for publication.

Biographical sketches of early residents of Rochester, Indiana, which are mentioned by Dr. Brackett, appear in two publications reprinted by the Fulton County Historical Society: Kingman's *New Historical Atlas of Fulton County, Indiana* (1883), and Marguerite Miller's *Home Folks*. The latter, in particular, has anecdotes of early Rochester days in which Dr. Brackett is mentioned. The publications of the Jackson County (Arkansas) Historical Society provide a wealth of information about the situation in Jacksonport during the war, and refer often to people Dr. Brackett mentions, such as Miss Mary Tom Caldwell and her grandfather, Thomas Todd Tunstall.

Thanks to Civil War Confederate historian Ed Gleeson for his intensive review of the manuscript in its various stages, and for offering significant comments and additions that were critical in helping to pull the work together.

A number of other people provided helpful comments as this book reached completion; among them, Brick Autry of the Fort Davidson State Historic Site in Pilot Knob, Missouri, and author Curt Anders, who reviewed the final manuscript. I am grateful to the following individuals and institutions in Arkansas: Charlotte Plegge, Curator of the Jacksonport State Park

Courthouse Museum; Evelyn Griffin of the Phillips County Museum; the State Historical Society of Missouri; and Susan Hamilton of the Phillips County Library; and also to the Missouri Historical Review for their cooperation in providing illustrations.

The existence of the internet has made this publication possible. Not only is it an infinite resource for historical research, it is also the avenue through which I first learned about Guild Press of Indiana, Inc. My intensive editing communication with my publisher and editor, Nancy Niblack Baxter, has been greatly streamlined by the use of e-mail. I am deeply grateful to Nancy for her faith that we could, in fact, turn this mass of material into a readable book, and to all of the staff at Guild Press for their efforts in the elegant production of *Surgeon on Horseback*.

James W. Wheaton
December 1998

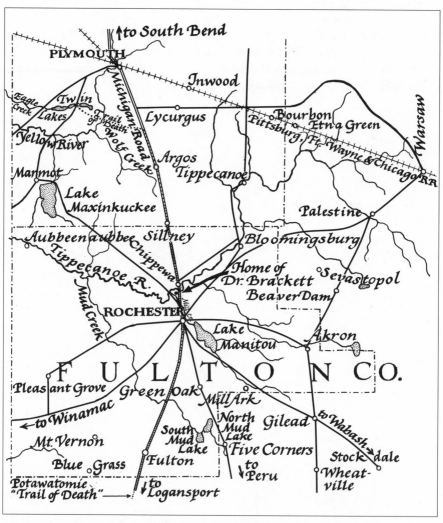

The Brackett farm was located just north of Rochester, in the northern part of Fulton County, Indiana. (Map by Richard Day)

ROCHESTER, INDIANA

★ ★ ★

THE CIVIL WAR OPENED with the firing on Ft. Sumter on April 15, 1861, and an America flourishing in stable rural and urban peace and security was suddenly ripped into two parts. Dr. Charles Brackett was building a medical practice while farming ninety acres just north of Rochester, Fulton County, Indiana. Rochester was a typical Midwestern farming village. Located in Indiana's lake district, it was settled late in the frontier period—the last of the Potawatomi Indians had been marched west at gunpoint only twenty-three years before. The land was moderately productive, opportunities promising. The sincere and moral Brackett, like hundreds of thousands from both North and South, left it all behind, volunteering patriotically for military service with one main goal: to serve his country.

In April of 1861 Dr. Brackett attempted to raise a company of eighty volunteer soldiers from Rochester in answer to Lincoln's first call, and was elected captain. Governor Oliver P. Morton quickly filled the state's quota, and some units had to be turned away, including Dr. Brackett's (see letter of August 1, 1861, following).

Dr. Brackett evidently decided that obtaining a commission as a physician was a more practical way of serving his country, and invoked the aid of Schuyler Colfax, a fellow member of the Odd Fellows Lodge. At the time, Colfax was a member of the House of Representatives from Indiana, and became Speaker of the House in 1863. He served as Vice President in Grant's

1

first term, but his political career was later ruined by his involvement in the *Crédit Mobilier* scandal concerning funding for the Union Pacific Railroad.

South Bend Ind
June 3rd 1861.

His Excellency Govr Morton
    Dr C Brackett of Rochester Ind is a candidate for Surgeon of one of the Inda Regts, and I very cheerfully bear testimony to his superior qualifications for the position. He is one of the very best Surgeons & Physicians in Northern Ind has had sixteen years of experience; has one of the best sets of Instruments for field practice in the State; speaks the German fluently & his Appt as Surgeon or Asst Surgeon would be a great acquisition to the service.

Respt yours
Schuyler Colfax

Copy of letter from S Colfax to Govr Morton June 3, 1861. Forwarded June 8th 1861

THE COUNTRY WAS NOT PREPARED for the immediate necessities of raising an army. Governors were put in charge of enrolling and sending off military regiments recruited from counties in their own states. The details of a confusing summer of recruitment plans put together by Governor Oliver P. Morton but gone awry for Charles Brackett are obvious in this letter.

Rochester Fulton Co Indiana
August 1st 1861.

Adgt General Laze Noble
Dear Sir:
    I hope you will give the following an attentive perusal for the sake of knowing why I do not attend with the Company of Volunteers who left this place yesterday under Mr Minor.[1]

---

1. Milton A. Minor, Captain of Co. A, Twenty-Sixth Regiment Indiana Volunteer Infantry, Colonel William M. Wheatley (Kingman's *New Historical Atlas of Fulton County, Indiana*).

In the first place from "General Orders No 13" I learned that "Companies will not be permitted to march to the rendezvous without positive orders from the Adgt General."

Next in answer to your order of the 9th July requiring me to be at Camp Morton by the Monday following I wrote you asking for ten days time to convene the company, & as I recd no answer from you I concluded that the Regiments were all full & that we were not wanted: therefore I did nothing further than to stick to the terms of your orders, & to those of my call of June 29th (a copy of which I herewith send), & which I pray you read.

Mr Minor represented to the men that he had orders to march, & that I had turned over my roll to him; to me he represented that he was satisfied that we would be recd from your parole agreement with Mr A McDonald & that we should be "recd if ready in twenty days" from the time that McDonald said he saw you.

I told him if I recd an answer from you to that effect I would then work to have the men ready, but that no consideration would induce me to represent to men that we were received unless I knew we were: that the company I raised in April last was raised from Gov Morton's promise made to J H Stailey, & to Judge Schryock that if I would raise a company it should be recd; that he wished to commission only those he knew to be true; On the strength of this parole agreement I represented to the men that we were sure to be recd into service, though my own knowledge of things told me that more companies were ready than would fill the regts for the state service, & for the three months men. I was terribly deceived, & felt the mortification keenly; & had no desire to repeat the blunder. It was represented to the men just gone that I was going with them untill yesterday, Although it was known from all I said, & from the handbill issued that I would not convene the men unless positive orders were received.

If the Company should be received in a Regt I would be very desirous of a place in the Regt any where except under Minor as I consider him to be (to say the least) too excitable, & to have represented affairs (in relation to the Company) in a different light from the true state of the case.

If you will show this to the Governor (if you think it proper) it will much oblige me, as I would like to have him know, as well as yourself, that I am yet inclined to enter the service, & wish to obey orders as nearly as possible to the letter.

I am asking very much of you, yet a regard for my reputation prompts me to it & I hope at some future time to be able to repay the kindness.

With much respect I am your Obtservt

Charles Brackett.

HIS ATTEMPT TO RAISE A COMPANY having been rejected, Dr. Charles was invited by his younger brother, Captain Albert G. Brackett, to join (as assistant surgeon) an Illinois cavalry regiment he was raising in Chicago. Dr. Charles's older brother, James W. Brackett, also a doctor, was evidently favored by Albert for the post of surgeon. Dr. James's letter below is not exactly a warm invitation to join Albert, James, and another brother, Joseph, in the Ninth Illinois Cavalry Regiment.

Relations between the various Brackett brothers were often clouded by money problems. Charles owed Albert some money on a note and could not pay, and Albert got a judgment against Charles. Eventually, Charles would join the Ninth Illinois Cavalry. In the summer of 1861, however, he elected to go with another cavalry group from Indiana.

Rock Island Illinois
August 12, 1861.

Dear Charles,

I presume you have received both mine and Albert's letters before, and have determined what you will do relative to your company or receive the position of Assistant Surgeon in his Regiment.

I suppose you would prefer acting as Captain of your Company to acting in the capacity of Assistant Surgeon.

I wrote to Albert previous to the receipt of your letter that I should prefer Wm˙ White of Iowa City or Dr. Bulkley of Washington City to any other men for my Assistant but should you wish the position you would receive it before all others.

Albert said he would send my orders in a week or ten days and then if nothing prevents I will see you, although your best way will be to go directly to Chicago and see the Captain and make such arrangements as you see proper.

The Captain will be Colonel of the Regiment and has the disposition of the offices and officers of the Regiment.

Joe will be QuarterMaster and you and I Surgeons or I Surgeon and you Captain—as you may elect.

Matty[2] thinks of going on with me should I go on, as well as my Family to visit Mrs. Wright and your family.

Albert's Regiment will be raised from Illinois, Indiana, Iowa and Michigan.[3]

> Your brother
> James W. Brackett.

From the Journal:

August 16th 1861—Left home at 9 PM for Indianapolis. Rode all night, and reached Peru at daylight

August 17th—Reached Indianapolis & recd Commission as Assistant Surgeon of Cavalry Regiment. Was ordered to join immediately at Evansville. Compelled to lay over for Cars till Monday.

Ind 5 50

Evansville 6 25

Indianapolis Saty August 17th 1861.

Dearest Margeret,

I arrived here in good time today. Reported myself to the Governor & Adjt General. Recd my commission & was ordered immediately to Evansville where my Regt is under Col Baker; thence Monday the 19th inst we start for St Louis. Associated with me as Surgeon is Dr ____* of Evansville. So you see I am off for the war without delay.

You must write me at St Louis, directing your letter to Chs Brackett Surgeon of First Cavalry Indiana Volunteers. I shall write you at short intervals. I have not procured my uniform—this I will do at St Louis. When I have it I will send you an Ambrotype. Have

---

2. Albert's wife, Martha Tolman Briggs. Dr. James was married to Sarah Ann Work Brown.

3. The actual origins of the companies were: A: Rock Island; B: Geneseo; C: Cambridge; D: Chicago; E: Logansport, IN; F: Chicago; G: Valparaiso, IN; H: Kewanee; I: Belvidere; K: Princeton; L: Chicago; M: Onarga. (Davenport, E. A. *History of the Ninth Illinois Cavalry Regiment*. Chicago: Donohue and Henneberry, 1888.)

*probably Dr. Isaac Casselberry.

yours taken at the first opportunity. You need not send it to me, but keep it, & if your death should happen before we meet I would get it if Alive. At any rate the children would have them.

You do not know how I was affected this afternoon when I found, on opening my satchel, the little presents which I supposed my darling Louisa put in for me the bit of paper with the verse of the "Star Spangled Banner." Tell Louisa that father will keep it, while he lives, as a treasured keepsake from his loved daughter.

I cannot think much now of business for a few days, but when I write again will give you such directions in regard to business as I think will be of service.

Tell the children all to be good & that Pa will try & bring them something nice when he returns. Everything is activity here, & business brisk. Soldiers are to be met at every step, & now & then one minus an arm or a leg, or pale from the exhausting discharges from wounds from Bullet, or Sword; Stern determination however sits on their brows, & though cripples yet they are undaunted. I took dinner to day with Geo W. New Surgeon of the 9th Regt. He has many interesting trophies from the Enemy's camp. His son was with him during the three months trip to Virginia. The Regt is again nearly organized for the war be it long, or short. Had I known what I now know I would have brought my large instrument case with me. There are none so good instruments here. Do not lend my large case. If it is needed you can lend my medium sized Amputating case, or the small operating case.

Once more love to the children. Write often giving me all the news. Tell Esther I will remember her among the rest on my return; have her with the children attend school when it begins.

Be sure & write soon & often to your affectionate husband
Charles Brackett

Indianapolis Sunday
August 18th 1861.

My Dear Daughter
I am now at the Palmer House in my room No 58 Alone, & thinking of my loved ones at home, & especially of my good daughter Louisa. You are now getting of sufficient age to begin to write, & I want you to write me a letter If you can as often as your Mother writes, & she will direct yours, or enclose it with her letter to me.

Indianapolis Iat'y
August 17th 1861.

Dearest Margaret,

I arrived here in good time to day. Reported myself to the Governor & Adjt General. Rec'd My Commission & was ordered immediately to Evansville where My Regt is under Col Baker; thence Monday the 19th inst we start for St Louis. Associated with Me as Surgeon is Dr _____ of Evansville. So you see I am off for the war without delay.

You must write me at St Louis, directly Your letter to Chs Brack H Surgeon of first Cavalry Indiana Volunteers. I shall write you at short intervals. I have not procured My uniform- this I will do at St Louis. When I have it I will send you An Ambrotype. Have Yours taken at the first opportunity, You need not send it to Me, but keep it, & if Your death should happen before we meet I would get it if Alive. At any rate the Children would have them.

You do not know how I was affected this afternoon, when I found on opening My Satchel, the little presents which I suppose

It is uncertain when I may see you again but whenever it may be I hope to find you improved in everything that is good. Let the motto "In God is our trust" ever be yours, & at all times energetically use the power, & talent that a good God has given you to perfect all that you undertake; even to the least of your duties.

Do not depend too much upon others to assist you in the performance of your duties. Attend to each duty without delay; if you have a work to perform that will take but ten minutes of time, use the first ten minutes to perfect the work, then play, & if you have only an hours work for the day let the work be done during the first hour you have, then it may be off your mind, & your whole course through life, thus spent, will be easy, & you can accomplish wonders, without ever being hurried.

Your little present affected me very much & will I trust do me much good in the future. "Little deeds of kindness, little words of love", make up the sum total of our happiness on earth, & the one who gives is generally more blessed, than the one who receives; yet your little gift of a simple verse without doubt will be a great blessing to your father.

You never saw your father cry probably, yet when I looked at the Flag with the little verse accompanying it, I sat down and cried like a little child (probably as I have never before done), & all for joy that my daughter by her little present thus directed anew her fathers attention to his duty to his God & his Country. Be assured your little gift shall be carefully guarded while I live as a talisman for good.

Tell Lyman, & Rosa to be good children, that father thinks very much about them, & hopes to hear good accounts from them.

I cannot get to Evansville till tomorrow, as there have been no trains leaving for that place & will be none till tomorrow morning at 7 AM. If no accident happens I will reach Evansville tomorrow at 7 Oclock PM. & on that night or Tuesday we will start for St Louis whence I will write your Mother again. I wrote to her yesterday, & the letter (yours, & hers) may arrive by the same mail.

I am eating occasionally of the large Red Apples you sent me: From which tree did you get it? It is a very good one. I look at the apples as one from you, one from Lyman, one from Rosa, one from baby Mary, & one from Esther, & when I look at any of them I think of you all, & of Mother & GrandMa.[4]

---

4. Margaret's mother, Ann Dary Wilson, 1786–1863.

"Home sweet home" seems dearer as I am further seperated from it, not particularly on account of the place itself, but because all I love are there.

It may not (I hope) be long before we all will meet again at home; but if death (the common lot of us all) takes any of us before that time my trust is that we may all meet in the Spirit land where partings, & sorrows are no more, & all is love, peace, & joy. "In God is our trust" Let that be our Motto, loved ones all.

Your affectionate Father,

Ch Brackett

P.S. Tell mother to get a barrel of salt so that the stock can be salted regularly, & that if Mr Bearse is there to borrow a Gun let him have the Double barreled one. Do not lend Old Bundy to any one, & when you make a sale you may sell all of the Guns except Old Bundy. That is for Lyman.

★ ★ ★

DR. CHARLES BRACKETT was about to enter a seething cauldron of a state—not a "theatre of war," but an arena for bitter political factionalism. Missouri had been divided about evenly on the eve of the war, and although the state had a pro-Confederate governor, it refused to secede. A Federal garrison stood outside St. Louis: would the governor seize guns at the Federal Arsenal, and force secession?

Washington was taking no chances and replaced the garrison commander in February 1861 with a young firebrand commander—a captain, soon to be made brigadier, Nathaniel J. Lyon. Lyon and Congressman Francis P. Blair, Jr., who were both rabid Unionists, stripped the St. Louis arsenal, moving its weapons to Alton, and infuriating moderates as well as pro-Confederates. Lyon, still rampaging for the Northern cause, disbanded and humiliated militiamen west of St. Louis on May 10, thus causing a riot that killed twenty-eight and injured many more. It is important to know this background because Lyon's and Blair's extreme action outraged many Missourians and set them implacably against the North and into guerrilla warfare.

Lyon went on the move against "all Confederates" in Missouri during the summer of 1861, and drove partisan and guerrilla bands to the southwestern part of Missouri. It was at this point, with bands of partisans roaming around the south of the state shooting their fellow Missourians, and the Northern army trying to "secure Missouri," that Dr. Charles and his unit reported to the training area.

ST. LOUIS, MISSOURI
First Indiana Cavalry

★ ★ ★

Dearest Wife

We arrived here last night, late, from Vincennes, much tired. Had a good sleep in the open air (in the Fair Grounds) Four miles from the city, & this morning feel in best health & spirits. St Louis is not now as it was when you were here; Regiments are encamped in all directions in, & out of town. Heavy, sixty-four lb Columbiads are being mounted on defences in all exposed parts as if the powers that be feared an attack from the Rebels now in heavy force at Springfield (Two hundred miles from here) where the Secession flag is flying. Fremont[1] is here, & troops are coming in daily to the number of one to three thousand. Our command numbers eight hundred All mounted men. We brot our horses with us from Evansville & you may think we made quite a load for the cars. We had no accident except since we came here we have had two men wounded from their horses kicking, & one thrown & badly hurt. Last night I lay down by one wounded man to give him a part of my blanket, till his com-

---

1. Major General John C. Frémont

rades should relieve him, & I was so tired that I fell asleep till broad daylight. Our wounded & sick shall not suffer from any neglect of mine.

I have just finished my requisitions on the Government for Hospital stores, Instruments &C, write a list of articles which if I get will do for all probable emergencies.

It is possible that I may send, or go home to get two horses. I am entitled to two, & a hand to take care of them. I thought I would like to hire Dave Edwards to come with them, but I am told here that I had better hire where labor is cheaper than there. Can you get along alone well? Let me know truly how you feel about it. I hope to be able to send you some means every month probably fifty dollars . . . I shall look daily for a letter from you. Direct to Chs Brackett Ast Surgeon of the First Cavalry Regt Indiana Volunteers, Col Baker, St Louis Missouri. (See this last word how to spell it correctly)

Write often. I wish I had Little John[2] here, or if Lyman was even as old as Louisa I would have him. He could earn twelve dollars pr month & his board as well as not. Garland Rose is here & he says my best way will be to take a contraband as the cheapest & most faithful. I would prefer a white boy on most accounts. I have to keep two horses & a servant for which the Government pays. I am using now one that Dr Casselberry furnished me at Evansville.

The Doctor is a very pleasant man, & I doubt not we will get along well together.

Fremont is just here reviewing some Ohio & Indiana troops each side of us. It will be our turn soon before which time I must have a uniform. I would not get any if it was not obligatory on me. I could do my duty just as well in citizens clothes, but we would not be able to recognize Officers unless some marks of Distinction were adopted.

I shall not dare, or be allowed to take any part, in an action, except such as belongs to my profession. I feel a little awkward about it, but it is for the best that a part must be detailed to take care of the wounded.

The city is under martial law, & as quiet & orderly as is Rochester. More so. Our train loaded two of the largest boats to transport over the River. When the men were mounted, & baggage train all

---

2. Dr. Brackett's nephew John Ely Brackett, about fifteen years old, son of his late brother, Dr. Lyman Brackett. "Lyman" is Charles's son, then seven years old.

ready it made quite an imposing appearance. I had an ambulance with one wounded man, one sick one, & a soldier, & his wife who is going as a nurse. We will have several women to each company to act as nurses & laundresses. Some ten of the Sisters of Charity came with us, though I do not know as they will accompany our Regt as nurses. They are nursing the wounded in the hospital, of which there are one hundred & fifty from the battle of Springfield; they are mostly only slightly wounded except two who are shot through the head, & I think they will probably die.

I am making most ample provisions for all probable contingencies in the care of the men of our Regt. They are mostly good young men, sober, attentive, & industrious & if they are ever in an engagement will tell a good story for themselves if the Officers are all right. The greatest difficulty with the Officers is that they mostly have their duties as military men yet to learn. This is my only cause of fear for the Regt. It is barely possible that I may be sent back to the other detachment of our Regt (six hundred men at Madison) to go on to Washington. If I am I shall try & come around by home where I hope to find my dear ones all well. I think at every leisure moment of "Home, Sweet, Sweet Home" & my loved ones there. I feel sure however that I shall meet you all again alive so sure as one can feel on an uncertainty . . .

We have a very good, pleasant man for our Chaplain, one that I feel I shall like.

Now I must bring my long, rambling disjointed letter to a close, by wishing you my Dearest wife & children all happiness, & may the Good God be with you always.

Love to all enquiring friends, from your Affectionate husband
Charles Brackett

From the Journal:

Saturday 24ᵗʰ—In hospital Henry Tieder of Chicago Dragoons, Capt Theilmann, dislocated clavicle fracture of Acromian [?] Scapula

Use for hospital one of the buildings in the Fairgrounds. Very good for this purpose.

Sunday 25ᵗʰ—J Grampstein of Chicago Dragoons, with hoarseness and Cough eight days duration

Camp Blair near St Louis,
August 25th 1861

Dearest Wife

Though it was but yesterday that I put my last letter to you in the PO at St Louis, yet I must employ a little leisure I now have in writing you again.

My time is much taken up in Hospital duties. We have besides our own Regt of Cavalry some detached companies of Dragoons & Artillery who are not supplied with Surgeons, & who attend our Hospital for medical & surgical aid. I want to make ours a model Hospital & unless something unforseen occurs will do so.

We are in the midst of a vast camp which is being prepared for thirty thousand men, the largest in this country. You cannot see from one to the other side of it where the lines of the Barracks make their Angles. The Regts that are now immediately about us I do not know. Besides our camp there is one at Carondelet or "Vide Poche" down the River & others located at places nearby that I do not know. I have been in the City proper but once since my arrival here. That was yesterday when I was in making requisitions for Instruments, Medicines, Hospital Stores, Furniture, &C.

I was materially assisted by GDRose our State Marshall who was sent on by Govr Morton to assist & look after the interests of the Indiana forces.

Congressman Shank, from the 11th Dist of our State, who is now one of Gen Fremont's Staff was also as kind as a Brother & afforded me much valuable information.

Shank & Rose stay at the Planters House where I had a most excellent dinner. Quite a treat for one from the Camp where for a few days Old Bacon & Seabuscuit were our only fare. This hard living was a consequence of some men assuming duties with which they were not thoroughly acquainted & will not again recur unless a sudden march to the interior should be ordered. We are throwing up some defences, mounted with sixty-four lb Columbiads, at the most exposed Points. Ben McCulloch[3] the Rebel leader says since the battle of Springfield that he will have St Louis or go to Hell, & as we are satisfied that he cant get St Louis we think the Devil is sure of him; that is if Mr McCulloch is a man of truth & veracity.

---

3. Brigadier General Ben McCulloch of Texas, later killed in action at Pea Ridge commanding a division of two brigades.

There are many wounded here from Springfield.[4] Poor fellows they have a dejected look even where their wounds are not very serious, as at this season other sickness hides [?] in their depression.

From all best accounts, our loss at Springfield, killed, wounded, & missing was about twelve hundred. The Rebels numbering five times our force lost not less than two thousand—this shows they fought well, as indeed they should have done when they anticipated from their overwhelming numbers an easy & sure victory. McCulloch told his men that they would be sure to kill half of our troops & take the balance prisoners, but they failed miserably nearly four thousand of our boys through an orderly retreat conducted by Siegle [Sigel], & Sturgis, getting off in safety.[5]

I walked this morning along our lines over two miles, yet did not see even one half of our Camp. The Camp of our Regt is directly north of the fair grounds on a line with an Ohio, & a Kansas Regt of Infantry. The fair ground here is the finest I ever saw anywhere. Statues, Fountains, beautifully arranged walks, & Roads, through grounds of native forest trees, Buildings for all purposes necessary to such an institution all ornamental in their Character make a delightful place of it. We are arranging our Hospital in one of the Central buildings on a fine eminence. I stay at the Hospital a part of the time messing with the soldiers & occasionally taking my meals at a German Hotel near the Front Gate. We are very careful where, & what we eat. As many as four soldiers have been poisoned by these Chivalrous Seceshers.

One of our Guards, a mere boy from Ohio, while on his lonely rounds was approached by a friendly looking, smooth tongued villian, who after a little talk with the Guard asked him to partake with him of his Pie; the innocent boy accepted the offer with thankfulness eat of the Pie, & was directly thrown into spasms by what

---

4. Lyon fought a Confederate force under McCulloch near Springfield, Missouri in the southwest corner of the state and was killed in the bloody stand-up battle (the Battle of Wilson's Creek, August 10, 1861, a victory for McCulloch). A new commander had been put in place by this time for the entire troubled state by President Lincoln. The well known western explorer John Charles Frémont (Major General) had been given instructions to bring the state under Union control and he was at once accused of not supporting Lyon—thus adding to the bitterness of Unionists.

5. The combined Rebel forces were approximately eleven thousand, twice the Federal force; each side suffered approximately twelve hundred casualties. Dr. Brackett's statement is typical of the rumors that circulate in every army, and which were particularly intense in Missouri.

proved to be a large dose of Strychnine. He may recover but probably his mother & sisters have made him their last farewell. So it is, but I hope we have no more men, or boys who will be victimized in that way.

We have many German Soldiers here, & since Yesterday morning when I set a broken bone for a wounded Dragoon of Capt Theilmann's Company Chicago Dragoons, it seems as every German in the Crowd knows me, & I am met by greetings in all sorts of Germanic Dialects at nearly every turn . . .

The street is thronged with gay equipages, Ladies, Men, & children all as merry as crickets; they do not seem to know, or care for what is in the future. We have a Chaplain from Evansville. He preached today at the Camp, but as I had eleven pages of copy to make of our Requisitions which must be in early in the morning I did not hear him. This makes nineteen sheets I have written today besides my morning duties at the Hospital. My love to all enquiring friends Kiss the Children all for Pa & for yourself accept the best wishes of your affectionate husband

Chs Brackett

From the Journal:

Monday 26th—Three shirts & Handkerchief to wash at Tavern in Camp Blair Fairground near St Louis. Visited a member of the Ohio Regt (near us) who was shot by a Guard through the breast; the ball entering near the Sternum on the Right side, about third or fourth rib. Wrote a letter to Judge K G Shryock of Rochester, Inda.

August 29th—Thursday About thirty patients in the Hospital, & twenty Outpatients. All doing well.

Hospital At Camp Blair Near
St Louis Mo Thursday August 29th 1861

Dear Margeret

I believe it is now near a week since I wrote you, & (as I have a little leisure) with thirty patients lying about me will spend it in letting you know how I get along. Since I left Evansville Agst 20th my bed has been the soft side of a plank with my old coat for a pillow & my shawl for cover. I sleep soundly & am in tolerable health though I have suffered some from a cold contracted during our passage here. We were at the junction near Vincennes some six hours, but I had no chance to go out to find Brad Brouillette whom I should have been glad to have seen.

There are several Indiana Regts here. Two were sent out last night to Jefferson City where it is surmised that McCulloch is making an advance. The boys with knapsacks slung, & plenty of Ammunition started off in high spirits. One of our guard shot a man, one of the Ohio troops, who was trying to break the guard. The bullet went in the right side near the breast bone, & came out through the shoulder blade of the same side. The poor fellow I saw the next day, & I presume he is before this time dead. No blame attaches to the Guard who did his duty. Another one was shot dead for trying the same trick, the bullet going through his head entering between his nose & eye. These were troublesome, overbearing men unwilling to perform their duties. Yesterday I was in the city to get our Mds, Instruments, &C. There I saw the remains of Genl Lyon[6] being escorted to the Ferry by Cavalry, Artillery, & Infantry several Regts. The hearse was the most elegant thing of the kind I ever saw. The flumes at least four feet in length, mounted on high Gilded bearings, & all other parts of like elegance, & corresponding size. The coffin was wrapped in the Star Spangled Banner. One hundred prisoners (taken at Springfield) followed in the procession. Surrounded by files of soldiers, & without arms, soiled & travel worn they were pitiable looking objects. They were mostly small, weakly men with many boys. I presume the weakest of the Rebels who were in the action. I saw one Captain of our forces who was wounded there; the ball struck him in the left breast over the heart, & running around the rib came out near the backbone. He was able to be up & walk about. He said the surgeon stuck one finger in the wound in his breast, & one in that in his back & was able to make his fingers meet in the wound, so you may judge what sort of a hole a minnie ball makes.

I may send in a few days for some horses, & if I do will want a good boy (Dave Edwards if he will come) to take care of the horses for me. Have you recd the letters I sent you? I have heard nothing from home since I left, & it is full time that I should hear . . .

Once more Farewell write often to your loving husband
Charles Brackett

---

6. Brigadier General Nathaniel Lyon, killed at Wilson's Creek, August 10, 1861.

DR. BRACKETT IS IN A HODGE-PODGE of a military camp, units arriving, drilling of "green" regiments, supplying amateur warring in its glory, but without its officials having a very clear knowledge of the deep and sincere split in the city of St. Louis and the region around it. Partisans for both North and South agitated the people constantly.

Hospital at Camp Blair
near St Louis Sund Sept 1st 1861

Dearest Margeret

Your very welcome letter of the 23rd ult reached me yesterday, & as I had written on Thursday or Friday I thought I would not answer till today. I have nothing specially new to write, matters are going along without change, we are all the time busy with our sick, & are getting somewhat tired of the delay in getting our arms & equipments. Affairs are very quiet. The City, & State are now under martial law. Yesterday the Good Ladies of St Louis sent to our Hospital a large four horse wagon load of mattresses and bedding. A very acceptable donation to both sick & well. Last night I lay on a mattress with my good shawl above me, & an army blanket for lower sheet. I sleep well & dream sweetly of Home, Wife, & Children. Tell Lyman that Pa wishes that he was here. We have one little estray boy here without Father, Mother, Friends, or home except now our Hospital & its inmates. We call him the child of the Regt & mean to take good care of him. He is a bright little fellow, & all take a lively interest in his welfare; it makes the tears of gratitude well out of his large bright eyes when words of encouragement, & praise are spoken to him.

I am now boarding entirely in the Hospital. We have plenty now; the Ladies visiting our Hospital every day to ascertain our wants.

In regard to the House for the renter I think if he intends to put it off till spring that it will be time enough then to make the plan.

I intended to build a Chicago frame 14 ft square, story & half high, Gables East & West, with leanto or porch at one side, & cellar, boarded with vertical siding like the new milk house, & if built this fall battened but not plastered till next spring, the boards will then be better seasoned & the walls (plastering) less liable to crack. I should prefer that Mr Culver build the house, or at least supervise,

& assist. In that case it will I know be well done . . .

Did Mr. Jethrow New[7] go with the Volunteers? I am sorry he was not elected Captain though Collins makes a good choice. I have hopes of being appointed Surgeon of that Regt. Tell Keith to write the Governor in regard to appointing me Surgeon. It will increase my pay about six hundred dollars pr year. Worth trying for. Write often God bless you all, & with much love I am ever your affectionate husband

Chs Brackett

Planters House St Louis
Wed Sept 4th 1861

Dearest wife

As I wrote you a few days since from our camp four miles from the City, & doubt the proper transmission of letters by our Regimental Postmaster who has not yet become perfect in his business, I will write again where I can mail my letter in person.

We are getting along finely though the equiping of our troops is a slow process, & the men are getting to be impatient at the delay.[8]

Tell Lyman when I get home I have a good many stories to tell him about the war how the men have been hunted, & shot at; & how they escaped. Stories I have had from the lips of the men who were actors in the scenes. The Union men of this state are coming rapidly in from the North & West in detachments of from one to ten companies & they all or nearly all have some tales of wrong & suffering to relate of which I have heard enough to afford entertainment for the children for an indefinite time after I get home. I am writing from the room occupied by Col Chenk [Shank?] one of Genl Fremont's aids. He is taking much interest in the welfare of the Indiana troops.

I believe I wrote in my last a long string of duties for you to have done. I feel anxious to know how you get along, & if you will be able

---

7. Jethro New was one of the men whom Dr. Charles recruited back in April, and had been elected second lieutenant of the proposed company. The roster of Company D of the Twenty-ninth Regiment, recruited in Fulton County, shows both Joseph P. Collins and Jethro New as captains.

8. The delay is caused by more drilling for a green outfit.

to manage affairs so that you will all be comfortable during the Winter. Let me know all about it.

I enjoy myself very much though I cannot say that I sleep here with a sense of perfect security as at home. We had at camp last night some incidents which excited the men considerably. I felt that if our guards did their duty that we would be in no great danger, the night passed without Alarm after midnight, & I slept well dreaming of wife & children at home where all I hope is peace . . .

Little John E Brackett could get along first rate with all that would be necessary & would enjoy it right well. You can speak to him about it. It would be a trip he would like right well I am satisfied. There are a good many boys with the Officers smaller than John & they enjoy themselves hugely. If Lyman was only five years older I would want nobody else but him, or at least would want him.[9] Tell the babies all to be good & kind to each other to mind what their Mother tells them at all times. I feel best when I think that they are all good children & that they make no unnecessary trouble. Be good to grandma also all of you. Make her as comfortable as possible.

I wish you could have some of the fine fruits that St Louis affords. They have the finest Peaches here I have ever seen. Still no fruit that I find tastes so well as that at home, & if such fruits as the Peach, apricot & nectarine flourished better there I believe I would never wish to exchange our home for another, but we cannot tell what a year or even a few months may bring forth . . .

Chs Brackett

From the Journal:

Wednesday Sept 4th—There are only a few serious cases remaining in the Hospital.

Wednesday Sept 11th—Sent to wash undershirt, Shirt, & hand-kerchief. Sick & wounded are doing well except two typhoid cases. Some soldiers were poisoned yesterday by pies sold in the barracks by Negro women.

---

9. Dr. Charles still considers war to be a pleasant enough adventure, and is considering inviting his seven-year-old son Lyman to join him. His attitude would change in time with the dangerous realities of battle. Military camp was no place for boys. General William T. Sherman's son died of typhoid after coming to his father's camp.

Prepared for Expedition as follows— Field knapsack with

Sod BiCarb	Ether sul Lot
Ipecac	Sub micr Hy
Quinine	Aloes
Opium	Rhes
Tr Opium	Ammon Acqua
Morph	Cupricum
Chloroform	Enip Adhv
Collodion	Bandages
Whiskey	Muslin
surgeons silk	Carb Ammon)
Thread linen	Strychnine)
Wax	Field Case)not ready
Pocket Case	Sash)
Cesate	
Lint	
Pins	Citric Acid
Sponge	Olive Oil
Tourniquets	Writing paper
Batting	Jvd Potass
Ammonia	Ext Blk Pepper
Capsicum	Sul Zinci
Belladonna Ex	Jvd Jydrz P____
Blankets 3	

★ ★ ★

Camp Blair near St Louis
Wed Sept 11th 1861

Dearest Margeret

. . . I am writing in the Hospital, & can't get along very well.
We have some fifty patients here sick with all sorts of disease. Yesterday two men of our Camp were poisoned by an old black & a
white woman. It was difficult to keep the soldiers from killing them
when caught, but they will have a fair trial & such a _____ as shall
be just I hope.

I am detailed to a scouting party or detachment to some place
in the interior. We will start tonight on horseback. I have my instruments, & mds all ready. Possibly Dr Casselberry will go as being
senior Officer—he has choice. I shall do as ordered, though I had

hoped to have started for home this week. This will take us ten days after which if I live I hope to see you soon for a day or two.

I will write to the friends when I can. We have thousands of horse here now, & thousands of Infantry, & more coming every day.

Do not neglect to write often, I wrote Keith today. See him on all matters pertaining to business. I would like to be commissioned with Dr Humphreys. Write to Colfax to that effect. I am better acquainted with him & prefer by far to be with our 9th Regt.

God Bless my Dear Wife. Tell Rosa Pa will write her when he returns from his scout. Our Men are surrounded by the Rebels as I hear, & on this acct we go.[10] If I do not go I will write you. Once more good bye wife & dear Children, & I hope to see you all again. At any rate I will write often when possible. Write at least every week to your loving Husband

Chs Brackett

From the Journal:

Started September 12th Thursday—Rode all afternoon, returned to Camp at 9 PM. Were reviewed by Fremont & recd his compliments. I suffer much from Diarrhea, low fever & cold in head—Hemicrania from Cold contracted in Hospital.

---

10. Incorrect. The Federals, not the Rebs, are winning the fight for Missouri. "The Pathfinder" Frémont had extended martial law through all of Missouri by proclamation, and in a highly inflammatory section of the proclamation of August 30 had freed Confederate slaves in the state. In spite of Frémont's disastrous mismanagement of the Missouri war effort, misappropriation of funds, and clashes with Lincoln, the North was inexorably gaining ground. Lincoln would remove Frémont the third week of October 1861 and send seasoned General Henry W. Halleck to clean up Missouri.

PILOT KNOB, MISSOURI
First Indiana Cavalry

★ ★ ★

From the Journal:

September 13th—Recd leave but, as detachment was ordered out I stayed to go with them. My leave was to date from 16th inst for ten days—But I could not allow myself to go home when part of our command were going to meet the famous Hardee while waiting for the cars on Iron Mountain Road.

At the corner of Plumb & Main Streets, was very kindly treated by Mr Frittochle (a Baker) we waited till 11 PM at which time I am writing this.

Sept 14th—Arrived at Pilot Knob at 10 AM.[1, 2] Hardee reported with his vanguard a few miles out. About noon the Picket Guard came in reporting the enemy coming on the Town. We prepared for action, under Arms for about an hour when it was ascer-

---

1. On September 14, 1861, the First Indiana Cavalry was transferred from Camp Blair (named after General Frank Blair, a future corps commander) to Pilot Knob, Missouri, a Federal outpost. The real war was far away. Dyer's *Compendium* describes the "interior scouting" venture of the First Indiana Cavalry as "skirmish at Black River Ironton." Dr. Brackett evidently didn't go out until the next afternoon, and returned to Camp Blair at 9 P.M. Then, according to the next letter (September 14), they immediately left at midnight and went to Pilot Knob and Ironton (two miles south) and stayed there.

2. Union troops and supplies were moved south from St. Louis eighty-six miles via the St. Louis & Iron Mountain Railroad to Pilot Knob, the end of the line at that time. Thus, possession of the railroad was strategically vital to the Union war effort. Pilot Knob earned its day in history in September 1864, when Brigadier General Thomas Ewing, Jr. defended Ft. Davidson against Sterling Price.

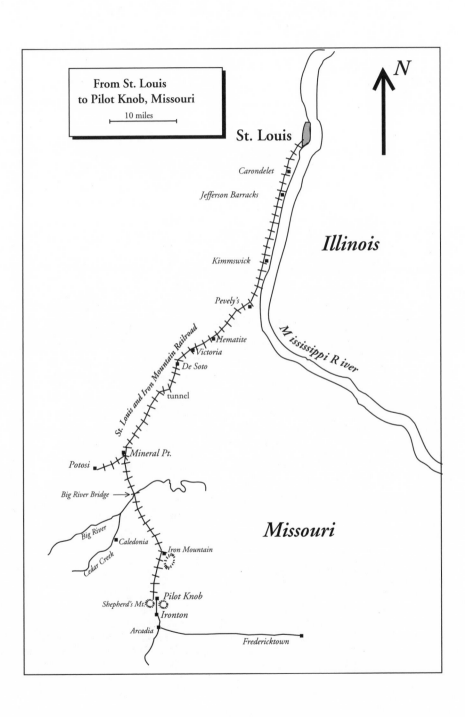

tained that a detachment of scouts (300) from Ironton were mistaken for the enemy. Went to Ironton for quarters.

Pilot Knob
Ironton Co Missouri
Saty Sept 14th 1861

Dearest Margeret

Yesterday I got leave of absence to go home for ten days, but just last night one half our Regt was ordered here, & I came with them. We started at midnight & without sleep or food we just arrived here, a most romantic spot encircled by high hills called the Iron Mountains. The Rebels[3] want the place & their General Hardee[4] has his advance of fifteen hundred [men] ten miles from here with a reserve of from seven to thirty thousand as the various estimates make it, forty miles below. Nebraska & Indiana troops[5] are here in possession & will try & keep it.

If I should live till peace is restored I would like to come here for a residence. Iron smelting is the chief business, though they make some lead for this part. The Confederates must have it (if they can get it). Our Regt will be the advance guard between the Rebels & our Infantry. They are now moving down while I sit here in the shade thinking of home & its dear ones all. Tell Lyman that I thought a good about him last night, & that if I should not live to see him again that when he grows to manhood, & his country is in danger from any foe that he must be a good soldier & defend his Country with all he has & when peace reigns over the land then to return to civil pursuits. Yesterday, at 6 oclock PM I expected to have been in Logansport & home sometime Sunday, but when orders came to move here I gave up my leave for the time. I wanted to get

---

3. The various scouting parties were looking for partisans from the Missouri State Guard, not the Confederate Army.

4. Rumors over the next month seem to be placing this well known Rebel general, William Joseph Hardee (1815-1873) in Arkansas, sometimes when he was in Tennessee and elsewhere. Hardee did command troops in Arkansas, but not on September 14, 1861. On October 7 he relinquished his command of the Seventh Arkansas to his colonel, now Brigadier General, Thomas Hindman. Hardee then accepted command of a division in the Department of the West under General Albert Sidney Johnston. He was at Bowling Green, Kentucky at Johnston's headquarters from October until the Battle of Shiloh.

5. Also present were men from Illinois, Wisconsin, and Missouri.

Dave & the mares. If I cannot get off & it is advisable I will send by express some things to you & money for Dave to pay his way hither with the mares. I shall try & come home after Dr Casselberry joins with the balance of the Regt. We were out day before yesterday on a scout with four hundred men & horses but nothing occured worthy of note. I had everything in my department well prepared. The Col when we started sent me a large navy revolver which was all the offensive weapon I had, & it was enough to defend myself with if I had been attacked. Our way hither was full of interesting incidents which I will tell you all about when we meet again . . .

Chs Brackett

From the Journal:

September 16th—Sent Stephen Lewis to General Hospital; of Co C—

At 1 Oclock PM we are started south to hunt secesh.[6] I strove hard to have an ambulance to go with the train but our Officers would take none though I found a good one . . .

Sept 17th—at a farm just deserted by its people . . .

Wednesday Sept 18th—All safe this morn. We bivouacked at 9 last night on a deserted farm where provisions were abundant. We can find no people, all are hidden. Started at 6 ½ with part of our prisoners, & the horses & mules that are worth taking. Broke most of the guns. All but the best ones. Found a woman's skirt filled with powder & lead. Talbert escaped yesterday.[7] His son was sick, too sick to be taken; was sworn; left two mules [?] & colts to one of the women, & one to a widow. Prisoners are tied on the horses. 9 AM Stop to make Prisoners at a fine farm in the valley.

Talbert escaped yesterday through information of our advance being made to him by a secesh friend living not far from where we bivouacked last night. It is said by our prisoners that he got off

---

6. The Secesh being hunted are the fellows of Jeff Thompson's nasty band of partisans. These people are civilians, though soldiers in the Federal army in Missouri often mistook them for Confederate regulars. Dr. Brackett is describing the actions of an invading army of occupation without realizing it. No one really understood any of this at that time. The First Indiana Cavalry is on detached service here, foraging for supplies, and not yet attached to a larger unit.

7. Captain Daniel Talbert has yet to be identified further through historical sources; he may have been an officer in Thompson's command.

with about forty men poorly equipped. Ten minutes later all
would have escaped. A half hour earlier we would have saved all—
Where we now stop the Old Man, & boys take the oath. Two sons
are in the southern army. They murdered a union family last July
near this place. We bought bacon of the old man. Just beyond this
one of our horses was shot by ____ who was afraid of being apprehended. Camped at 10 M ready for a start at 4: hope to make
Ironton tonight distance 20 miles

Reached camp just midnight Slept with guide in wagon; Rise
6 AM Thurs Sept 19th

Nine shots were fired on our train at the "Ozark Mill" on our
return trip no damage. Captain Talbert's commission, haversack,
& confederate scrip was seized by our boys.

FROM THE FOLLOWING LETTER we can conclude that the previous action
described in the diary was to scare off a single company of the Missouri State
Guard, the Missouri Seventh Regiment. This is not a pitched battle, but a
Civil War within a Civil War.

> Ironton Iron Co Mo Thursday
> Sept 19th 1861

Dearest Margeret

I wrote you a few days before this, I believe the day I got here.
Since then I have been very busy, & on the day we got here (last
Saturday the 14th inst) after I had written you all the news, & put
the letter under seal, we were alarmed by one of our pickets who
came in saying that a long line of Hardee's men were coming to the
attack. All were prepared for action in a short time, & we lay under
arms behind Railroad tracks, Breastworks made of Baled Hay, & entrenchments made of Brush & dirt for more than an hour when our
Scouts reported that the force was the Missouri 7th Regt which was
scouting in two parties from Ironton, one mile below Pilot Knob
where we then were; so ended our first experience in war. On the
next Monday the 16th inst we started out to hunt up & Rout one
Captain Talbert of the Rebel Army[8] & I will write the notes I made
on the trip. "At 1 oclock Mond Sept 16th we were started south to

---

8. Talbert was not part of the Rebel Army, but a partisan. This experience was not a
battle; and the First Indiana Cavalry was not part of a Federal army as yet.

hunt "secesh." I strove hard to have an ambulance go with the train but our officers would not take it after I had found one. I ride in a wagon drawn by six mules. (We have two six mule wagons in train & three hundred, & fifty men) all mounted, & armed with navy revolvers & sabres. Road very Rough & hilly. Secesh houses on the Road mostly deserted, men being off in southern Army.[9] The union men who had been able to stay at home treated us well, & furnish freely all we ask; halted a while near "Ozark Mill." Near here one old man thinking us to be secesh said that he would give all he had for the secesh cause, & did give us for Capt Talbert one horse & rifle signing a paper at the same time that he was their friend, & would furnish freely what he had & himself as soon as the hurry of work was over. Corn through this region very good. At Greenville it is known by scouts that Hardee has left for Arkansas, & is near Doniphan with a force variously estimated. Passed Big Creek nearby which we Bivouacked at Six PM, five miles from Big Lick, & fifteen from the supposed location of Talberts Camp.[10] Started at 9 PM & traveled till 1 AM & Bivouacked at Days farm just deserted by its people. I slept here on the wagon without cover a couple of hours. The boys mostly lay on the ground by their horses. Started at daylight, men feeling some sore & stiff from fatigue. Road mountainous, Rocky, & little used. Broke one of our wagons, & leave it. Our next stream is Black River, country very little settled & houses through the hills mostly deserted. A new Guide joined us last night, one who has been driven from his home by Talberts men. Road obstructed by felled trees making progress slow. Our advance is now 8 oclock AM a half hour ahead of us. We could easily be all cut off by a small party in Ambush. After getting over the hills on the Black River Valley we pass two good farms where we get apples & peaches in abundance. Reached Black River at 10 AM forded it several times, & at 12 ½ oclock broke our wagon in the middle of the River. Our Lieutenant of the Guard then rode forward to find our Advance, & our Guards, Guides, Servants horses mules & all lay down to sleep. No guard is out as I know, & I (having one of my hardest attacks of

---

9. The Secesh would evacuate their homes and then return later.

10. Dr. Brackett sincerely believes that he is in the heart of the "war." The First Indiana Cavalry continues to protect its camp from partisans. The real war is about to happen in the East. Bull Run now being over, Major General George McClellan was building the Northern Army to over one hundred thousand men for a move south which would be extremely slow in coming.

sick headache) feel very little anxious about the matter either way. It seems that I feel as careless as the rest as to the result. Two & a half PM. Part of our advance return & report that they have surprised Talbert & his men two miles from the ford, killed two of his men, wounded one, took twenty Prisoners Forty horses & mules, all his camp equipage even to his Commission & southern scrip, & about forty guns. Our Boys broke & bent the guns about the trees except a dozen of the best which we keep. One of our Guides H___ by name shot one of the men & it is uncertain who shot the others. Bivouacked tonight at 9 PM five miles from Talberts Camp, on a deserted secesh farm where we find provant of all kinds plenty. Slept in wagon again. Men lying in all directions on the ground with the Blue heavens, Bright with glittering stars & silver Moon for their only cover & so on we went & returned here last this morn at about 1 AM. I slept again in the wagon with a Guide & the boys took their tents already spread for them, & the hot coffee, & soft Bread was ready for us through the thoughtfullness of our cooks who heard us on the Mountains a half hour before we came. We were fired on frequently after night but no one hurt.

Now as I am tired I will close by wishing you all love & a kiss for the children each.

7 Oclock PM. Since I wrote the above, which I intended as a copy of my notes taken while we were out, but which I did not wholly transcribe I have been engaged moving our Hospital Quarters to a more pleasant location. I occupy now the house of a man who is a secesh Captain, his wife left & locked the house about two months since. It is a pleasant house with two large front rooms three bedrooms, kitchen & porch below, with hall, & two rooms above with closets & all convenient. I have taken the north frontroom & bedroom for myself, & Judge Moore who is Hospital Steward. The judge is from Warwick Co Editor of the Boonville Democrat, & Circuit Judge. He is over sixty years of age, & dyed his beard & hair in order to pass inspection. He went with us on our scouting expedition & was one of the first in the fray. It wondered me how he could stand it, nearly sixty hours in the saddle, yet he got through with less complaint than most of the others. We have a large number in Hospital on account of the fatigue. We took no coffee, & you may know how I stood it. I thought often of my good wife, & how soon a good bowl of strong coffee would be ready for me at home. Our cool milk house & its contents I wished for often. I found yes-

terday morn a crock of milk in a spring, & spite of thoughts of Poison used it. I had a teaspoonfull of sugar with me to sweeten a cup full & with a piece of Pilot Bread thought myself well off. It is now reported that we return to St Louis early tomorrow. If so I will send the letter & maybe follow it soon. We may be ordered on to Washington as Fremont is sending several Regts there. I presume a great battle must come off there soon. The people here fear much to have us leave. They say they have not felt safe till we came, & to think we would go fifty miles south towards the Arkansas gave them all hope in the Hoosier Cavalry. There is no doubt that we did a good job . . .

I have been taking my board here at no regular place, eating now with a mess in camp, & now at a tavern. Today I dined with the Brigade Surgeon[11] at his quarters But I get no where as good fare as at my own home . . .

There is nothing like sleeping in open air to make sleep refreshing. Two hours last Monday night laying across the tops of a couple of barrels of Pilot Bread in the wagon with only my shawl thrown over me appeared to be plenty of sleep. I think tonight instead of sleeping on the floor in the house I will lie in the mule wagon as I have for a few nights past. Insects of Divers kinds are so numerous in these houses that one can take little comfort sleeping in them. The further south one goes the worse they become.

I will now look to the sick & perhaps write more before I sleep. I left at the Hospital at St Louis John D Ball, a son of Calvin Ball of Newark in our County. He is in a Missouri Regt of Cavalry under Colonel Merrill. He was brot to the hospital at midnight with the cholera morbus. I recognised him & after he was able to get about kept him as a nurse in the hospital as long as I stayed. I did what I could to get him a leave to go home, but do not know as he got it.

The sick ones are all asleep. I find that nothing does more to restore those sick than plenty of rest, but my ideas are not considered orthodox, & we have some clashing of prescriptions. The Senior Surgeon is not here, but I have as an assistant a Scotchman, private in one of our Companies. We get on well together, as he is a worker all the time . . .

CB.

---

11. Not officially "Brigade Surgeon," since Colonel Baker had not yet been assigned to a brigade.

From the Journal:

Frid 20th—Moved camp back to Pilot Knob

Saty 21st—Two men of Nebraska 1st Regt shot by accident & brot to hospital.[12] Recd letter today from Capt Collins of 29th Regt Ind Vol. Answered same day—Young man died PM 3 oclock buried darkly at 9 PM Attend burial with Dr. Patterson. He was a most estimable young man, son of a widowed mother residing at Superior City. His last words were "I am going home now." The shot traversed right kidney, caput coli; then passed through left thigh of a comrade, & hit right thigh making a blue spot, then fell spent to the ground entirely uninjured. 1st Nebraska leaves at 12 midnight for St Louis. Leaving four patients in my care. I get breakfast for them at tavern this morn.

Sund Sept 22—Slept cold last night on a French field cot I bought yesterday of Dr Low, Surgeon of Nebraska 1st. Sent Ironton paper to Louisa this morn . . .

Pilot Knob, Missouri
Monday Sept 23rd 1861

My Dearest Margeret

I want my Pill Bags mended; the Bottles not disturbed, but the Pocket Case I will not want. My case of Surgical Splints I want put in a good strong box. Let Culver make one strong & light with strong rope handles in the ends & on the top & sides Painted "Chs Brackett Asst Surgeon 1st Regt Inda Cavalry Hospital Department USA" & "C Brackett 1st Inda Cavalry Hospital Department" on the Pill Bags. I want the tooth extracting Instruments left in the Pill Bags.

I wish you would see Keith to have him write to Lazelle Noble for a pass to send on my Horses, the Instruments, & Dave Edwards, & Little John as far as St Louis, & if you get the pass let me know, when I will send further directions. If I had known in the beginning

---

12. Friendly fire in camp! Several regiments are being kept around at Pilot Knob with the First Indiana Cavalry to protect from Missouri partisan raids. Another is the First Nebraska. This is a picket duty assignment.

there would have been no trouble about getting them passed, & now if I cannot get a pass I can charge in my bill for transportation so that it would amount to the same thing only that I have no sure way of getting the money to you to pay their expenses. It makes a great difference with the amt of my Pay having the horses & servants if I have all my pay will be over two hundred dollars pr month.

I want you to look in one of the middle pigeon holes in my desk for a commission as Surgeon or Ast Surgeon that I recd from Governor Wright of the State of N York. Let Keith mail it to me, & if he thinks best have it recorded so that if lost I can make proof of having had it. It will make about seventy dollars pr month difference in my pay. You do not write often enough. I look every day but am almost as often disappointed.

I have kept sixty dollars in gold sewed in my undershirt, part of my pay for the past month of August. I wish you had it, but by the next payday I hope to send you some Treasury notes that will be safe to transmit by letter.

I want Johnson to make me a piece of Blue Indigo Blue Cloth as soon as he can make it. I want an uniform & would like one of his or Jo Hannas make. Blue Cloth is wonderfully high. A full dress will cost near Two hundred dollars. I wear an undress uniform which only cost me ten dollars. You be sure have one of them make me from ten to twenty yards of finest stuff.

C Brackett

My Dearest Margeret

P.S. I enclose five dollars at a risk. You did not tell me of the recpt of five I sent from St Louis.

[The following was enclosed with the above letter.]

I enclose this to let you see the Prices of uniforms & generally poor stuff at that; this is a letter written to the Asst Surgeon of the 1st Nebraska Regt that left here day before yesterday. They had two of their men shot the day they left one of them is now under my charge, the other shot through the kidneys died a few hours after the shot.

It was hard to see the poor fellow die so young. He was the youngest of four brothers all in service, & sons of a widowed mother living at Superior City. He recd the morning of his death a long letter from her exhorting him to be a good boy, & brave; that she hated to give him up, but that it was best to be ready always for the defence of his country. His last words were "I am going home now." I attended his funeral at night & It brought to my memory the lines written on the burial of Sir John Moore who was killed at the battle of Corunna in Spain I believe. One verse is thus

> "We buried him darkly at dead of night
> The sods with our bayonets turning
> By the struggling moonbeams misty light,
> And our lantern dimly burning."

Thus we buried this young man the moon was just rising in the East its light strugling through the broken Clouds. I shed many tears over his grave for his poor mothers sake. Once more Dearest God bless you & the dear children all.

Charles

P.S. Write as often as you can & I will endeavor to let you hear often from me. When you see in the papers an account of the battle of "Black River" or "Talberts Camp" it will give you an idea of what I believe I wrote you before I was in CB.

[*Letter enclosed*]

New York, August 2, 1861
Dr Wm McClelland
Omaha City

Sir

Yours of 20th July is at hand—we enclose business card of our Army tailor—with request that you would answer the question propounded which you can easily perceive are important for well fitting garment.

The following are prices of articles ordered

Coat $28 Pants $12 Vest $6.00 Shoulder Straps $5 Epaulets for Surgeon rank of Major $32.50 Asst Surgeon Capt $30 Sword $25 Sash $15 Belt $5. Sword knot $2 50—Uniform Hat for Surgeon $14 Asst Surgeon $13—Forage Cap complete $5.00—We can send cheaper epaulets if desired.

The Coat, pants and vest will not be the most expensive but good goods and *well* made—We can forward the goods in from 2 to 3 days after your answer Is received

Very Resptfly
Warnock & Co.

★ ★ ★

IN HIS JOURNAL ENTRIES for September 24–27, 1861, Dr. Brackett complains of illness, and mentions that the sick have begun to receive a "comfortable" diet.

★ ★ ★

Pilot Knob Missouri Thursday Sept 26th 1861

Dear Wife

Troops are daily coming in & going out on the cars. Our boys are out day & night, bringing in prisoners at almost every trip. It is however a trivial business seemingly as most of them are sworn & sent home, & generally are worse than before as they have less fear of us. Our loss at Lexington[13] gives us the blues especially as many think it might easily have been avoided. I think it is all for the best as Price now there will be surely taken with his whole command unless relieved by McCulloch. There seems now but little fear for this place though I think that diversions of troops to other points might turn Hardee's attention again this way. I have no doubt from my own observation that he is better informed of our forces here than I am.

Last night about this time (9 Oclock PM) we had quite a little excitement;[14] we heard some shots fired down at Ironton (a mile & a half below this) & then the drums as we supposed beating to arms. As a matter [of caution?] I had the Hospital lights all put out, & the attendants to go & make observations. I stayed in the Hospital, & the men soon returned reporting all quiet. We have not yet learned the cause of the alarm but presume that it was some firing on our Pickets.

Here where anarchy, ruin, desolation, & death have come upon the people from their own neighbors there is some just ground of complaint. Crops destroyed, stock driven off, houses burned, & men women & children shot down at their own hearthstones have been matters of everyday occurrence, & no idle tales. The worst of these

13. Confederate Major General Sterling Price (1809–1867), ex-governor of Missouri and at that time commanding the pro-Confederate Missouri State Guard, determined to root out Northern sympathizers. He beseiged Lexington on the Missouri beginning September 12, and eight days later Colonel James A. Mulligan of the Irish Twenty-third Illinois Infantry had to surrender.

14. The Missouri State Army (pro-Union irregulars) fight the Missouri State Guard. The First Indiana Cavalry has no part in this except to witness the devastation.

traitors have however had the tables turned on them, & have fled in dismay. The ride of the Indiana Cavalry fifty miles through the country of the worst of these outrages gave me a fair chance to see, & learn what an attempt at disunion has brought upon the people of this region. The secessionists of Missouri are as a class no worse men than the secessionists of Indiana,[15] & of Fulton Co. The same opportunity there would have been followed by like scenes of houseburning & murder. Talberts men that we routed on the Black River would compare favorably in appearance, & manners with the anticoercionists of Fulton Co. The same class of half bred lawyers, Pothouse Politicians, with the Rabble of ignorance & malice make the mass of the ungodly horde. About the same in all the states . . .

Charles Brackett

Saturday 28th 6 Oclock AM.

I have been unable untill now to write. I feel better this morning than I have for some time past. The greatest trouble is with our cooks who are taken from the ranks & our officers take them away whenever the caprice takes them. We have the best of cooks in the ranks & are entitled by law to one for the Hospital. Yet the mass of our Officers ignorant of their newly assumed duties do not in all cases do just as they ought. This is to be expected, & the less grumbling about it the better . . .

You said nothing whether Albert had a Regt formed or not, or whether Jas was going with him.

Write soon & often & believe me ever yours truly

Chs Brackett

Pilot Knob, Iron Co., Missouri
Sunday Sept 29th 1861

Friend Frank[16]

As I have the afternoon of this pleasant day to myself I will employ the time in writing you a few lines. I have been troubled most of the time since I came into Camp, with the Camp Diarrhoea.

---

15. Dr. Brackett refers to the "Copperheads," Knights of the Golden Circle, or just southern sympathizers, of whom there were many in Indiana.

16. Francis K. Kendrick was Charles's brother-in-law, married to Margaret's sister Anna Wilson.

It did not make me sick enough to give up till after a trip we made from Ironton onto the Black River, forty miles below, to break up a camp of Hardees men in numbers variously estimated from one hundred to two hundred & fifty, under the command of a Captain Daniel Talbert a terror to the whole country . . .

[Action of September 16–18]

We reached home the next morning at about 1 Oclock AM having ridden all night. We were fired at from the hills & ledges of Rock that bordered the Road but no one was hurt except one of our horses was shot by a horseman that we tried to take, but he escaped, how I do not know for it seemed that he must have been shot for there was a perfect storm of bullets sent after him. Our foremost man would have caught him had he not shot his horse, he turned in his saddle, our man about ten paces behind him, & fired running stopping our mans horse by a bullet through his neck. Some of the boys followed him on a bye path after that more than two miles.

That ride I think brought me down, as I have not been able to mount a horse since, & for three days was hardly able to sit up.

If I am able to get about much before leaving this I will express to you some geological specimens amoung others that would interest you most & of which there is plenty here the magnetic oxide of Iron. with some peices of which you can pick up a whole keg of nails so strong are its magnetic powers. You may let Culver have a peice when I send it . . .

C Brackett

St Louis Wed Oct 2nd 1861

Dearest Margeret

. . . I am writing now from Esqr C Colmans office N E corner of Fifth & Chestnut Sts not far from the Planters House. Mr. Colman was from Cherry Valley N York, an old acquaintance . . .

You talk of my using your letters to light my cigars. I smoke no cigars. Since I had such a severe attack of Piles I smoked the pipe for its medicinal effect with much good resulting. I never gained strength so rapidly as within the past two days. I came here from Pilot Knob for medicines, Hospital stores, &C. The climate about

Pilot Knob is bracing & extremely healthy. Our men gaining rapidly while there. I do not like the air about St Louis. At the Knob the hills are almost solid Iron ore. The whole chain is called the Iron Mountains; in some places the ore is of the magnetic variety so much so that when you lay a gun or sword on the ground it will stick there with some force. A peice of the ore as large as your fist will lift up several pounds of nails in a string. I will send a peice one of these days.

The streams are said to be stocked with speckled trout, & I hope to have some leisure to fish while there. John & Dave could have fine sport fishing If they were with me. If Dave can't come I believe John could come by himself, but I will try & come after them soon.

I found at our camp here a good many sick. They are taken good care of getting all that is necessary for their comfort.

I think I told you that our regiment was divided, one half here under Col Baker the other half at Pilot Knob under Major Gavitt. We hope to be reunited soon, & until then I will not be able to get home.

The morning commenced rainy, but it is now clear & very warm. Bad weather for the sick.

Our General Fremont has gone on to Lexington to try & repair the loss sustained there.[17] We have wonderfully bad success from many causes, the chiefest of which is the lack of arms, & may be much is from lack of experienced Officers. There is not of that love of country evinced which I had expected from them mostly. They are made up in too many instances from small fry politicians. Yet we expect almost miracles from our Commanding General, & I fervently hope our expectations may be realised. Yet I must confess that I fear much with all my hope . . .

Do you know anything about Albert's Regt whether he has it full &C. I have heard nothing about him, or the rest of them since I left home. I have been expecting that when his Regt was full it might come to this Department, but from hearing nothing of it either by the Papers or otherwise I have thought that he had met with poor success.

I notice that I have commenced my letter on one sheet, & have

---

17. Frémont, under investigation for spending money without War Department authorization and in high disrepute, was trying to fend off disaster by restoring his military reputation.

written its continuation on another, but I will fill them both out at the risk of becoming tedious. The news of camp life is about the same thing day after day. At the Knob we get good milk, & butter the only things that we need specially except what Government furnishes. We get the best sugar cured hams I ever ate. In fact I eat almost exclusively raw ham, while sick. We have potatoes plenty, sugar, coffee, tea, bread, pork, rice, vinegar. Other things that we want we have to buy. Our Hospital fund enables us to get such other delicacies as the sick require. Everything requisite for the sick & convalescent we have. Occasionally for a few days, our regular rations are delayed by moving, or a failure on the part of the commissaries, & quartermasters in attending to their duties. On the whole we have nothing to complain of. The men getting better attendance, when sick, than they could at home, & when well wholesome & good food in abundance. There is now a proposition from Gen McClellan, under consideration to furnish rations of tobacco. This would be a good thing, I look upon tobacco as being as necessary as tea or coffee. In truth men accustomed to it are nearly worthless deprived of it.

Hoping this may find you all well, with love to Grandma, Kendrick & Anna, & that you may write often I am ever truly yours

Charles Brackett

DR. BRACKETT RETURNED TO PILOT KNOB on October 4 by train and was reunited with the First Indiana Cavalry on their outpost duty. He hears rumors about distant battles, but is pessimistic. These are Union victories under Generals Blair and Samuel Curtis, not Frémont. At the beginning of the war, many officers and men were led to believe that Southern civilians were really pro-Union.

Pilot Knob Iron Co Mo
Monday Oct 7th 1861

Dearest Wife

. . . I am now boarding with a Methodist Clergyman by the name of Barth for the sake of quiet & better nursing than I can get in camp. I commenced day before yesterday, & feel already the Advantage of it, in an increase of strength, & improvement generally. I believe I told you that a severe attack of piles was the greatest difficulty following & accompanied by a vexatious camp diarrhoea.

It is a pretty location where I board up the steep hill a few rods back of our Hospital, & commanding a fair view of the whole valley, & village & all the entrenchments & batteries except a couple that are masked by bushes.

We hope that Col Baker with the rest of the Regt will join us today, if so there will be a strong probability of my coming home for a few days, but you must not be expecting me so that diappointment will come to you. The Paymaster is down, & I will send you my monthly after I get it, if I do not bring it. It must be sent by express as far as Plymouth. I will send to the care of Chs Reeves, & direct him to forward it to you. Will you have your pigs in the pen fit to kill by Christmas; they will make very nice pork. I wish you could have some of the small sugar cured hams that we get here. They are as tender & sweet as when first killed. Each one is tightly sewed in canvas which is white, or rather yellow washed. If you can have all the pigs in fair order you better preserve the hams in that way. The recipe for curing is the same as that I use except that you take eight lbs salt to the hundred of meat. Thus meat 100 lbs, salt 8 lbs, sugar lb i, saltpetre oz iv. After the hams are cut in shape rub them well with dry salt for a few days, let them drain clear of blood a couple or three days then either put them in a pickle of the above ingredients for a few weeks or rub it in dry; then smoke, canvas, and whitewash before the weather begins to get warm in spring. Then further to be absolutely sure of saving them pack them in boxes with charcoal. Maybe I can be at home to help you at this but if not we will hope that I may help eat them next summer. I would not winter any but the large sow, the spotted one. Kill all the rest. You do not say whether you have had the threshing done or not. Better have it done soon as possible. It wastes in the stack.

How would you relish the idea of removing to St Louis? I can make very good trades for St Louis property. Dr Patterson has just brought in your letter of the 30th ult. You are doing as well as could be expected, & comfortably I hope. The hay makers, that is one part of them I expected nothing good of, & if they have not stolen it all they will probably before spring unless you keep things under lock & key you will loose more than when I was at home . . .

I should be much pleased to see you here, & if I supposed that we would remain here even for three or four weeks I would send for you. You would be much benefitted by the trip, & I am sure that I should be not less so. Mrs Barth just brought in an excellent grape pie, which Dr. Patterson & I have been eating. I find the grapes cooked are very advantageous to me. I am not so particular about the seeds as I used to be, I can eat all now with good relish. Their astringency is not only of benefit to me medicinally, but it suits my palate. With all my sickness my appetite has been good . . .

The Officers wives from Evansville were most of them at St Louis. They stayed in Camp, had been there about a week, & were intending to return home today when the balance of the Regt intended coming down here.

I am glad you are seeing to the making of the blue cloth, as I prefer that of home manufacture. It can be sent directly here by express from Plymouth or Peru. I hope to find one of Kendricks cheese in the package when it comes. I was too unwell while at St Louis to sit for my Ambrotype, you will get it one of these days. The weather is exceedingly pleasant, the air clear, bracing, & cool.

Night before last we had a heavy rain drenching everything in the tents. Yesterday one of our cannon commanding the Greenville road was spiked by some bold secessionist; this strengthened the idea which is prevalent here that we are about to receive an attack. There is a force of nearly two thousand men at the Mingo Swamp a few miles from the scene of our little skirmish on Black River forty miles below. This Mingo Swamp is between Greenville & Cape Girardeau on the Mississippi River. If attacked I do not think we will be found napping; yet I cannot say that I feel as safe as if we had Officers of more extensive military experience. They are all brave enough however, & what they lack in skill may be made up in bravery. It was a bold deed in some one spiking a thirty two pound gun almost in the midst of our entrenchments, & it shows that the enemy are perfectly acquainted with our camp. We are all very anxious about Fremont. There is so much grumbling about him from men high in rank, & our losses at Springfield[18] and Lexington following each other in such rapid succession give us good grounds for belief that treason & imbecility both have places in our midst. Yet the masses are right, & it may take many sad losses on our part to bring out the right men to conduct the war to a perfect restoration of the government. An end that will come whatever reverses may happen to us.

---

18. Frémont would be removed within two weeks of this letter. However, rumor and lack of information cloud the picture. Springfield is a minor skirmish; casualties light.

Our Brigade Surgeon, Dr Stephens of St Louis, has his head-quarters at Ironton (a mile & a half below this). His wife & family are with him. He is a very gentleman in all respects, he has been for twenty years a resident of St Louis, but he says that he does not know that he is worth a dollar in the world. All depends on the success of our arms. Dr McDowel one of the wealthiest men of St Louis is in the Southern Army.[19] All his St Louis property is confiscated, sol-diers occupying as barracks his splendid college buildings, such are the fortunes of war. We must not complain if our lives are spared to each other. Let our secession friends sacrifice our property if they will; a better day will dawn upon us if we live to see the end of the war. Kiss the children all for Pa. Love to friends, & many many kisses for my beloved wife

Chs Brackett

P.S. I will send some fresh seeds of Persimmon Plant in garden half inch deep cover with leaves, & brush & mark place well.

Pilot Knob Iron Co Missouri
Saty Oct 12th 1861

Dearest Wife

. . . I am gaining slowly: for the past week have been boarding with a German minister of the Methodist Church south. It is a pleas-ant place, as pleasant as any I can find here. Unless I gain faster next week I shall endeavor to get an absence on sick leave. I know with my Margeret's good nursing I would gain faster, & my good children to wait upon me. Many times each day I sigh for a bowl of cold milk & nice bread from the hands of her I love best. It seems as if a bowl of milk from the new milk house, with bread prepared by my own Dear Margeret, with the children to stay by to see when I want more would strengthen me more than all things else that could be fur-nished in Missouri, or anywhere else than home. I am writing with my paper resting on my lap, with no rest for my arm, & elbow. This will account for its irregularity . . .

You will hear from me again in a few days if I live, & am well. The bal of our Regt arrived from St Louis today, but I have not seen the Colonel; There is only one thing that will now determine me to get a leave of absence, that is the condition of my health. I thought

---

19. Support was probably fifty-fifty in St. Louis.

that the expence of going home better be dispensed with, but I shall incur it if I get no better. Getting my pay regularly, & keeping well I could in a few months ease off all our debts. My accounts must be made in notes I do not want to rob my family any longer, or be preyed on by those indebted to me. Let them give notes if they cannot pay. I am entitled to interest, as I pay it to those I owe.

Let people understand this. I have been always too easy suffering imposition upon imposition, but it is time now that this way of doing business should be changed . . .

your Affectionate husband Charles Brackett

From the Journal:

Tues 15th 6 AM—Am less weak this morn, than since I was first taken sick. Morning beautiful; neglected my morning prayer, but now return earnest thanks to the God of Love for the health & blessings He confers on me one of the least deserving of all his children. Recd letter from wife of 8th inst in answer to mine of 2nd inst. All well at home. Jeff Thompson[20] reported coming in on Farmington Road. Two Regts sent out to meet him. The train for St. Louis is returned from near Mineral Point where our men guarding bridges have been driven back with some loss. Wires cut, & bridges burned. Expect an attack here tonight. Many wounded of Normal Regt brought in by rail. Four of our companies went out last night to Potosi where we hear now 5 PM there has been hard fighting since daylight. All very quiet here. The stillness preceeding the storm.

Wed Oct 16th—All quiet yet here Col Baker not in from Potosi. Only Big River Bridge burnt so far as certain—Some Indians reported by guard to be with attacking party. Our guard drawn into ambuscade. We wait impatiently to hear from our Colonel. Has returned 3 PM with six prisoners, & six horses Major Gavitt starts with six Co's for Fredericktown on which road last night & this morning we lost six of our pickets. All quiet here yet. Cars in from burnt bridge mail from St Louis all right.

---

20. "Swamp Fox" Jeff Thompson, an extraordinarily aggressive, hard-riding, hard-drinking, hard-fighting cavalryman, was being seen everywhere, because he now had two brigades, one of Missouri state troops, the other of Arkansas state troops.

Thurs 17ᵗʰ—Send letter to J H Stailey written yesterday. All quiet. No further fear of an immediate attack. 3 PM Scout in from Major Gavitt fighting hard thirteen miles out. Hospital moved to Millert's Tavern. Have joined with the Surgeons of the other Regts in one general hospital.[21]

4 ½—Reinforcements from St Louis just in, messengers say fighting hard, but retreating slowly toward town. All things now ready for wounded men cool & ready for the fight even those who are unable to go out of town.

6 PM—John Arnold finger shot off Co F. wounded four miles this side of Frederick. Sergeant McRannells [?] shot through left side. Other wounded not in. Another detachment of Wisconsin men now in all cheery.

Major Lunt now in with five companies. All safe at St Francis Bridge. Dr Paterson makes interesting report of fight, & his interview with Dr Gaulding of New Orleans & Dr G. S. Passin [?] of the Missouri Confederates. They come out with flag of truce to get their wounded. I have been on my feet all day kept up by excitement. Retire at 11 PM . . .

Pilot Knob Iron Co Missouri
Saty Oct 19ᵗʰ 1861

Dearest Margeret

. . . I put the letters all together yesterday. I have missed getting three of yours. Direct to Pilot Knob Iron Co Mo till further orders.

Tell Mr Long that I will pay him when I come home if you do not before. Tell him that I want him to make me another pair of Boots, for I cant get such as his elsewhere. If I make what I hope to out of my Commission my pay will be Two hundred & twenty-seven dollars ($227.00) per month. With this I will be satisfied. It is the pay of an Assistant Surgeon of Ten Years standing. This is for yourself. If I get home I can have a week or two to stay. I would come now if I had my money. The Brigade Surgeon says that I should have

---

21. Wounded were coming in from battles in Lexington, Jefferson City, and Springfield. Doctor Brackett had work to do. The First Indiana Cavalry remained out of the action, still camped at Pilot Knob. These are skirmishes, but they are taking their toll. Indiana regiments in the Greenbriar Valley in western Virginia and other outposting places in the early days of the war are also frustrated at the irritations of inactivity and Southern sympathizer harassment.

six weeks leave of absence. I contracted the Piles during our trip to Black River. It was a tedious ride . . .

Now for the news. We have been fighting Hardee's advance forces under Jeff Thompson at & near Fredericktown on the St Francis River for three days.[22] They first Burnt the Big River Bridge & destroyed the Telegraph & then marched in force from Frederickton six thousand strong with five Rifled Cannon. The Indiana Cavalry three hundred & Hawkins Mo Cavalry fifty men went out by night drove in their Pickets & they retreated over the Bridge. Our men were all right under their Battery of five Guns but the Fog was so heavy they could not see us.[23] As it cleared up Major Gavitt ordered a retreat & our boys just got out of Range of the Guns as by a miracle; then seeing our force so small by day light, they again pursued. We retreated as fast as horses could run four miles till we met a thousand of our Infantry & two pieces of Cannon. Gavitt immediately made an ambuscade, & led the Cavalry into it, but before they got to the cannon they saw our men in the bushes & turned to flee.[24] There were of the Rebel Cavalry about four hundred & though they were not fairly in the ambuscade before they received our volley which killed thirty of them. If our men had lain a little closer we would have killed & taken all; then it was their turn to Run & run they did clean back to Frederickton, leaving the Road strewed with men Blankets horses & saddles. How many were wounded we do not know but of our wounded only two have died. Had they such guns as ours nearly every man of ours that was hit would have been killed some thirteen in all, but their little round bullets of the old fashion with poor powder they have made but small wounds, while our heavy minnie balls weighing an ounce killed or mortally wounded every man we hit. They shot first rate, hitting our men

---

22. Hardee never fought "under Thompson," of course, though Thompson was ranging through the area sometimes with or near Hardee's troops. William J. Hardee is an Old Army Regular; Thompson is a sort of free-lance Missouri trooper. Hardee organized and led an Arkansas company early in the war before he began his memorable career, which led him to the status of lieutenant general in the last of Sherman's campaigns. He was not present at this time near Pilot Knob because he had moved on to Bowling Green, Kentucky to join Albert Sidney Johnston's army.

23. Elements of the fearsome Thompson chase off Federal scouting parties of the Federals bivouacked at Pilot Knob, including a few companies of the First Indiana Cavalry.

24. All of this is very much exaggerated, typical of soldiers' comments about brief skirmishes early in the war. Thompson's instructions from Price were to make war against U.S. government property.

about the head & face & breast. Capt Hawkins horse was shot with thirteen Rifle balls yet was able to come home; the Capt was hit several times but not hurt. He got a rebel horse with the Pistols taken from his two Pickets (taken by the Rebels two nights before). One of our Lieutenants is dying now. He was struck over the eye with a ball that run round under the skin & lodged in the nape of his neck. He kept his horse during the whole fight laughingly saying "they could not hit him in the same place again," & though he looked like an Indian from the blood flowing freely over his face, he kept fighting wiping the blood, as it filled his right eye, flowing over his brow. Sergeant McReynolds shot through the left breast kept his horse till he had executed the order (in doing which he was shot, then rode up to Capt Heinman gave him his Pistols said he "had no further use for them", then fell from his horse, but thank the Good God he will get well. Dr Casselberry took out the bullet, which lodged against his rib breaking it, & prospects are fair for him. I could not but shed a tear for him so brave & no complaint he took my hand, & I told him that his wound I did not think mortal he smiled pressed my hand & went to sleep. It is not so a Coward takes his wounds.

Dr John S Gaulden of New Orleans Brigade Surgeon of the Arkansas Brigade, & Green S Passin [?] Surgeon for the Secesh Missourians came out with a flag of truce after their wounded men; they came out about a mile from Frederickton where Dr Paterson (the Scotchman I told you about) was with Hawkins wounded. The Doctor ordered them to halt, which they did, then went in looked at the wounded asked for some whiskey (of which they said we northerners had almost entirely deprived them); they were sorry that the two sections were at war, & told the Doctor that they hoped to meet when all should be peace again; They forgot their errand & went back without any further search for their wounded. They said they had lost sixty, but they had run off to the mountains for at that time we had only shot a few Pickets of those who were furtherest out. The ambuscade was made after that & four miles this side, or five.

We have reinforcements of men to the number of seven thousand with light Artillery plenty, & I think an attack is meditated for the morning early. I shall take a spring wagon & go out with them if they go, & the next news will be that Jeff Thompson with all his force are prisoners in our hands. That is if we have the luck we expect. If we make the attack we will start this afternoon so as to be upon them by daylight; then if our other column is in the right place we will have them in a net from which is no escape. Write soon.

Charles

P.S. . . . I have a comfortable place to board with the Preacher. Searjeant Wilsey Rooms with me; his health has been poor since the "Black River Fight" & at my suggestion he came here to recruit. It is about a half mile from the Camp & Hospital. With many kisses I am Dearest ever your Affectionate Husband

Chs Brackett

Sunday morn Oct 20th

We did not go out last night on acct of Orders to wait for the rear force to come up from Cape Girardeau (as I suppose). I have a little story for the children.[25]

When the excitement was highest, & our men of Indiana were retreating, or falling back, & report said that we must be defeated. A long train came in with the Wisconsin Eighth Stalwart brave intelligent men, brim full of fight, On they came, & such cheers you never heard. The Wisconsin boys jumped off the flat cars, & forming rapidly they started at double quick time for the scene of action, unfurling their beautiful silken Banner with a bundle of gilded arrows across the staff, a pet Eagle as soon as the banner was flung to the breeze, flew to his perch on the arrows over the flag, & as the soldiers hurrahed the noble bird would spread his wings as if he understood the whole matter. It is a noble bird that the men have taught to take his place on the banner, & spread his wings whenever they cheer. This noble Regiment with this noble bird coming just as they did infused the best spirits in our boys, & made all feel safe except the secesh citizens who before exultant, now were downcast & sad; perfect types here of the secesh in Fulton County. News good for the Rebel cause makes their faces all smiles, & they run together like so many swine to a corn pile; but news of an opposite character gives them all the blues, & soured, & snappish with elongated faces you can only get from them a surly grunt.

I wish Lyman could be here to see the nice encampments white with snowy tents, & enlivened by the soul inspiring music from their martial Bands. I went to sleep last night with soothing strains (of

---

25. There are many legends about "Old Abe," the mascot of the Eighth Wisconsin, but, in fact, his wings had been clipped repeatedly since his earliest days.

Hail Columbia from a good brass band just below the house) soft-ened & tempered by the distance, bringing soft sleep to my weary, lids. There is much of pleasure, & comfort with all the horrors of war, & I would like much to have my boy brought up to a camp life, at least so long as I am out in the field. There are many boys of not many more years than he has with their Parents in camp. The boy I told you of at St Louis is with Col Baker well clothed, fed, & cared for . . .

I send the last paper (St Louis Democrat) you need not be un-easy at the news it contains. We are safe unless a large body of Price's men & Rosses Indians make an attack from the west. I know Ross the Chief. He is well educated & I dont believe the news of his join-ing the secesh.[26]

C.B.

THE WOUNDED WERE COMING into the hospital from various units that were in Missouri skirmishes like that of Fredericktown. Dr. Charles hears stories about distant battlefields. He is shocked at the realities of battlefied or skirmish casualties, an attitude often seen in the early days of the war. Soon most men—and doctors—would necessarily become inured to suffering and death.

Pilot Knob Iron Co Mo Sunday Oct 27th 1861

Dearest Wife

. . . Our killed of the 21st amounted to only six (6), & wounded fifty-eight (58) The Rebels had killed about three hundred. The Catholic Priest had a list (day before yesterday) of two hundred & ninety he had seen buried, & more have been found dead. Some would be shot through leg, or arm & get off a mile or two before dying. The hogs eat some of their dead. Men who had taken the oath

---

26. John Ross (October 3, 1790–August 1, 1866) was Chief of the Cherokee Nation for almost forty years. He was the son of Daniel Ross, a Scotsman of Loyalist sympathies who had settled among the Cherokees in Georgia at the close of the Revolution. His mother was also of Scotch ancestry, but was one-fourth Cherokee. The Cherokees were forcibly removed from their lands in Georgia in 1838, and settled in Tahlequah, Oklahoma. At the outbreak of the Civil War, Ross sought to keep the Cherokees neutral, but in October 1861 was forced to sign a treaty of support for the Confederacy, which he repudiated in 1863. He was always a Northern supporter and officer. Whether Dr. Brackett actually had met Ross personally or only knew him by reputation isn't clear.

here were among the number partly eaten by hogs. Men, & boys were among them from all parts of the country. Some from New York. They (the Wounded & Prisoners brot in) cried like children. Their wounded will almost all die. They are shot by the minnie ball which in all cases makes a fearful wound.

Our wounded will nearly all get well. Major Gavitt & Capt Heignman fell leading one of the rashest charges ever made by men. Of the Forty (40) who were in the charge on the cannon, Thirty fell dead & wounded plenty of them were cut in shreds (as to their clothing) and their bodies not touched. I told you that Sergeant Wilsey roomed with me at Mr Barths; the sergeant was sick but rode in the foremost column of four & he alone of the front & second column was unhurt. All the rest fell. his horse had five bullets through him, & his clothes were riddled with balls. You may judge . . . Two thousand men lay in the fields in ambush.[27] The road is not more than thirty feet wide & in front was the battery of four cannon the balls from which cut trees clean off, as large as my body. These cannon were firing on our boys, & when they were in the ambush two thousand rifles, & shot guns opened their deadly fire on them some at a distance of not more than sixty feet & you may know how thick they were in the fields from the fact the Illinois Infantry flanking them in the field at the left of the road shot ninety (90) before they could get out of the field. Think of it ninety men killed in one field & that a small one from the fire of two or three companies. Forty of these men were shot through the head, & with skulls split open, & Brain thrown out some of them lived on the field two days, & one is yet alive in Hospital. Their Colonel Lowe was shot by a minnie which split his skull leaving his brain bare & clean—but enough—make me a pair warm pants, some drawers, & the rest I will tell you about when I see you. You better get the accts home & mayhap you can post them; but if not I hope to help you at it before long . . .

Your affectionate husband Charles

27. On October 15, Jeff Thompson's partisan cavalry operating out of Fredericktown attacked the Iron Mountain Railroad bridge over the Big River. When Thompson returned to Fredericktown he found that about 4,500 Union troops were closing in on him. First withdrawing, he decided to attack Union troops, ultimately along Greenville Road, where cannon lay in ambush (as Dr. Brackett reports, though numbers are vastly overestimated). Thompson put the number of his killed at 20, with 30 captured. Union soldiers said they buried 160 Confederates. Union forces probably had seven killed and 60 wounded. Thompson withdrew from the area successfully and Federals occupied and torched the town.

From the Journal:

Mond Oct 28th—Clear, pleasant, felt better than usual. Slept well last night.

As our troops marched through Fredericktown some secesh ladies reviled our soldiers saying they would come back in more haste than they went out, & they hurrahed for Jeff Davis. After the battle the house (a brick) from which these secesh had cursed our men was speedily burned in spite of all the officers could do to prevent; some eight houses were burned, & the rest were saved only by the officers representing that they belonged to good union men in our army, or that they were occupied by widows. The Soldiers were sure that the people had lied to them about the whereabouts of Gen Thompson & that they were intentionally leading us into a snare.[28]

MISSOURI PARTISANS HAVE INFLICTED CASUALTIES on the First Indiana Cavalry in the skirmish at Fredericktown. Oddly, or perhaps predictably in the confused situation at Pilot Knob, Dr. Charles picks up the general dissatisfaction over guerrilla warfare in Missouri and wants out. Like his fellow officers, Charles is anticipating that Curtis will drive the Rebels out of Missouri into Arkansas. But in order for this to happen there will have to be a pitched battle, which was not occurring.

Pilot Knob Missouri
Wed Oct 30th 1861

Dearest Margeret

I suppose that before this time you have expected to see me at home, but I shall not start before I am paid off which I hope will be in a few days. Our Regt is much demoralized since the battle at Fredericktown. Some of our Officers were killed & some wounded so that their places must be filled, & general dissatisfaction reigns supreme. I shall resign my commission having no wish to remain where so much clashing of opinion prevails. Whether I resign immediately or not I will be at home to visit you for a few days. I have

---

28. What seemed "lying" to Northerners was "patriotic protection" of the troops to Missourians. This was Rebel country. Jeff Thompson was their No. 1 hero.

a leave of absence for a month but cannot leave till the paymaster comes which I think will be soon. There is some prospect for me to get control of the Brigade Hospital. The Brigade Surgeon (Dr Chs Stephens) of St Louis is dissatisfied not getting his pay as he thinks he ought. He wants me with him & sent word that he should be up today. There are one hundred & ninety-nine sick, & wounded there. Plenty to do. I shall not accept unless it will pay, & in case I do will have you & the children to stay with me. I am tired of being away from my family. Money does not compensate for the loss of the companionship of wf & children.

And a residence here temporarily I will not accept except the pay is sufficient, & regular. I am willing to serve my country without pay either with musket, sword, or professionally. Yet I want while others receive pay to be on a par with them. On a par so far as getting paid for my work. There is much to find fault with, & it is an easy matter to find fault, & not so easy by a long way, to remedy existing faults, & further the more a man tries the Utopian scheme of perfecting the actions of his fellow men the more he will fail. The only way is to begin at home, there a man may do much with the divine assistance which will come to every man who seeks earnestly.

I am now getting heartier than usual, in many respects, though I have been excessively weak. We are having beautiful weather clear cool & bracing looking every day for a movement southward to the Arkansas line. We lost Jeff Thompson, & his crew from Fredericktown except about five hundred killed & wounded. Their wounded are all dying. Ours are all doing well. Our big balls seem to kill wherever they hit. Our men shot through & through get well without trouble. We lost in all only seven & about sixty wounded, while of their dead the Priest had a list of two hundred ninety buried, nearly as many were in Hospital wounded, but how many wounded have died since last Thursday I do not know. One of the boys of our Regt found his own cousin among the wounded Secesh lying on the battlefield;[29] the poor fellows cried like children while holding each other by the hand. The wounded secesh were all very penitent, but many would do the same thing over when chance offered . . .

Chs Brackett

P.S. Direct your letters to Pilot Knob Missouri, not to St Louis

---

29. Of Fredericktown.

DR. BRACKETT RESIGNED his commission on November 1, 1861, and returned to his home in Rochester by way of St. Louis, Indianapolis, and Vincennes.

★ ★ ★

From the Journal:

Saty Nov 2nd—Paid fare to Indianapolis 8 50 Start at 3 PM. Paid omnibus fare on board, & on car. Conductor Wm. H. Finkbine took it from me without ceremony, & as usual I let it go with few words. Very much of gentlemen some of these conductors. Arrive at Vincennes 10 PM Stop at American Hotel by Mrs. Clark. Paid at Everett 3.50 for one breakfast, & nights lodging. Wonder how much was made by leaving Valley Hotel for Everett? See & stop with Brad Brouillette over Sunday.

Sund Nov 3rd—Feel much better this morn none of that tired feeling of yesterday. Find Brouillette at home stay with him till night. Return to Hotel for Lodging, Breakfast for "Poor Soldier" as the Landlady said, only .75. Wonderful Patriotism.

Mond Nov 4th—Clear warm Pleasant. Diarrhoea this morn. "Poor soldier" again only pays .75 for bed & Breakfast. Had very pleasant visit with Brouillette. Mrs. Brouillette very kind; gives me Bottle of Blackberry Cordial which she says will make me "very much health"

> *Vin to Ter Haute* 58
> Ter H to Ind 73
> Surgeon Blair of 58th
>> St Louis to Vincennes 148
>> Indianapolis to Logan <u>70</u>
>> 349

[*Activities at home.*]
Saty 9th Amputat Toes for Jas Martin $10.00
Recd cash Heffley $1.00
Visit Wm Riell (?) Ind wife & boy 1.00
Sund Nov 10th Dinner at Kendricks
Mond Nov 11th Wrote Stailey
Govr Morton
Hon Wm H Seward

C Weicht Angola Steuben Co.
Colonel G. D. Rose
Jas W Brackett
Visit Miss Long $1.00 . . .

Pilot Knob Nov 15th/61

My Dear Doctor

You by this time are [convinced?] that I am careless, but we only returned to night from a 20 days scout in the Swamps. the trip was a pleasant one, without any accident. We took Green[ville] & Poplar Bluff without firing a shot, & our men & officers distinguished themselves with their usual bravery. the Charge on poplar Bluff was magnificent, not a drop of whiskey was left our Officers [ought?] to be [noticed?] particularly for their gallant conduct at the grocery. With what horses, prisoners, bed clothes the men stole . . . made quite [a haul] . . .

yours
Sincerely
J. J. Paterson

P.S. do not fail to write me

[*Dr. Brackett answered on December 12.*]

THE FIRST INDIANA CAVALRY PERFORMED scouting and skirmishing duties in Missouri and Arkansas throughout the remainder of the war, seeing action in the vicinity of Helena, Little Rock, and Pine Bluff. The regiment was mustered out on May 31, and discharged on June 22, 1865.

★ ★ ★

[*Letter from Charles's brother William, four years older, who went to San Francisco early in 1862 and remained there during the war.*]

Chicago Nov 25 1861

Dear Charles,

I understand you are home once more, after seeing something of the stern realities of War in Missouri. I should like to hear an account of your adventures & "hair-breadth escapes by flood & field," which, I have no doubt, have their serious as well as comical sides. Sometimes, I think this war is the hugest farce that ever was enacted, then again, I think it is something the most melancholy & calamitous the world has ever witnessed—so does our fancy "sway us to the mood it likes or loathes" . . .

Do you intend going into the Army again? I would not do it, if I were in your place, unless I were first surgeon in the Regiment. You ought to have the first place or none. I would not enter at all into this War, unless I had a place of both honor & profit. In most wars, if I went at all, I would go as a private.

Your aff. Brother
William

AS DR. BRACKETT TAKES A SICK LEAVE (actually resigns from the First Indiana Cavalry for reasons he describes in a later letter), his younger brother, Albert G. Brackett, completes the process of forming a regiment of cavalry at Camp Douglas, Chicago. Albert sheds light on the new regiment in a letter to their cousin, James S. Brackett, in Lancaster, New Hampshire.

Chicago, Illinois
December 4th 1861

To Jas. S. Brackett
Dear Cousin:

It has been years since I have written to you but you must not think from this that you are forgotten by me. William does the correspondence for the family & I always enquire of him how the various members of it are getting along.

My own movements are so uncertain and changeable that I seldom find time to write or get settled so as to live with any considerable degree of comfort.[30]

---

30. Albert was a professional soldier, away from home for many years. He was born in Cherry Valley, New York, on February 14, 1829. The last of the seven Brackett brothers, he was four years younger than Charles. Albert received a commission in the Army in 1847 and served with distinction in the Mexican War, after which he published the book *With General Lane's Brigade in Central Mexico* (1854). After a career as a newspaper publisher in Rock Island, Illinois, he rejoined the Army in 1855 with the Fifth (old Second) Cavalry, and served in Texas. When Texas joined the Confederacy he escaped with his company by steamship to New York via Key West and Cuba. Refitting his

I am now here as Colonel of the 9th Regt of Illinois Cavalry, & have a fine body of men, one thousand & fifty in number, collected to do such service for our country as we can. Brother James W. is Surgeon of my Regiment. Charles was Asst. Surgeon of the 1st Indiana Cavalry, but for some reason resigned. Another Brackett, probably one of Uncle Joseph's sons or at least a grandson is Captain of a company of Minnesota Cavalry. Our name seems to be doing pretty well in the present contest.

I wish you would send me a long letter, as I think you have more time to spare than I have, and give me the family news. Besides which you write a much better letter than I.

Tell me if your kind mother is still living & how many children you have &c. I like to hear about family matters, and hope some day to have a home of my own. In that case I shall expect to have you visit me with your flock.

Give my respects to all of our family, your wife in particular & believe me

your aff. Cousin
A. G. Brackett

DR. BRACKETT HAD RESIGNED instead of going on sick leave or leave of absence. Unschooled in the ways of the Army, he is surprised to learn he cannot be recommissioned in the First Indiana Cavalry. Having a brother commanding a regiment in a different state came in handy.

Rochester Fulton Co Inda
Decr 14th 1861

His Excellency Govr Morton
Dear Sir: By a letter from the Adjt Genl Noble of the 5th inst I

---

company at Carlisle Barracks, he was ordered to Washington, crossed the Potomac River with the first Federal troops in May 1861, and participated in the battles of Blackburn's Ford. His cavalry company was General McDowell's escort at the Battle of Bull Run, July 21, 1861.

He raised the Ninth Illinois Cavalry as Colonel in November 1861, as served with it for three years, afterwards assuming responsibilities at the brigade level. He remained in the Army after the war, serving in numerous commands in the West and contributing to various historical journals. He is the author of *History of the United States Cavalry*. He retired with the rank of Colonel in 1891, died on June 25, 1896, and was honored by burial in Arlington National Cemetery.

learned that by my resignation I had forfeited the right to be again commissioned in the volunteer army. I did not resign intending to leave the service, but having a sick leave for forty-five days (on account of disability incurred in a trip to the Black River in the expedition under Major J G Gavitt, I thought I would resign in order that our Regt might not be deprived of an assistant for so long a period, & also (having strong assurances of a promotion) that I might so direct affairs in regard to the sick & wounded as I thought best for their welfare. I was not allowed to participate in the operations on our wounded, & the only amputation of a leg (in our Regt) was performed by the Wisconsin Surgeon. This was too much for my State pride & I grumbled about it among other things; Dr Casselberry was also dissatisfied with me from some cause, intimated as much & importuned me to resign which (as I was sick at the time & had my sick leave) I was only too glad to do when I found we could not remain together without unkind feelings. He wanted another assistant & as soon as I found it to be the case, having a good excuse in my then disability from horseback exercise, I resigned my commission, not for a moment doubting that I could return to service as soon as health returned to me. Now I lay these facts before you that you may know that I did not resign to get rid of the service, but that in the words of my resignation "my Regt might not be deprived of an assistant by my absence, which from the nature of my disability might be of long duration, that I did not resign because I wished to get out of the service."

If by the order from the War Dept I cannot again be commissioned I wish you to understand that I have not resigned from a lack of Patriotism, & I took pains in wording my resignation to have that understood. I have spent the past season doing my best to prosper the cause of the Union, & if I thought I could not be put in a situation where I could do more I would do as I did last spring enter the ranks as a Private.

Hoping that my case may not be hopeless I await your action with much solicitude.

Respectfully

Your Obt Servt
Charles Brackett M.D.

CHICAGO, ILLINOIS
Ninth Illinois Cavalry

WHILE CHARLES BRACKETT WAS SERVING with the First Indiana Cavalry, his brother Albert had organized the regiment he had intended. It had come together in the autumn of 1861 at Camp Douglas, Chicago, and by January 1862 was ready and eager to head to "the seat of the war." It was at this point that Dr. Charles joined them. The original authorization for the Ninth Illinois Cavalry was given by Simon Cameron to Albert G. Brackett.

★ ★ ★

WAR DEPARTMENT, 6th August, 1861

Captain Albert G. Brackett, of the Second Regiment United States Cavalry, is permitted to go to Illinois, or any other of the Western States, for the purpose of raising a regiment of volunteers to serve during the war. Whenever ready, they will be mustered into the service by companies, and subsisted, clothed, and equipped by the United States. For this purpose a furlough of one month from the 10th inst. is allowed him.

[*signed*]
Simon Cameron,
Secretary of War

" . . . The first company to arrive at the rendezvous was Company A from Rock Island, September 15, 1861. Then followed B and C from Geneseo and Cambridge, Ill., D from Chicago, E from Logansport, Ind., F from Chicago, G from Valparaiso, Ind., H from Kewanee, Ill., I from Belvidere, Ill., K from Princeton, Ill., L from Chicago, and M from Onarga, Ill., and thus was gathered at Camp Douglas, three miles south of the Court House, and mustered into the volunteer cavalry service for three years or during the war, as fine a body of men as any in the army that helped to save our beloved country from disruption . . ." [Davenport, pp. 14–15]

THE REGIMENT BEGAN TRAINING at Camp Douglas in September 1861, and by the end of the year they were anxious to get into active service. Albert wrote to Governor Yates on this subject:

HEADQUARTERS CAMP DOUGLAS,
Chicago, January 10, 1862

To His Excellency Richard Yates, Governor of Illinois:
Sir: The Ninth Regiment Illinois Cavalry, which I have the honor to command, is now full and ready to take the field. I am most anxious to go into active service, and this feeling is shared by every officer and man in the Regiment. I would, therefore, most respectfully ask of you to telegraph to General Halleck, to move my Regiment at once to St. Louis or Cairo, or to such other point as you and the General may think best.
I am, your most obedient servant,
Albert G. Brackett,
Colonel Ninth Illinois Cavalry
[Davenport, pp. 20–21]

Saty Jany 25th 1862.
Headquarters Col Bracketts
Illinois Cavalry Camp
Douglas Chicago Illinois
My Dear Wife
I shall be unable to see you today as I promised from the fact that I spent the day yesterday in camp consulting with my Brothers who are all very anxious that I should accompany the Regt with

them. All are going except Wm who says that the southern confederacy must be recognized & maintained. That they cant be subdued with much other secession nonsense. He seems to be sincere all sincerity & no spark of Patriotism. Sorry I am to write this, but perhaps he is more sincere, & honest than others who thinking the same thing speak differently. I know that we will succeed.

I do not know yet what I shall do. Hospital matters in this Regt are altogether different from those I have elsewhere seen. I will not (if I go) be exposed as before, & will not go except as I wished to go, & this is the desire of the Colonel, the Doctor, & Joseph who is in the Quartermasters Dept . . .

I found Wm at the Richmond House where he is pleasantly situated. He had an oyster supper at his house - present all his brothers, Alberts wife, Her Brother Chaplain Briggs & wife. None others.

We had a very pleasant time I wished as did all the rest that you had been there, but it will be as well another time.

There are no particular directions except that you better pay Keith twenty dollars when you return, & do not keep any money about you except government money. Pay out other money instead of that. Our own State Bank Paper is also good & safe. I shall not if I stay be able to send home much money untill after my first payt. You know how the Colonel is in regard to the *appearance* of his Officers, & men & as they all come up to Regulations I will not be behind in this Respect. The Regt is the best appointed, & equipped of any I have seen, all in perfect order Barracks as comfortable as any home Hospital very comfortable, divided into wards, & away from the Surgeons quarters the length of the Parade Many officers are members of Churches even now in the next room Family prayer is going on by the family of one of the Officers.

Albert is a total abstinence man now, & I am truly glad to say that he is improved in all respects He would taste nothing of the liquors at Williams last night, & with his wife is more pleasant in every respect . . .

Camp Douglas Near Chicago, Illinois
Thursday Jany 30th 1862.

Dearest Wife

It is one week today since I came here intending to return on Saty following, but the best laid schemes gang aft aglee, & I am here yet, waiting anxiously to hear from you in answer to mine of last Friday the 24th.

It is very uncertain when this command will leave this place. Albert is now Commanding Officer of the Post.

I want the Colts sent up here; I spoke to Ward the Stage Agent & he said that he could take them to Plymouth & ship them on the cars to Chicago. It better be done next Tuesday Feby 4th. If you wish to keep the old mare do so, if you please trade her to the Scotsman Robertson for the watch which trade to Kendrick taking his note drawing interest from date. If I go which is yet uncertain I will send my clothes home with such things for the children as I may be able to get. I shall want you to come up for a few days if we stay here long, though we have a great deal of trouble through the marching among officers wives servants &c . . .

Love to GrandMa, & for yourself the kindest wishes of
your ever loving husband Charles

THE NINTH ILLINOIS CAVALRY was to be sent to Arkansas with Brigadier General Samuel Curtis's Army of the Southwest (Missouri and Arkansas), but they would not see action for many months.

Headquarters 9th Illinois Cavalry
Camp Douglass Chicago Illinois
Saturday Feby 1st 1862

Dear Margeret

Many weary days I have been anxiously waiting to hear from home, & during the time I have written twice to you. I write weary days. In most respects the time has rapidly passed for I have been quite busy. My Quarters are away from the Hospital, & I visit there morn, & night. I room with Joseph who is Battalion Quartermaster. Pay 138 dollars per month. Jas has good quarters but his wife is now with him so that I room with Joseph. The Barracks are very comfortable, & the Officers all keep at the same table paying $3.30 per week . . .

Albert is now Commander of the Post. He says if I cannot be recommissioned (on account of resigning) that he will continue hiring me as he now does at $80 per month, & $100 per month when in the field. Probably I will get a Surgeons Commission, in fact

I am quite certain that I can by going before the examining board of this state.

The Assistant Surgeon (Knox) has resigned & the acceptance of his resignation was read to the Regt this morning . . .

Doctor Gregg of R Island is Captain in an Infantry Regt lying next to us. Doctor McVickar whom you will recollect is Post Surgeon. He could not pass an examination before the state board of examiners, & then went before the board of examiners at Washington, & passed . . .

Our board is moderately good & the bill of fare of one day is a sample of all other days. Many of the soldiers have their wives with them they get along very nicely. They have quarters assigned them in the Barracks where in their own room they have almost the privacy of home, indeed fully as much as the tenants in the crowded tenant houses of the city have . . .

Headquarters 9th Illinois Cavalry
Camp Douglass Thursday
Feby 6th 1862

Dearest Wife

Your two letters of the 28th ult & 1st inst came to hand on Monday night or rather Tuesday morn Though suffering from a cold settled in my jaw, & eye I went to the Depot of the Fort Wayne Road & made arrangements for having the mares cared for when they came. Yesterday they were brot to camp none the worse for the ride on the cars. I paid six dollars for their transportation. I have not been out to the stables to see them yet on account of my cold which was rendered somewhat worse by my exposure on Tuesday night & day.

They have had several parties in town since I came here to which I have been invited, & particularly (by Albert & Martha) been urgently solicited to attend. Albert freely offering me the use of his wardrobe from which to dress untill such time as I may have an outfit of my own in military style—To this party given in honor of Col Paddock who was commander of the Post before Albert assumed the command they were specially urgent that I should go & our Chaplain Mr Briggs came to me Tuesday morn & wished me to take his wife under my charge, as he would be unable on account of sickness himself to go. So I went to the Taylor who is to make my suit, & got a suit for the evening, & attended the party which was a grand affair got up in the best style that the city could afford (at the Sherman House).

You would like Mrs Briggs very much. She is so perfectly free from all affectation, & withal the handsomest woman at the party that evening. Yet I wished often that one more engaging to me in all respects had been there to have enjoyed the pleasures of the evening. Martha payed you a very pretty compliment: at a time when some parties were praising the sparkling vivacity of her (Mrs Briggs) eyes, saying that Dr. Brackett would loose his heart & such like nonsense Martha replied by saying there was no danger as I had left at home a wife whose eyes would out dazzel those that they were praising. I had nothing to say on the subject, yet I thought Martha was wholly right, & I knew she spoke it from her heart. There now I find myself spreading on the flattery a little too thick, but when I assure you that it is only a rehearsal of mere fact I know you will be satisfied.

I intended to have kept one of the bills of fare which were on the supper table but lost it. About three hundred Ladies & Gentlemen were seated at the table. The Gentle all shining in the newest brightest of Regimentals, & the Ladies of course rigged in most fashionable style. We marched from the reception room up stairs to the dining room to the music of the Regimental Band; then marched several times around the room before seating ourselves. After supper Toasts & Speeches were in order Col Mulligan made a stirring speech in answer to a toast. Dr McVickar also made a very lengthy speech, & one not very well suited to the majority: it (the speech) was altogether too much proslave.

After leaving the table at midnight Dancing commenced, & as my partner did not dance, she, & Sarah (the Doctors wife) with a few other Ladies & Gentlemen spent the time in looking on & in conversation. Poor Sallie was very disconsolate she could not dance on acct of her religion & wanted the Doctor to go home with her; this he would not do so she left with Mrs Briggs (escorted by one of the Majors). Mrs Briggs had intended to leave directly after supper & so had I; but when the carriage was ready the Porters could not find my cap & coat. So I had to stay an hour & a half longer before it was found; by this time (after Two Oclock) the dancing was finished & all returned to camp well satisfied with the Party. I enjoyed it very much, the only drawback to my enjoying it perfectly was that you were not there to enjoy it with me.

I feel anxious to get off from this place toward Dixie Land where

I think is the proper place for Soldiers. If I have to be away from my family I want to be where I can be of some benefit in putting the rebellion in the quickest possible manner. Money does not compensate me for the loss of the society of my wife & children: however much I may have appeared to chafe at the prospect of staying at home during the war my home is dearest yet to me of all other considerations except only my country. Our free constitution once destroyed; our homes are rendered valueless, & our children & ourselves become the slaves of whichever military _____ has for the moment the strongest party with him.

Some of the time I feel almost discouraged & think to myself that I can be of no utility to the Government, & then again reflect the army that must subdue the rebellion is composed of units, & that the strength of individual members combine to make up the whole strength of our powerful army. I become cheered by the thought & encouraged to persevere against all obstacles till victorious peace shall crown our righteous efforts . . .

C Brackett

Headquarters 9th Regt Illinois
Cavalry Camp Douglass Chicago
Illinois Mond Feby 10th 1862

Dearest Wife

Yours of the 7th inst is just recd. It found me quite busy. My cold is better though it keeps me blowing my trump[et] pretty constantly. The mares came all safe.

Martha, & Sarah left last Friday; the prospect is that we shall soon move if so you will have no chance of seeing us. There is a possibility that this regt may not be moved at all; if so I shall go home. I am Asst Surgeon of the Regt with same pay as I had. The hiring arrangements was to cover accidents that is to pay me for staying till I could get an appointment. We will draw no pay till the end of this month. My uniform will cost me eighty dollars. Jas cost one hundred & forty. Mine will look just as well. We have a great chattering in the room, so I will wait till the room is quiet before I write further.

I have just had my dinner & now have the room to myself. I board at the mess house with most of the other Officers Jas has gone to a hotel nearby, because he says there are more women there. His ways are coarse & disagreeable to me in many respects. His profanity & coarse indecent vulgarity appear each day worse to me . . .

The [dentistry] work I saw in the city done by W J Lawrence is the best I ever saw. The teeth so reinforced by an extra rib of gold as to render them very strong; the improvement (of his own invention) very simple is of great extra benefit . . .

The women are leaving the camp with the expectation that it will soon be broken up. If I could know just when we were to leave I could then tell better how to shape things. I may want my pocket case, & large compact case of instruments with the splints. Tell Dave that if he wishes to go with me that I must know it by an answer yes or no. I can pay him Thirteen dollars per month & board him & find him in some other matters of necessity . . .

THE REGIMENT FINALLY RECEIVED ORDERS on February 15 to proceed to Benton Barracks, St. Louis, for final outfitting. "The start was made February 16th, the very day of the fall of Fort Donelson, which was that day surrendered to the then coming man, 'Unconditional Surrender Grant.' The movement of the regiment occupied three days, one battalion each, the Sixteenth, Seventeenth, and Eighteenth, via the St. Louis & Alton Railway. It required one hundred and thirty cars to transport the nearly eleven hundred men and almost twelve hundred horses, and the stores belonging to the regiment." [Davenport, p. 22]

★ ★ ★

Camp Douglass Illinois
Sunday Feby 16th 1862

Dearest Margeret

Your very good letter just reached me with this one from Stailey. I am to be commissioned by the Governor of this State as Surgeon; though I shall act with this Regt as Asst Surgeon for the present. I had my examination so that is all right . . .

Charles B.

From the Journal:

Start for St. Louis
Monday Feby 17th—Recd from Joseph $10.00 on way. Lieut

Col Paddock died on way at Bloomington

   Morn of 18th—(Tues) Breakfast & Dinner at Springfield 1.00.

   _____ at Springfield 1.00 Reached Alton & took boat to St. Louis

   Wed morn 19th—Returned on *David Tatum* to Alton with sick: Came down Wed night on *Meteor* Left Carpet Sack on *D Tatum*. Reached Benton Barracks Wed PM 19th inst. Lost one man overboard from D Tatum night of Tuesday. Meteor stuck on Sandbar Wed night. Dine .50

Benton Barracks Mo.
Friday Feby 21st 1862

Dearest Margeret

   Your very welcome letter of the 14th inst just came to hand, & was gladly recd. We left Camp Douglass on Monday the 16th inst, that is I with the first Battalion. The Colonel & Lieutenant Colonel were along. On Tuesday morning the Lieutenant Col Paddock died from cold contracted during our night ride on the cars. It was exceeding cold, & we were left on the Prairie in the night, the Locomotive having to go alone off for wood.

   Instead of getting through to Alton in fifteen hours (as is the regular time) we were thirtysix hours; the first night was exceeding cold & I expected many of the men would die. But the Lieut Colonel, to appearance among the heartiest, was the only one. We sent his body back to Chicago where his wife, & three orphan children will receive it. After many mishaps we reached St Louis safely. I then returned with the boat to Alton for a second load among who were many sick whom I wanted to care for. Also to see to the getting on of Jenny Lind, & Dolly [the mares]. Poor things they were over forty-eight hours without food or water yet stood it very well, though Dolly seemed some weak from her long fast. Night before last she, Dolly, was put alongside of a vicious horse & was kicked to death so she is gone. Jenny Lind is like a bird, about the brightest animal among the whole eleven hundred of our Regiment.

   The last (third) Battallion came in this morning, & all is bustle among us; We are rigging up a secesh house for a hospital A three story brick with hot & cold water to every room.

   At Alton I saw many Prisoners taken at different places in Missouri & in Kentucky Among them were Major Genl Tilghman[1] & Staff. The General is a noble looking man, & his Staff was also composed of smart looking fellows. The rest of the Prisoners were a hard looking set. Boat load after boat load of prisoners are continually arriving destined for various places in Illinois . . .[2]

GENERAL HEAD QUARTERS, STATE OF ILLINOIS
Adjutant General's Office
Springfield, February 22nd 1862
Colonel A. G. Brackett,
Commanding 9th Ills Cavalry,
St Louis,

Colonel:

Enclosed herewith I hand you commission for Charles Brackett Surgeon of Ninth Cavalry Regiment, Illinois Volunteers, which please deliver to him,

Yours, Respectfully

Allen C. Fuller
Adjutant General

From the Journal:

Feby 22—Lost Jenny Lind, taken from Stable yesterday. Wrote wife, & Dr. Patterson yesterday. Recpt to QMaster for Horse blankets 8 recd but 7 (seven). Mare Dolly killed in Stables Thursday 20th inst. Men without fuel, suffering from Rheum in Con. Report to Commanders & to Colonel. Missed celebration in town. Said to have been grand affair.

Quarters assigned No 10 Officers row Adjt Waterberry, & Hospital Steward S Miner room with me.

Feby 23—Six Cos report before 10 AM 45 men Take my break-

---

1. Brigadier General Lloyd Tilghman was inspector of Forts Henry and Donelson in Tennessee early in 1862, and did everything he could to prepare them in the face of Major General Ulysses S. Grant's advance up the Cumberland. He was captured after the fall of Fort Henry.

2. Many of these prisoners were Confederates also taken at the fall of Forts Henry and Donelson, an important Union victory earlier in February. Some would die while imprisoned at Camp Douglas.

★ ★ ★

ILLINOIS STATE MILITIA HEADQUARTERS

Springfield Ills. February 22^{d} 1862

To all to whom these presents shall come
Greeting:

Know ye that Charles Brackett having been duly appointed Surgeon of the Ninth Cavalry Regiment Illinois Volunteers, I Richard Yates Governor of the State of Illinois and commander-in-chief of the Illinois State Militia for and on behalf of the people of said State do commission him to take rank as Major from the 15th day of February 1862.

He is, therefore carefully and diligently to discharge the duties of such office, by doing and performing all manner of things thereunto belonging; and I do strictly require all officers and soldiers under his command to be obedient to his orders, and he is to obey all such orders and directions as he shall receive from time to time from his commander in chief or superior officers.

In testimony whereof I have hereunto set my hand and caused the Great Seal of State to be affixed.

Done at the City of Springfield this 22nd day of February in the year of our Lord one thousand eight hundred and sixty-two and of the Independence of the United States the eighty-sixth

By the Governor: Richd Yates
Commander in chief
Illinois Militia

O. M. Hatch
Secretary of State

Registered in Book A. Page 157
Allen C. Fuller Adjutant General I.S.M.

fast 10 AM restaurant .35 cts No news yet from lost mare. No coal yet for men in Barracks. Much suffering in consequence.

" . . . There [Benton Barracks] we received our first arms, a regulation sabre, and Colt's navy, and the Remington, revolver for each trooper, and about one hundred Hall's carbines." [Davenport, p. 23]

Benton Barracks near St Louis
Mo Sunday Evening Feby 23rd 1862

Dearest Margeret

It is now near 9 OClock. Joseph & our Quartermaster Sergeant are heating up the stove for cooking a can of oysters so while they are at work I will write you a few lines to pass away time. I am now rooming with the Quartermaster, & our room of Rough boards warmed by a coal stove is crowded with Saddles, Boxes of Boots, Shoes, Boxes of Nails & Horse Shoes & all sorts of Quartermaster stores.

James has rooms in the Hospital, an elegant Brick residence, Secesh, & I stay in Camp which is a half mile from the Hospital. I took dinner there to day, & had breakfast at a restaurant a half mile from the camp west. Part of the time I mess with the men & part with the Officers, not having any permanent quarters. It is all confusion here Regiments moving in, & out every day We will move I think next Wednesday the 26th inst; where I do not know. Direct your letters to me at Benton Barracks 9th Regt Illinois Cavalry, & it will reach me wherever we go. You must write often. Joseph just got a letter from his wife & little Mary. Tell Louisa that she must write; not mind how it looks; let me know how the stock gets along, chickens, turkeys, & pigs all is interesting that comes from home. Lyman must also learn to write as fast as possible so that I may get letters from him, & you must write for yourself & the babies.

Read the news of the battles to the children I want them to hear & recollect all about them. How our brave boys fought, bled, died, & conquered at Forts Henry & Donnelson, & how our Gunboats went up the Tennessee River into Alabama & found all the way thousands of Loyal Southerns who hailed the Stars & Stripes with wild delight. How Curtis has raised the Old Flag in Arkansas & how my Old Regt the 1st Indiana Cavalry cut down the Rebel Rag, &

hoisted the Flag of our Union in Doniphan where Jeff Thompson & his crew have so long held the people in terrible subjection. Let Lyman learn all this, & swear to himself always to remain true to his country, & when necessary be ready to shed his blood like water in her defense. I am sure he will never be a traitor to a good Government. "Tattoo" is now sounding, Drums & Bugles making the cheery call. After the lapse of half an hour "Taps" will sound when all lights must be extinguished in the Barracks, & when all must roll into their bunks.

I wish you could spend a week in camp with me, but at present it is out of the question; we may bye & bye be stationed where you can come & spend a while with us. You would like it much. Joseph has just set before me a big dish of oysters so I will stop for a while, though I may after eating be too lazy to write. I have seven horse blankets for my bed & sleep sweetly every night. I was presented with an elegant pair of white mackinaws in Chicago, but they are among the Hospital luggage which is yet unopened.

Oysters eaten: Quartermaster Price has just sent in word to Joseph to have the Company Smiths to put up their forges early in the morning to shoe all the horses; this looks like business, & without doubt we will soon be off. Jo is alive with excitement & is telling what he *will* do.

I would not be much surprised if our destination was for New Madrid by boat down the River, if so I will be again after Jeff Thompsons crew, & hope this time he will be bagged with his marauding crew. At any rate we will soon be among secesh, & as this is what all the boys have been praying for they will doubtless all be pleased . . .

Kisses for the babies, & a Kiss for you from Charles.

From the Journal:

Feby 24th—Six Cos report with 27 men on sick list. In Hospital six men. Fair, pleasant. Report says we are to leave Wednesday 26th inst. Recd pair shoes, & Pants from Quartermaster. Dined to day in Quarters on Tender Loin of Beef brot in by P Master Marshall—Excellent. After dinner put on woolen shirt bot of Sutler. My Carpet Sack with shirts being lost—pd for shirt $1.50. Very comfortable. Columbus taken, as report says. Take instruc-

tion in Sabre exercise. Make out papers for discharge of Sam'l P
Webb Co I.

Feby 25—Five Cos report 23 sick. Vist & prescribe for 10 others not reported in order. Cold, Cloudy. Made requisition for ambulances Transport carts, & horses for our Regt.

Wed 26th—9 Men of first Battalion (which left today) left,
whom I directed to post Hospital. Co A Capt Burgh left four men
Irving, Axtell, Rathbun & Fulham, with descriptive lists. The rest
had none. At noon find Killner, Co H, in back room of Officers
Quarters. Blind with Erysipelas. After much running got him a
place in post Hospital after night. Impress on commanders of
companies the necessity of making descriptive rolls of men left on
moving. Stay at Hospital. A stylish residence belonging to a secesh.
Very tired with my days work. Dr [James] stays out. Things all
packed, but no requisitions made for transportation.

Feby 27th—Cloudy, cool. Five Cos move today, with five yes-
terday leaving two in Barracks. No more sick on list; those of yes-
terday better. Went to town to attend to settlement of old accts.
Lawyer not at his office. Met Dr. Dodd veterinary surgeon at
Colmans office. Missed cars returned to Hospital after night.
Wrote wf & sent home cotton seed.

★ ★ ★

MOST OF GENERAL SAMUEL CURTIS'S ARMY of four divisions was coming
down from Northwest Missouri, pushing General Sterling Price into Arkansas, where he linked up with General Earl Van Dorn.

"Everything being in readiness in a few days, February 26th, five
companies of the Ninth left St. Louis by the Iron Mountain Railroad
for Pilot Knob, Mo., one hundred miles southeast. On the 27th, five
more companies moved out, and March 1st the last of the regiment
(having been obliged to wait the return of the cars from Pilot Knob)
were sent forward. Here we completed, as far as possible, the outfit
of the regiment, two hundred and four mules, thirty-four army
wagons, and general quartermaster's supplies. This being the last
outlying post, we here organized our mule train for the first time.
To the most of us, it was amusing in the extreme to see the men who

were detailed as wagoners and teamsters capture the mules in the corral; some had to be caught with a lasso, and then harnessed to the great army wagons, six mules to each." [Davenport, p. 23]

Colmans Office
St Louis Mo Thursday Feby 27

Dearest Margeret

As you see by the heading I have not yet left. Ten companies have gone to Pilot Knob, & with the rest (two) I will start for the same place tomorrow; that will bring me to my old range. I have not been in the city (till today) since the next day after my arrival here, & came in this afternoon to arrange my old account with the government. I hope to be able to get an allowance of about two hundred dollars. I have recd no pay yet. My commission came this week from Gov Yates, giving me the rank of Major;[3] though I shall for the time being continue acting Assistant Surgeon. I divide the pay with James who is acting Surgeon, thus giving one hundred & fifty dollars pr month instead of one hundred & twenty-eight which I recd before. I have had bad luck loosing both the colts; Jenny Lind having been stolen from the Government stables, & I have not much hopes of ever recovering her. I also lost my carpet sack with my clothes, & papers; this not from carelessness, but from an attentive devotion to the sick of our command; I left it on the David Tatum while I went onto another transport to assist the sick. So with all my loss I feel that I have done my duty, & will in the end not be a loser by it . . .

It is possible that I may go down to the Knob to night in a special train with the Colonel. Joseph went with the first Battallion day before yesterday when I ought to have gone, but to assist James I waited. We have all matters well arranged.

I send you a few seeds of the cotton plant. Soak in warm water twenty-four hours then plant in a box with garden soil, & keep in the house; plant them all as many are defective. It makes a very pretty house plant. be careful about frost; try & have a few plants of early cucumbers, & tomatoes; as I hope to take dinner with you by the

---

3. Charles has the rank of major; most surgeons started out as captains, while most assistant surgeons started out as first lieutenants.

fourth of July. Home is dearer to me than all else, & I hope will ever be, although I enjoy myself in the performance of my duties anywhere.

I hope the children will be attentive to their studies, though I wish them to take plenty of exercise, work, play, & go to school each in turn. Tell Lyman not to be about the horses alone & to be careful in all his play. I will bring home my boy a drum, a good one if I am well on my return; unless Chamberlain brought one for him (which I told him to do if he got some money from Wm which he thought he would have.)

I will send you some money when we are paid off, though probably not much the first month.

I am now wearing Government shirts & stockings which are first rate. I have also a pair of Government pants; these things I can get, having the amount stopped from my pay. The pants are very nice, & will save my dress pants which I will only wear on parade . . .

Your affectionate husband

Chs Brackett

PILOT KNOB, MISSOURI
Ninth Illinois Cavalry

★ ★ ★

DR. BRACKETT RETURNED, interestingly, to Pilot Knob and the camp of his old unit, the First Indiana Cavalry.

★ ★ ★

From the Journal:

March 1ˢᵗ 1862—Leave for P Knob 7 AM. Just above Irondale one of our men killed by falling from cars, of first Battallion. Taken on our cars. James Denney Co L Capt Booth. Died Feby 27ᵗʰ 6 PM Two hours after amputate left leg. Enlisted at Chicago. Says he has sister in NYCity. Clark Cr by Amt of Waybill at Planters House. Arrive at Pilot Knob at 1 PM. 1ˢᵗ Ind Cavalry just left. I find Capt Brown of the 1ˢᵗ yet here. Take Quarters with Post Quartermaster (Dr Dyer) very comfortable. Hosp [Steward?] Dr. Miner borrowed of Dr. Drake of 38th Illinois Qui Zi Acet. Morph Zi. Sub Zinc Zi. Tinct Iod Zi.

Rain with thunder & Lightning last night; the day foggy & damp.

Sund March 2ⁿᵈ—Wet, Cloudy; hard rain with most severe thunder last night. The bal of ours arrive this morn. Learn that Capt Hawkins is now Major. Col Carlin yet commander of Post. Visit sick in tents prescribe & administer med to twenty-four. Direct five to Post Hospital. Recd letter from wife with ambrotype of children. Ansd letter, & wrote letter to R Toland Argus. Cannot get meds for sick men except such as I have in Pocket Case.

THE NINTH ILLINOIS CAVALRY was now moving slowly down the west bank of the Mississippi in Southeast Missouri heading into Northeast Arkansas. Their destination is Jacksonport, a strategic town that controlled access to both the White and Black Rivers and was near a saltpeter deposit. It was a town that seethed with Southern partisanship. The armies of Curtis and Van Dorn were gathering for a battle in Northwest Arkansas.

> Pilot Knob Mo Sunday
> Sunday March 2nd 1862

Dearest Margeret

. . . Many acquaintances here have died since I left. Many left, & a few here. My Old Friend Capt Hawkins is now a Major, & a terror to Secesh. I am occupying a room with Doctor Dyer, Quartermaster of the Post. Every one of his family, here, is very pleasant. Two sons about twenty, himself, & wife. The rest of the Officers, & men of our Regt are in their tents the Colonel having issued stringent orders that all should begin camp life in earnest. The order is excepted only in my case, there being here no tents for me yet. Jas with his Hospital stores is not yet here. We had one young man killed, on our way hither from St. Louis, by falling from cars; he was a bugler, enlisted under a false name, & would have no word for his parents or friends before he died. A singular mystery hung about him, but poor fellow he payed dearly for some matter either of his own or friends: he fell from the cars at three Oclock AM, & was not missed till the next day; he rolled himself from the track, his legs hanging by strings only to his body & remained there during the cold rainy night till next morning, five hours, before he was found; he tied his neck handkerchief about the thigh and twisted it tight with his pistol to stop the blood, from loss of which he repeatedly fainted. Of fine appearance, & good education some dark mystery had driven him an exile from home, & prevented him from sending a single word of greeting to those he left behind. May my boy, & children so live that they may never be ashamed to own their friends & home, & may they with pride speak of parents untarnished.

The 1st Indiana Cavalry left yesterday about an hour before I got in. A few of the Regt were left behind; these few I have seen; they have gone to Greenville whither we will soon follow. They had a slight brush there a few days ago, a detatchment under Major

Clendenning being driven back by a small force, for a distance They lost only one man, & overrated the strength of the rebels, who were shortly whipped back by a small force of Missourians.

Write often I will close now by wishing you a good night, & kisses for yourself & babies.

Charles

Sunday evening March 2ⁿᵈ 11 OClock PM The wind is blowing cold & cheerless out, & I have just finished reading the papers, & not feeling sleepy will write you some lines more . . .

The Surgeon of the 38ᵗʰ Illinois was much surprised at seeing me as he said that he did not think I could live long when I left last fall. The past winter has been the most sickly of any for many years past, that is among the citizens of the place, many of whom have died. Carlins Regt leaves tomorrow for the South. Albert is in command of the post for the present. We will probably not be here long as they are hurrying up transportation; the day having been spent in breaking mules getting them ready for the wagons. In the Hospital Dept we have twelve Ambulances, & four transport carts for carrying our hospital stores, sick & wounded, &c. We number eleven hundred & fifty mounted men. This of itself is a small army. The cost to the government is enormous. Army movements are now positively prohibited from being published, & I am not permitted to write anything about our operations. This rule strictly enforced will do much to increase our efficiency & perplex secesh. Too much has been done in the way of informing the enemy of our movements. It is time enough for them to know, when we are upon them. The boys are (most of them) anxious to be at work though some seem to be more anxious for Quarters further *from* the scene of actual hostilities, saying that they would prefer being sent out to fight Indians. I want no Indian fighting till treason is all extinguished, then I want to return to my home . . .

Good night my Dearest Margeret Kiss the children for Pa, & believe me yours affectionately

Charles Brackett

SOMETIME BETWEEN MARCH 3 and 11, the Ninth Illinois Cavalry was assigned to a brigade of Brigadier General Frederick Steele's division of the

newly promoted Major General Samuel Curtis's Army of the Southwest. As the result of Curtis's March 7–8 victory over Van Dorn at Pea Ridge, the Confederates evacuated all of Missouri and Northern Arkansas.

Curtis with two divisions of six brigades became the army of occupation, as most of his army was moved east of the Mississippi to fight with Grant.[1]

"From Pilot Knob, Mo., commenced our first field experience March 6, 1862, and our march into Dixie began. As we wound our way on those pleasant spring days, how little it really seemed that we were actually in the enemy's country. The long line of cavalry, with their sabres and arms gleaming in the bright sun, the handsome standard of the regiment, the gay guidons of each company, then the long line of wagons carrying a large amount of ammunition, camp equipage, and stores, formed a picture long to be remembered.

"The first objective point was Greenville, Mo., and a train with supplies started in advance for that place, with an escort under the command of Lieutenant Blakemore. The remainder of the regiment soon followed, and arrived at Reeves Station on the Big Black River, March 13th . . . Reeves Station, where the regiment remained for some time, is fifty-five miles from Pilot Knob and thirty-five from the State of Arkansas.

"Here we were assigned to the Third Brigade of Gen. Frederick Steele's Division, serving in the district of Southeast Missouri. The Brigade as formed here was composed of the Fifth Illinois Cavalry, Colonel Wilson; the Ninth Illinois Cavalry, Colonel Brackett; the First Indiana Cavalry, Col. Conrad Baker (afterward Governor of Indiana); the Thirty-third Illinois Cavalry, Col. Chas. E. Hovey; and the Thirty-eighth Illinois Infantry, Colonel Carlin."[2] [Davenport, pp. 24, 25]

---

1. After Pea Ridge, the Second and Fourth Divisions of Curtis's army were transferred east of the Mississippi, leaving him with the First and Third Divisions only, a command of about sixteen thousand officers and men.

2. A "legion," a mix of cavalry and infantry. This is the brigade of Brigadier General William Plummer Benton of Richmond, Indiana, who commanded the Eighth Indiana Infantry at Pea Ridge.

From the Journal:

Mond 3rd—Cold, light snow. Carlins Regt leaves for South at 10 minutes before 11 AM. Go with high spirits. Twenty-two men on sick list—from Co A 8, Co E 10, Co H 4. Col Brackett Commander of Post. [Visited] Post Hospital at invitation of Brig Surgeon Burke. Patients well cared for: 12 of 9th there.

Tuesd March 4th—Cloudy, cold. Co L.G.E. & A report none in order, Twenty-seven men examine [?] fourteen other straggling in at anytime before [?] AM locate hospital in the Barth house on Hill. One man John Dolquist Co C shot sf through foot with pistol. Get goods up to new Hospital at top Sheppards Mountain where is magnetic ore. Found one family living in Ore cabin. Had some good specimens of ore: Return at sundown quite tired.

Wed 5th—Cloudy, cold. Twenty-three reported sick One of our Pickets shot last night through calf of left leg. was fired at by two men. Called to see him at 12 oclock & 15 minutes last night. Private in Co L Capt Booth. Name Wm Shepperd.

Thursd March 6th—Start with Battalion for Greenville. Bivouac 9 miles S of the Knob near the Sinclair farm occupied by a widow of that name. road today rough & [many] watercourses. Stay on Marble Creek. Sleep with some others at Widow Sinclairs on floor with Brackett & Yates.

Frid March 7th—After march of 15 miles Bivouac on Crane Creek Pond [Crane Pond Creek] Have sick headache. Major Humphrey takes care of me at his fire.[3]

Saty March 8th—Clear, beautiful morn. Slept well, with the skies for canopy. First night of my bivouac: feel uncommon well this morn; Camp near Wm Williams farm—near Crane Pond. Travel 10 miles today & camp near the English place. I have visited today some sick on the road. One soldier among them.

Sund March 9th—Cloudy warm Boy comes in camp with pies to sell. Says that they can get no salt or powder: that probably is the reason they are so peacably disposed. We tried to eat a pie that Charley Yates bot on road yesterday, but made without salt or shortening gave it up as a bad job. Start this morning at 8 AM,

---

3. Dr. Brackett did not seem to know that Curtis and Van Dorn were fighting the Battle of Pea Ridge in Northwest Arkansas. As a result of this battle, Missouri was lost to the Confederacy. Although Curtis didn't know it, that general was now in position in Northern Arkansas to take the entire state.

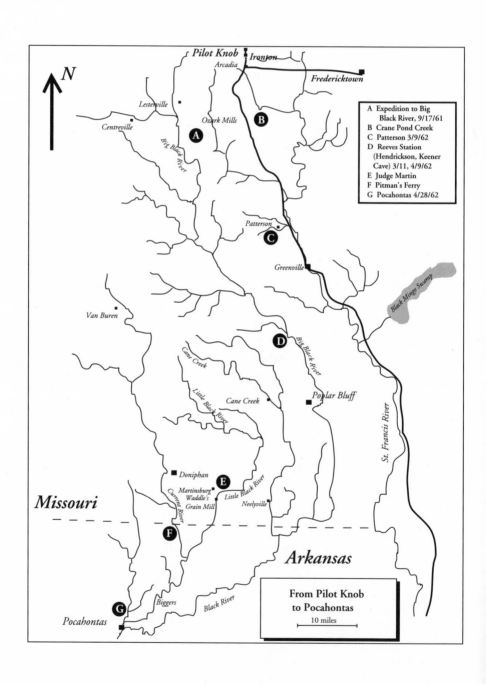

N

A Expedition to Big
Black River, 9/17/61
B Crane Pond Creek
C Patterson 3/9/62
D Reeves Station
(Hendrickson, Keener
Cave) 3/11, 4/9/62
E Judge Martin
F Pitman's Ferry
G Pocahontas 4/28/62

Pilot Knob Ironton
Arcadia
Fredericktown

Lesterville
Centreville
Ozark Mills **B**
A
Big Black River

Patterson
C

Greenville

Black Mingo Swamp

Van Buren

D *Big Black River*

Cane Creek

Little Black River Cane Creek

Poplar Bluff

St. Francis River

Doniphan **E**
Martinsburg *Little Black River*
Waddle's
Current River Grain Mill Neelyville

Missouri

F

Arkansas

Biggers *Black River*

G
Pocahontas

**From Pilot Knob
to Pocahontas**

10 miles

leave Sergeant Holton Co B Houghton (Orchitis). Pass through Pattersonville Wayne Co; bot tobacco of Dr. Black. ten cents for small leaf. Left sick in Charge Dr Jas L Wood. Take one of Hawkins men, who was left at Pattersons to Hawkins Camp— Stop at Maxwells on the Donophan road & pay for chicken shot by my orderly John Davison—Mr Maxwell says he had his horses taken by Hawkins men & his Gun—55 miles to Pitmans Ferry one mile below the Missouri line. Stop for the night on Otter Creek a half mile below Mr Joiners: Mr J is sick gave him some med . . .

AFTER PEA RIDGE the Confederate War Department virtually abandoned the Trans-Mississippi. Brigadier General Thomas Hindman commanded the Department; Brigadier General Thomas Churchill commanded the District of Arkansas with a single cavalry brigade of six regiments. Four companies of Arkansas State Troops (partisans) operated out of Little Rock. Van Dorn's entire Army of the West headed east of the river into Mississippi, as wounded soldiers trickled into Dr. Brackett's camp. Curtis sat in Batesville with Steele's three brigades (Northeast Arkansas), afraid of a rear attack from Missouri by the fearsome Jeff Thompson. Hindman sat in Little Rock with the state troops. Churchill stayed in Helena with his two Arkansas regiments of Confederate regulars, the First and Second Mounted Rifles. Curtis missed his opportunity to quickly move south. Meanwhile, his troops were sitting targets for Arkansas Rebel guerrillas.

Camp on Black River Mo
On Military Road to Pocohontas
Tuesday March 11th 1862

Dearest Wife

After an exceeding hard travel I take this the first leisure to write you. We are now on Black River a few miles below where we had the pleasure (last fall) of breaking up Talberts Camp, & report says that we have to make a fight with Van Dorn before reaching Pocohontas Arkansas. This may be so, & may not—Eight Companies of our Regt, with Hovey's Normal Regt the 33rd Illinois, & Carlins the 38th are on the south bank of Blk River. We have also one Battery of Light Artillery, & can give secesh a hard fight. Dr James & four Cos are back one day on the road. We are ferrying our wagons twenty in number with a crazy old scow which has sunk once this afternoon. I have one ambulance which is not yet over. In our own train we have twenty wagons each drawn by six mules, also six hundred & seventy two mounted men. We have had two shot on the way.

I took dinner today with an old Indianian Hendrickson by name. I had Joseph to go with me to his house. We had Fritters, maple syrup, milk, meat, corn & wheat bread, & all things that go to make a good Hoosier dinner.

I took today a Yellow Man for a servant from a N Carolina secesh, & he is not a slave though treated as such by the master; he was married to a slave woman & had quite a family of children, one a daughter with eyes as blue as mine. We had great difficulty to save his masters life & property from destruction.

I hope to write you when I have more time & a better table, (I am using my knee for one now sitting on the ground) for the last four nights I have slept on the ground with the broad heaven for my roof, except during a severe rain night before last when I slept in a tent. I was never in better health, & enjoy life as well as possible, hoping soon to return home with the conciousness of having helped to restore peace to our now distracted country . . .

I pitied the man we stayed near last night. Although rich in property negroes Lands, &c, yet he lived poorly & in dirt, worse than the poorest in our country—his own, & the slave children so mixed up that I could not tell the one from the other; dirt, & unkempt hair made all of one appearance as to color & looks. May the Good God preserve my wife, & children from the curse of living in a slave state . . .

HINDMAN SENT CHURCHILL'S other four regular Confederate Cavalry regiments (Third, Fourth, Sixth, Eleventh Texas) down to Arkansas Post to hole up in a Mississippi River garrison to be known as Fort Hindman. The four partisan companies of the First Cavalry Battalion Arkansas State Troops followed no orders from the Confederates, engaging in a brutal partisan war. Churchill ordered Colonel Charles Matlock's Confederate regular First Arkansas Cavalry Regiment Mounted Rifles to keep Steele busy at Jacksonport. (Dr. Brackett and many other Federal officers couldn't tell which Arkansas Rebels were Confederate and which were state troops.) Fearful of Thompson, Curtis used Steele's division (where the Ninth Illinois was) very cautiously. Fearful of Curtis, Hindman defended with Churchill's brigade very cautiously. After the April 6–7 Battle of Shiloh, both war departments would consider the Trans-Mississippi, especially Arkansas, to be useless to the war effort.

A major battle would be fought much later at Prairie Grove, Arkansas on December 7, 1862; this would be prove to be the closest Dr. Brackett ever got to heavy fighting. Except for Prairie Grove, however, there was not a single pitched battle fought on Arkansas soil between Pea Ridge and Arkansas Post; that is, between March 7–8, 1862 and January 10–11, 1863.

Camp on S Bank of Big Black River
Mo Thursday March 13th 1862

Dearest Wife

Yesterday we were ordered to the crossing of the little Black Twenty miles south, & were ready but the order was countermanded, & we must wait here for provision train to come from Greenville. This is vexatious as we are anxious to be traveling on to Dixie.

People have suffered here wonderfully but are patient, & hope for a restoration of law. Even the secesh (about one fourth of the population here) are tired, & sorry that an attempt has been made to disturb the harmony of the Government.[4]

I have seen several that were at the battle [skirmish] at Fredericktown, & escaped they have most exaggerated notions of the fight, & have been union ever since. They think now that the Yankees as they call all the union army, can do just as they please. The secesh here are *dirty* covered with vermin lying, cowardly dogs. The union men are the contrary, & if you wish to find a book or paper you need not go to a secesh house to find it. Men with a dozen negroes hundreds of acres of land, & cattle almost without number, & large houses, live in filth; have no cooking stoves, & their kitchens, & cooking utensils would put to shame the poorest among our people in northern Indiana. They are now more abject, & cringing than their negroes, & will obey the meanest order from the meanest union soldier, with more servile fear than you would think pos-

---

4. The population is mostly pro-Confederate. Many civilians told both sides what they wanted to hear, so that their property wouldn't be destroyed. Northwest Arkansas was pro-Union; Northeast Arkansas was not.

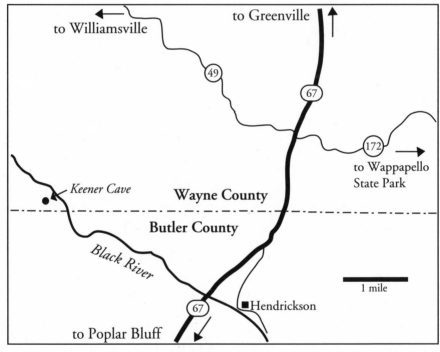

I have just returned from a visit to a singular cave two miles from here in the mountains . . . The roof was hung with beautiful stalactites of which I got many . . . [and t]here are many openings from the main entrance leading whither no one knows as it has not yet been fully explored . . .

After a rare opportunity to escape from his duties and do some "sightseeing," Charles Brackett described a visit to Keener Cave (*indicated in the map above*) in a letter to his wife dated March 22, 1862.

sible. Oh the chivalry, the noble southern Chivalry. So far they are a thousand times worse than I had ever supposed them, but perhaps Missouri does not afford a fair sample. The prisoners taken at forts Henry & Donelson (of whom I saw several thousand) are no much better.

I have just been in the River washing myself, & you may be sure I feel much better for the bath. One of the last battallion just in, in fording was thrown down the steep bank Sf, & horse, & went some distance down the stream before they could be secured. The weather is very warm & the soldiers are taking a general wash. It will benefit them. People are happier, & better in proportion to the amt of soap they use. Dirt & ignorance generally go hand in hand.

I think that if Lyman was here he would enjoy it; there is a little Logansport boy here, & a little girl about the size of Rosa. The father is a mule driver, & the mother a laundress; they are from Logansport in Capt Giffords Co. The little boy was sick yesterday & I met him today & he said "Doctor I must have a plaster for my side the pain is not out yet." The little girl does not talk much; they have the wagon for a sleeping apartment, & cook out doors. He is an old trapper, & soldier; trapped two years with Kit Karson,[5] & served five years in the regular Army, besides being in the Vol army during the Mexican War; he has been shot four times in as many battles, but is hale, hearty & able for any service yet. I think Lyman might want to see mother by times yet he would like to be with me. Dave missed it wonderfully, but it is too late now to lament . . .

Our Chaplain Briggs is in with the last Battallion.[6] He is a great busybody if reports are all true, & is making many enemies, by his foolish interference. I like him very well; in many respects he is an interesting man, but the fault of tattling is a despicable one. We are encamped in a piece of heavy timber a few miles below where we broke up Talberts camp last fall, & are on the ground then occupied by Hardees forces numbering seven thousand. The boys have fine sport killing squirrels which are very plenty. They are not allowed to shoot so kill them by shaking them off the trees. Many pay dearly for their sport by being bitten by the squirrels, who send their teeth to the bone every bite. They catch them often in their hands as they

---

5. Old Kit was the elderly (in his sixties) frontier legend who scouted for the Union Army in the Trans-Mississippi, mostly Texas.

6. Because it had not been involved in heavy fighting, the Ninth Illinois Cavalry was still large enough to be divided into three battalions, each of three or four companies.

fall from the trees. Turkeys, & Deer are plenty, & I expect to get some if we stay here long. My Indiana friend (Hendrickson) says he will bring me in one tomorrow. I have taken dinner with him twice. Yesterday Joseph, Major Humphreys, & I took dinner with him . . .

I have me a nice Sibley tent, which I occupy with my orderly (a soldier by the name of Davison). It is very large & comfortable, though I prefer in fine weather to sleep out. I had my hair, & beard cut today; Joseph says I look fifty pr cent better for it . . .

From the Journal:

Sunday March 16th—Vist at Log Hospital, Yenneke Co M in fever. Sturm Co C. pneumonia & Dyo___ Lt Thomas Co E. in fever, Dow Co E Diarrhoea & 9 others—with two to nurse & cook. Sergeant Rose Co L. has deserted, taking two horses as is supposed; the Sergeant was at first the loudest at praying &C of any other man in Regt, but lately the loudest swearer. Weather cool. Skies clear. Alexanders 21st Illinois arrives, with some Indiana cavalry. Island No 10 & Manassas reported in possession of our troops

Mond 17th—Clear Pleasant

THE ENTRIES AND LETTERS indicate that General Curtis or General Steele had posted the Ninth Illinois Cavalry all along the banks of the Big Black River. Since Colonel Albert has about one thousand troopers, it can be safely assumed that the regiment breaks down into many camps, with quartermaster's staff, medical staff, and commissary staff traveling freely from camp to camp.

Camp on S Bank of Big Black River
Reeves Station Butler Co Mo March [18th]

Dearest Wife

. . . I am in a very pleasant Sibley tent furnished me by the kindness of Quartermaster Dyer of Pilot Knob. I have it for my own exclusive use, & if I live till the war is over will endeavor to bring it home. For furniture I have a nice large field lounging chair as easy as a cradle. A half dozen boxes of md which I use for tables &c, a half hogshead to keep loose articles in, a pole laid across two forked sticks to hang my clothes on, & an empty barrel which I use to dispense mds on. I have a fire in front, & today all the blankets out on the brush to air. The sun is making the boys pull their jackets, & starting vegetation finely. We are now in the region of cane brakes, which grow here just of the right size for pipe stems. I am going to save some for Grandma. I had presented me a very fine Meerschaum pipe with an amber mouth piece, & nice case; this I carry in my pocket, & smoke occasionally I have just filled & lit my pipe since I commenced writing about it. Major Humphreys is just in & says that he has written to his wife that if he could only see her & the children once in twentyfour he would be perfectly happy, but that he looks at their likenesses, which he carries with him. Says May the Lord bless, & preserve them. I tell him that his is but the echo of my sentiments. My family is the most I have to think of & they are only from my mind when I am busy at my duties with the men. I am not home sick yet I pray the time to come when peace will allow me again to be with my loved ones at home. My tent fills up every few minutes with soldiers, complaining with cough, & other ailments, & I have to attend to them. I know how to pity sick soldiers, having suffered myself. We have one (a swede) that I am fearful will die. His wife is with him. There are a few women in camp, but the Col swears they all shall leave as soon as the men are payed off so that they can be sent. They make a good deal of trouble not allowing their husbands to attend to their duties. One (a Sergeant) deserted yesterday, leaving his wife who is expecting soon to be confined. Lieut Wilkinson is now in my tent, & wishes you to give his respects to A F Smith when you see him. The Lieut has been sick, but is gaining fast. I have just been out eating some bean soup, boiled chicken, & bread made in a frying pan (pan cake fashion). I would think it a bad bit of bread at home, but it tastes good here in the woods. Dr Patterson was over to see me this morning. The 1st Ind Cavalry, the 21st, 33rd, 38th & other Illinois regts are here on both sides of the River, & one Battery of Artillery. The Dr tells me that they killed the secesh Captain White, that I told you looked so much like me. He had retreated with his wife & two other women to the woods, where a few of the Indianians followed. He fired at them & they returned his fire killing him, & his horse. (So much for him) . . .

I am now writing in Joseph's tent also a Sibley; this with mine, & the Lieut Colonels make the only three in our Regt. Joseph has

his fixed in good style; I keep my papers all in his desk. I have no
trunk but will probably get one in the next town we pass through.
I told you in my last that Josephs wife was very sick; today he heard
from her that she was much better . . .

CBrackett

From the Journal:

Tuesd 18th—Cloudy cool—Co L 10 sick, Co A 2, Co B 8, Co
C 1, Co E 3.

Capt Stamposki Co F unwilling to excuse Jacob Hamilton,
who has diarrhoea, from duty—As Hamilton says.

At 2 PM dined with Capt Burgh Co A on Turkey shot yesterday by Lieut Blackburn. Excellent dinner. Mail letter to Wf in answer to hers of the 9th inst &C. One case of small pox in camp.
Recd letter from Wf of March 5th.

Wed March 19th—Wet during last night; morn cloudy.
O'Reilly Co L had prescription for Qui & morph & was given a
yellow powder which he said did him no good—Lyons Co L says
that his powders made him vomit & that his stomach is so sore he
can retain nothing. Prescribe for 43 sick at my tent & at the Log
Hospital. Mr Putnam DeWolf sick. I send prescription to the Hospital with following Recipe. "Flos Benzoin Jos XV. Three parts"—
H Steward Smith says to young DeWolf Co G that there is none. I
wonder? Reports of submission of the seceded cities, a flight of Jeff
Davis produces great rejoicing in Camp: possibly true.

Thurs March 20th—Morn breaks cloudy & cool Doctors
Casselberry & Patterson visit me this morn & make up party for
visit to cave to morrow.

Frid March 21st—Cloudy, cold. Four Co go out today foraging. Too wet to visit cave today.

THE REAR COMPANIES, including Dr. Charles and the medical staff, had not
yet crossed the Arkansas border with Generals Curtis and Steele. The Ninth
Illinois Cavalry was a *large* regiment, a thousand men and better than a thousand animals, plus the wagon train, so movement is of necessity deliberate.

Camp on Black River Reeves Station,
Butler Co Mo Saty March 22nd 1862

My Dearest Margeret:

I got a fine horse yesterday, & am likely to get pay for Dolly. We live finely. Our table is well supplied. Yesterday we got the honey from fifteen secesh hives; the old secesh tore out his hair by handfuls, & kicked about the chairs in his impotent rage; they are reaping now in the whirlwind, & the union patriots are having an easier time . . .

We are waiting here for our General Steele who will command the Brigade.[7] I had some acquaintance with him in our younger days; he is from Otsego Co NY. I spend the forenoon prescribing for the boys. After dinner take a short ride about the camps, get supper about dark, & before a rousing fire at our tent door Major Humphrey & I spin hunting yarns to a crowd of listeners who gather about our comfortable quarters, smoke our pipes, & about ten Oclock spread our blankets before the fire lie down to think of home wife & children drop off to sleep, & pleasant dreams, & awake at daylight refreshed, & strengthened for our days work; this is the ordinary routine of this camp. It is somewhat monotonous, only varied by occasional sallies of foraging parties who gather abundance from the secesh in the country about . . .

Our free man Dave is just in from a visit to his old master & his slave wife & children. I sent him there this morning with my orderly & Major Humphreys yellow boy. They brot in a couple of bushels of nice dried peaches (I wish you had them) & some cooking utensils; with other articles, useful in divers ways.

7 ½ PM I have just returned from a visit to a singular cave two miles from here in the mountains; at the foot of the cave a few rods from the entrance is a lake, deep, & dark. On the lake a canoe in which with torches to give us light I took a ride many rods into the mountain. We could not fathom the water. The roof was hung with beautiful stalactites of which I got many specimens some of which I will try to get home. There are many openings from the main

---

7. Brigadier General Frederick Steele, an officer from the regular U.S. Army, commanded a division of three brigades, not just a single brigade. After the victory at Pea Ridge, the Army of the Southwest had been stripped. Steele's full division of eight thousand men represented about one-half of Curtis's remaining force.

entrance leading whither no one knows as it has not yet been fully
explored, at least to my knowledge . . .[8]

yours ever Chs Brackett

From the Journal:

Saty March 22—Clear, cool, pleasant . . . Chs W. Chinweth
Co M died last night on river Bank. Sequela of measels. Visit cave
with a company of Officers: Find some boxes of Hospital Stores,
& an old saddle in field which I direct to be brot in to the tent:
One Box been opened & Bots abstracted.

Sund 23rd—Cloudy, cold, high W wind. Battal and Lieut Col
goes to Patterson. Maj Wallaces returns 10 PM from Current River

Mond 24th—Clear Cold still. Eight patients in Log Hospital
all doing well except L Storm the Swede of Co C & Talbert of Co
M.

Tuesday Mrch 25th—Clear, cold. Scout with five others to
Kitrells. Lieut Blackburn, Lieut Morrison, Charley Yates &C. Take
three prisoners, follow Kitrell two miles into woods, but do not
find him. Wallaces Scout to Current River Brot in fifteen prisoners
& same No Horses & Mules, & one White Jack. Lieut Blackburns
horse shot by Mr. Hill who intended to shoot Lieut - Wrote letter
for Yates. Took Breakfast this morn with Lieut Blackburn; had
venison potato, ham &C. Well cooked & well served. Louie John
Storm of Co C died about midnight from Dysentery, & Pneumonia. Patients all moved to Camp.

Thurs March 27—Storm who died on the morn of the 25th
was named Louis John Storm but on muster Louis G Storm. The
correct name I get from his widow. The day breaks clear, cool quite
warm by noon. Move my tent to River Bank. My orderly John L
Davison Co C, Paul Andersen Co C, Frank Holliday moved & put
up the tent: Major Humphreys also moves with me. Quartermaster Morrison of Battallion is also of our mess: make out certificate
for Lieut B O Wilkinson Co E for Sick leave for thirty days. Probably Lieut will not go as Capt is averse. Corporal M Peirce Co C
taken with fever with much cerebral disturbance. Am more than
ever disgusted with profanity so frequent among many from

---

8. Probably Keener Cave, off present U.S. Highway 67 on the south side of the Black
River. Not open to the public as of 1998.

whom better things should be expected. Day has been pleasant. Our new location for tents immediately on the bluff bank of the river is very pleasant, & much more convenient on most accts. QM Morrison brot in much leather from Kitrells: hope to get some for moccasins. Am wearing Major Humphreys. Most of the time. Munson Pierce Co C. Deranged.

SLOWLY BUT SURELY, Curtis was moving his troops down the Big Black, from Southeast Missouri to Northeast Arkansas, pestered here and there by partisans.

Camp on Black River (Reeves Station) Butler
Co Missouri Friday March 28th 1862

Dearest Wife,

As you see by the heading of this we are yet in our now old camp & so far as I know are likely to remain here; though Col Carlin says he thinks we may move southward tomorrow. My time is pretty much taken up by waiting on the sick & complaining of our Regt, though occasionally I get out into the country for recreation with a scouting party. I am going out with Lieut Blackburn, & twenty five men to take a couple of men who fired at the Lieut, & shot his horse a few nights since. They live about thirty miles west of this: we will start late so that by riding all night we may reach the house about three OClock in the morning. I have not yet got permission from the Col to go, but think he will grant it, though he has refused on several previous occasions; there is no probable danger in the expedition, & I shall go not only armed with a pair of good Navy revolvers, but also a long shooting Breech loading carbine with which by daylight I feel perfectly safe from any half dozen men armed with rifles or shotguns. If I go I will write you on my return, & this letter may not go till I do return. The General (Steele) is just crossing the River, this may interfere with our calculations; They are now firing salutes with the Big Guns, which make the very hills shake. The Eleventh Wisconsin came in last night: Our force when we move will consist of about fifteen thousand men,[9] with whom I

---

9. Dr. Brackett refers to the entire Army of the Southwest, divided into two large divisions. The brigades were being reorganized.

presume we shall move, through Pocohontas, direct to Little Rock (the Capital of Arkansas) . . .

The weather is beautifully mild though the rain from flying clouds is pattering on my well stretched Sibley tent, which I moved yesterday on to the river bank (a high bluff making a most pleasant location). I would like to have Lyman here; with my warm mackinaw blankets I could make him perfectly comfortable at night, & by day he would enjoy himself very much at the incidents of our camp life; I picked the first flowers of the season for you & Louisa some time since & have carried them in my pocket book ever since forgetting to enclose them to you. Now there are plenty, & I will enclose some for each of the children & for Grand Ma.

I found a copy of Hiawatha, & of a very copious collection of Irish songs, from ancient & modern authors. I miss the Bible you gave me, very much, but I hope it with all the other lost things will be found.

Read the "Famine," & the "White Mans foot" next to the last chapters of Hiawatha. The plant called by the Indians "White Mans foot" is the common "plantain" which only grows where white men have passed. The flowers I send you are of the "Miskodee(?)"

Read these chapters to the children, & when you read do so without reference to the metre; thus, "Peace be with you, Hiawatha, Peace be with you, & your people; peace of Prayer, & peace of pardon; peace of Christ, & joy of Mary." . . .

Our Regt is just filing past my tent I wish you could see them. The Wisconsin Eleventh is a crack Regt, & has better music than any other. I awoke at daylight this morning, & heard the "Drummers Call", then the "Revilee" played better I thought than ever I had heard it before.

Saty March 29th 1 OClock PM. I am yet here; the Col was unwilling that I should go out. The Lieut is not yet in; probably will not be till sometime during the night; having started yesterday at 4 PM. If he comes in before the Courier goes out I will let you know the result of his mission. We may be Brigaded with the 1st Indiana in one Brigade, & the Infantry in another. Scouts in from Pitmans Ferry report the roads almost impassable & that two Regts of Secesh crossed Current River yesterday & that they have a force there of twelve thousand. They have been so badly whipped lately that they are disheartened; but may give us a hard battle; this is not however probably. Most of the troops are tired of remaining here, & a change of location is desirable on most accts . . .

Chs Brackett

THE ADVANCE COMPANIES probably crossed the Arkansas border by the end of March, leaving Dr. Brackett with the rear still in Missouri for another three weeks.

From the Journal:

Tuesday April 1ˢᵗ—Pleasant, cool. Prescribe for forty-six, in tent, out patients—Private James Buford Co M Shot through second Phalanx forefinger Right hand by accident ? Dr. Jas W. is away & Instruments out of my reach & I do not know where to send for him: My instruments are over the River with Dr. Patterson so that I am forced to do up the wound with simple cerate till Dr. returns: Amputate at second phalanx at Articulation at 9 PM No ligature required. Ordered to Pattersonville with two ambulances to start at 7 AM morrow.

Wed Aprl 2ⁿᵈ—Clear, pleasant, high wind west. Rained hard last night

Get Jod Hudg & undershirt of Smith; for Capt Brugh get his invoices of QMBrackett. Left Blk River at 9 ½ AM & arrived at Pattersons at 4 PM 23 miles Took dinner with Joiner 10 miles from Black River. Examine at Hospital patients. Benj. P. Gallino Co L had Rubeola last Jany at Chicago. Bronchitis—Pulse 93. Irritation of mucous membranes generally—No of Pistol lent me by Bishop 119774. Cylinder numbered 9574—Give to QM for safekeeping. Discharge Wm E Earle Co K. & T B Butter* Also drop Hugh Beveridge

Thurs April 3—Pleasant, clear past night cold. Report to Col. & Surgeon acct of my doings to 11 AM. Send in ambul to Ironton Wm Earle Co K. Hen Woodbury Co L. John Mulligan Co K, Lieut J H Knox Co K—in all four, have six more to send to tomorrow, which will clear us of all invalids except two to stay till discharge papers come, & one Strong Co K unable to be moved.

---

* per Davenport's *History of the Ninth Illinois Cavalry*, the name is Thomas B. Batters.

Frid April 4ᵗʰ—Clear, pleasant. Sent seven men to Ironton— three yesterday—Five men sent down to be taken who had not been reported to me as sick: this disarranges all my plans—from Cos K, B & F—Lafayette Eving [?] Co L Thrown from & tramped by his horse S of Maxwells Found by Maxwell. I find him sufferinq from Concussion. Pulse regular 74 Pupils Dilated, & Contracted Alternately No Contraction below what would appear natural size for the light. Talks coherently of past matters. Occasionally acts as if still trying to relieve himself from pressure of hoofs of the horse. Fell during the storm, a slight thundershower. Dine at Maxwells— Excellent dinner—Peach trees in nearly full blossom. Take supper at Dr Blacks with Lieut Col Sickles. Large Sweet Potato Sweet Potato Biscuit, Fried Chickens, hot cake, regular good Virginia supper.

Camp at Pattersonville Friday
April 4ᵗʰ 1862

Dearest Wife

. . . I came here Wednesday by order of the Col to discharge some disabled men & to get all invalids at this post back to Ironton preparatory to an onward march south; this duty is done & tomorrow I shall start back to Blk River. The Paymaster is here, & I hope to send you some money (by express) to care of Chs Reeves Plymouth who will forward it to you. I enclose two dollars, for which I have no use here. You may find use for it . . .

I have worked hard today & am tired so will close by sending much love & many thanks for your kind letter & the Milainotype. Give the children many kisses for Pa & believe me ever your affectionate husband . . .

. . . The weather is beautiful Peach trees & flowering shrubs in full blossom. We have here sweet potatoes & everything good to eat. I took dinner at Maxwell's (a Virginian two miles from here) where one of our soldiers got hurt, & supper with a secesh Doctor (a Georgian) living in town. Roll call is sounding from the four Bugles of the four companies here.

The secesh pour into town every day in troops of ten & twenty to take the oath of allegiance.[10] I have found some who were in

---

10. Some take the oath several times during the war.

Talberts Camp last fall. One told me where he laid, & how he was tempted to shoot me from the weeds, but fear restrained him; he said he was so close to me he was afraid to run, & afraid to shoot because others he knew would shoot him. So he laid low in the tall weeds, & we were both safe. I saw a letter from Talbert to our Commander; he is in fear from one day to another believing that orders have been issued to troops to kill him anyhow, & anywhere. He writes in mortal terror & no doubt suffers all the pains of a cursed spirit; his guilt makes him fear "when no man pursueth" . . .

C.B.

From the Journal:

Saty 5ᵗʰ—Fair, pleasant—John Wifoat Co K. Shoot self ball entering about middle inner aspect thigh coming down, & lodging in calf about center outside—Cut it out this morning . . .

Sund March [April] *6ᵗʰ*—Clear, pleasant. Stayed with Mr Wm Patterson. Sleeping on a feather bed makes me feel lazy. Enjoy Virginia hospitality very much. Wm Slack of 5ᵗʰ Illinois Cav is sick here. F Lawson Co B who was detailed to drive ambulance from Black River left his horses at Pattersonville unfed & unattended told one of the men he "didn't care a dm what became of horses— Dodds Co I, & Wf, & Frank Allison Co L went to Ironton. Secesh say "wait till the leaves come & we can fix you" This even after taking the oath voluntarily; & for this they cannot be harmed, & so after committing the murder they may come in voluntarily, take the oath & must be protected in life & property by our army part of whom they have murdered, & all of whom they would destroy had they the power. Our hands are tied, we cannot molest, or make afraid any except, the man is actually killing one of us, & even then it must undergo an investigation. Secesh laugh [at] us & scorn & revile our Government as imbecile—The order of things, unless changed will protract the war indefinitely. 7 PM Dr Patterson, & Lieut Wilkinson in from Blk River. Break a bot of Bourbon for the Doctor. "For Auld Lang Syne" . . .

Camp Sickles (Pattersonville) Wayne Co Missouri
April 7th 1862

Dearest Margeret

    . . . Lieut Col Sickles (in command here) was ordered back to
Black River, & Major Humphreys sent up in his stead. I am also
ordered to return tomorrow. There are two companies here only.
Nearly all the secesh inhabitants here have taken the oath. About two
thirds have to make their marks, being unable to write.

There is now a better feeling among the people here than there
has been for a year past; all having sworn among themselves to obey
the laws & to protect each other; there are but very few here but are
glad our troops are here . . .

I am attending a young man a member of the 5th Illinois Cavalry Col Wilson. He has Typhoid Pneumonia; his father & mother
came down yesterday from Illinois to see him; he was gaining before
they came, but the excitement of their coming nearly killed him. He
is sick at Pattersons, & is well cared for by their family. I stayed there
night before last (Saturday night) the first time I have slept in a bed
since the first night of my getting into Chicago. As I have to get
ready for my morrows journey (23 miles) I will close perhaps to add
some more before starting.

Yours ever Chas Brackett

8 PM. I now have things about ready for a start in the morning.
Our escort will consist of about eighteen men besides teamsters. The
Asst Surgeon of the 11th Wisconsin will be with us. I came up with
only my orderly starting some time after the escort of twenty-five
men, but it is not safe & I shall not do so again. One Lieut was taken
today on the Road, or at least his horse was found shot, & he gone.
Also one of our soldiers is missing, & his horse found. There is no
safety for one man on the road, & foolish _____ should not allow
one to travel by himself. The Lieut was out to see one of the soldiers
sick at a private house. Our force is part of it now at Pitmans Ferry
in the edge of Arkansas. There was a force of secesh there but they
have fallen back to Pocohontas whither we are following them . . .
Good night

CB

From the Journal

Tues 8th—Cloudy warm. Get Free papers for Dave of Capt Booth. Col Wall of Doniphan killed a union man, & kept his head or skull (well cleaned) for a plaything for his children. Mondzeleski Felix orderly of Major Co F Stop at Maxwells to see L Irving Co L Sitting up but sore in head & chest. Stopped at Joshua Joiners to see his sick daughter, at 12 M. I have had sick headache.

Wed April 9th—Stopped last night 5 miles south of old Camp Rest moving. Thos Kay Co H. Piles, Incontinence urine, Piles. Stops & returns to old Camp Capt will send discharge Difficulty about kidneys five mos standing. Left at Sol Kitrells. Geo Prater [Prather] Co H. Chills. Left at Solomon Kitrell. Butler Co Mo Six miles South of Camp on Black River Reeves Station, on military road. Kays Pistol 119654. I take. Noon at Parson Eppes. Family deserted the house, & boys make themselves at home. Camp at night on Little Black Six Miles below Eppes. At Ponders Mill. Feed my horse at Wm Vandeveres, below the Mill.

Thursday April 10th—Cold, raw, cloudy. Slept in ambulance last night, used some Hospital Blankets. Dr Jas is very wrothy about it, says he will discharge every man that meddles with the Hospital blankets; that they must not be used till we get where they will not be dirtied. Dr R Holland four miles below Vandeveres invited me to take supper & stay with him tomorrow night.

Friday April 11th—Cold, Rainy. G H Sturm Co C detailed to drive two wheeled Ambulance by order of Col. Six men are down with disease mainly resulting from cold; are as comfortable as they can be made, remaining in tents. Our Hospital tents having been left at our Camp on Blk River from lack of transportation. Some Officers Complaining on acct of it. Had they been as mindful as perhaps they might have been of propriety, room for Hospital might have been made in the wagons. F Lawson Co B. took passengers from P Knob to Patterson Charging Fare, & leaving his horses unfed there. Wrote Wife, & sent to Louise secesh song "Run Yank or die".

AS THE RESULT OF VAN DORN'S DEFEAT at Pea Ridge in Northwest Arkansas, during March of 1862 the Army of the West evacuated not only all of Missouri, but also all of Northern Arkansas. All regular Confederate forces had already retreated from the area, except for one of Churchill's regiments.

Camp on Little Black River
Friday April 11th 1862

Dearest Wife

Our present Encampment is eighteen miles from the Arkansas line & eighteen below Reeves Station. Our Regt is scattered in detatchments from Pattersons to Arkansas, fifty miles;[11] we have troops above & below us all on the lookout for active operations; in one skirmish a few days since we killed five & took thirtyfive of Capt Tim Reeves, a brother of the Reeves who was our guide last fall to Blk River, & now an Officer in our Army, so you see it is brother against brother, Father against son.

Reeves men gave ours two volleys before we fired; they hurt none of our men, & only shot three horses. After our first fire they ran like sheep throwing away everything that would hinder their flight.

Kitchen with eight hundred men [partisans] is east of us hemmed in; so that he must cut his way through our lines, or be taken with all his command; we sleep on our arms, & believe we can hold him fast; but time must determine that.

I send you a secesh song that you may permit Mr Fuller to print in his Paper for the benefit of our secesh admirers, & as a specimen of secesh opinion of Yankees generally, Liberty, & Slavery. There are no secesh here they are all in favor of the "Old Constitution," & "Southern Rights." They say when asked about Northern Rights that they never have thought of that subject. They put northern rights, & negro rights on a par; i.e. neither have rights that a "white man" (a Chivalrous Southern) is "bound to respect" . . .

I was invited out to spend the night with a Doctor Holland, a Kentuckian living four miles from our camp in the edge of the great Mingo Marsh. The Doctor is a very gentlemanly man. I accepted his invitation conditionally, & as it has been raining a cold driving storm the whole day, did not go out. The Doctor is a very interesting man in most respects, & I would liked to have gone out, yet it is not

---

11. This statement has been true for a month; the companies of the Ninth Illinois Cavalry are strung out along the river, slowly moving south.

wholly safe, one of our men was shot while at a blacksmiths shop getting his horse shod, & two taken prisoners while eating their dinners at a farm house. These acts are done by scouting parties of marauders with which the country is infested. They never attack armed men openly, but sneak up & shoot one when unarmed, or off his guard.[12] I always take care to have one out watching, if I have occasion to stop at a private house for any purpose. I visit the sick in the vicinity of the camp, & we have occasionally one or two soldiers sick, or wounded at the farm houses whom I have to see. Our men are almost invariably well treated under such circumstances, & the more they know of us the better they like us . . .

I am writing in a cold tent. My own Sibley, & stove were left back at Reeves Station; but a train goes out early tomorrow, by which (on their return) I will get both. Our camp is in a narrow valley of timbered land. The hills on each side are rocky steep, & entirely destitute of undergrowth; the timber is mainly oak. A short distance east is the Mingo Swamp, mostly a cane brake with occasional islands of fine farming land. The cattle wintered in the cane are fat; from these we get plenty of fresh beef of good quality. Bear, deer, & elk are said to be quite plenty there, but it is dangerous hunting such sort of game now in that locality, where Kitchen & his men are on the lookout for Yankees. I saw a beautiful pair of elk horns, fully five feet in length taken from an elk killed there last fall.

It is now getting late, & my candle is almost consumed; the tramping, & snorting of the horses, the sighing of the wind among the branches, & the pattering of the rain on the tent are the only noises to be heard, even these are a sort of company. I make my bed tonight on a hand litter with some blankets, & will lie down bidding you good night & kisses for the children from Papa

Yours ever
Charles

[*The following was written on letterhead stationery with a portrait of General Wool.*]

Dearest Children

Louisa Lyman, Rosa, & Minnie I think you will love to get a short letter from Pa who thinks a great deal about you every day. I

---

12. Dr. Brackett is beginning to understand the ugly nature of guerrilla warfare.

Dearest Children

Louisa Lyman, Rosa, & Minnie
I think you will love to get a short letter from
Pa who thinks a great deal about you every day.
I saw to day the prettiest little negro boy about as
old as Minnie, he was a funny looking little fellow as
smart as a monkey, & he belonged to Mr Vanderen who
will sell him away from his mother when he gets big

saw today the prettiest little negro boy about as old as Minnie; he was a funny looking little fellow as smart as a monkey, & he belonged to Mr Vandevere who will sell him away from his mother when he gets big to pick cotton, or hoe sugar cane. Mr Vandevere will get money for him, & can buy with it some clothes for his wife, & other children. Don't you think that is funny to sell little boys & girls away from their mothers: but it is the fashion here, & people think it is all right. It makes the old negroes feel bad, & they think some time the Lord will assist them to be free so they can keep their little children, & have a home for them, & live with them all the days of their lives; they have an idea that they would love to live together where white men could not sell them apart. Maybe they are right: You must be good children, & thank your heavenly Father that you have liberty, to love & live with those you love during all the days, & years that you live.[13] Kiss Ma for Papa, & be careful not get hurt by going into the road to play. Do the Peach trees blossom yet? Write to Pa Good Night

AT THIS TIME the advance parties of the Ninth Illinois Cavalry were camped alone at Jacksonport on the Big Black River, serving as the Union occupational force, soon to be joined by Steele's other regiments.

From the Journal:

Saty April 12th—Clouds breaking: has rained most of night. Moving Hospital Stores over the River. Recd pay for Feby from Major 126 85. Have pleasant camping ground S of River below Mills. Our boys are running the mill grinding wheat & corn. Dr James W is very indignant that I slept under two of Hospital blankets. Swears he will discharge all Hospital attaches except Smith who he says is worth all the rest. I am tired of his vulgarity, & profanity, but will bear it a while longer. He entrusts the keys of all boxes to one of the drivers to whom I am compelled to go every time I want an article of med which is not out of Boxes: & nearly

---

13. Ironically, the Arkansas state troops that they would soon be fighting were prosecession but anti-slavery.

every day is intimating that meds, & stores are stolen, & that he can trust none but his favorite drivers. Regt Hospt Stores & meds exclusively for use of 1st Battalion as Smith said at P Knob when occupying Brick building as Hospital; I begin to think now that they are for exclusive use of a few of the heartiest & that sick have no claim . . .

Mond 14—Clear, pleasant. Discharge papers for Thos Kay Co H left at Sol Kittrells last Wed, & presented to Surgeon Jas W. Brackett certificate of Disability, who says "Kay is not sick" & he won't "sign the papers." New wall tent for cook put up today, & the Doctors four wheeled Ambulance brot to Hospital Camping place. Seven patients in Hospital. J S Hamilton Co F forced by his Captain to do duty when under my care for Diarrhea March 18th at Reeves Station.

I notice now that the bedpans are all here; but when L J Storm Co C was lying near to death March 18th at the Log Hospital with Dysentery & Pneumonia induced by exposure & neglect, Dr. Jas said they were broken & metallic one lost so poor Storm had to go to his death March 25th without even this small comfort. How much harm may we do by soulless neglect, of pressing, & special duties. D has removed all blankets except such as have been used by the sick into his own tent: some of the sick blankets have been brot in mine so that now at midnight I am forced to get up not able to endure the smell of the chlorine with which they are saturated. Will remove all hospital stores from my tent if I live till morning . . .

I took today as Physic zii Bals Copavia as a sort of experiment do not wish to repeat it. At first it created some heat in stomach, then radiating it passed in firey streams swiftly to extremeties leaving my feet especially very hot then two hours elapsing it operated freely, followed by another evacuation eight hours it made my pulse more frequent; tongue, & whole Canal hot, general feverish action, with some Dieuresis—I forgot to say that a spot of erysipelas on my right thumb observed this morn early induced me to try the Balsam especially as I have often noticed active erythema to follow the use of large doses of the medicine. Vomiting followed at bedtime with frequent & severe pains to relieve which I took dose of morphine, & iod; . . .

Wed April 16th—Rose at 4 AM. Cloudy, warm. rested very little during night Franklin M Scoville Co C Capt Buckles died at

Pilot Knob before we went to Patterson; his Descript Roll was with Hospt Steward Smith. How is this? I get above from my orderly J. Davison, & I saw at Patterson a number of such papers which I thought I should have been in possession of those to whom they belonged. I vomit frequently this morn, can take no breakfast; cold tea tastes best to me. Receive a mail, but I get a blank ticket.

Dr James seeing me reading a paper which lay upon his open desk in my office said I must let his papers alone & not overhaul them Papers that have been lying in his Desk of which *I* know nothing but which unlocked he leaves open to his Hospital Stewards Nurses, & all other employees about the Hospital. So I order one of his hands to take it out, & untill he can treat me with common decency he must leave it out . . .

Thurs April 17th—Rain at Daylight, & rain all night. Clearing 10 AM—Most of the whiskey loving men of the Regt sick this morning, & wanting orders for whiskey to sutler. very sick when whiskey can be had or a possibility of it. Jefferson Tappan Co L. bearer to me of present of apples & cherries from Jos Walton Bald Hill Laporte Co Ind.

[The patients] make me many troubles the demand for whiskey orders particularly the Irish boy with his living blarney, & "Cent mille failte" Other blessings of whiskey in a sutlers tent. Tent for whiskey, but not for the sick. Recd letter from wf of April 11th which I will answer this evening. Also one from Dr Durr of April 12th

Thursday eve, April 17th 1862

My Dear Charles

Your kind letters of the 4th __ & 7th with the money $2.00 came last night & were very acceptable, and now, 7 O'clock PM, I sit down to answer them. The whippo-wil sings at the door. The Babbies, Mary, and Rosa are sleeping soundly, the fire burns brightly- The Lamp is trimmed. The Table is drawn out. The Clock ticks on the mantlepiece. The kitten sleeps on the hearth, Grandma is here, too, with her knitting her cap as white as snow, her well patched apron her placid brow and cheerful smile. Louisa is reading an old number of "Harper's" and wishing she had something new to read or that Uncle Wm would send us the "Chicago Tribune," Lyman is sitting

Charles Brackett's beloved Margaret

by the fire, with knees crossed and hands folded nodding as he talks until some burst of childish laughter sets his dim blue eyes wide open again and he laughs till he is tired and goes off in a doze again Now as I have given you a peep at home tonight I will tell you something of the Farm & Orchard . . .

THE COMPANIES of the Ninth Illinois Cavalry were posted along a fifty-mile front from Pattersonville on the north, continuing to serve as the Union occupation force in Northeast Arkansas, in enemy country.

Camp on Little Black
eighteen miles from Arkansas
Thursday April 17th 1862

Dearest Wife

Your very good letter of the 11th April I recd today, with it came one from Dr Durr. It found us doing very well, our main force is north of the River, & our Hospital, mule teams, wagons, & cars on the south bank of the River; this is to protect the Regt in case of an attack. We have a large force at Doniphan west of this eighteen miles; two Cos of the Regt are at Pattersonville fortyone miles north.

We are picking up secesh occasionally. I found a secesh grave in the woods yesterday as I was rambling down the river banks to find some mint, or other vegetable that I could eat. How I long for a good mess of asparagus, or pie plant or something of that sort. But to the secesh, his comrades had dug a hole for him, & stuck in at the head to mark the place a big stick with the initials C. D. and after that the letters "OK". Poor fellow I suppose he had died true to *his* cause so they marked him OK, & "left him alone in his glory." I found the mint, but got a fine fish, a "redhorse" which had just been killed by an ill looking monster something like our crawfish in shape but large enough to kill a Red Horse over a foot long. I got the fish, & had it for supper, I also saw what I took to be an alligator. This ended my hunting for mint except for getting some pipe stems for GrandMa in that direction. I would rather see secesh than such reptiles. Jos wrote me that he had got a Mosquito Bar for me; this is good news, as insects are already very annoying.[14] My tent is nine long steps

---

14. In April 1998, they still are.

across & I have a stove in it, which some nights I heat up yet. I can put my cot in the centre & my mosquito bar hang over it & be comfortably protected from insects. He wrote he had one each for the Col, Jas, & me; the Col is very kind & studiously avoids anything of an unpleasant character, as to past matters. We have talked it over like two sensible men, without anger, & with brotherly love. I am much disgusted with the Doctor in most every particular, but try to do all I can to assist him, except to keep anything that belongs to him out of my tent, I put anything out that he sends me; tonight I talked with him first about the matter, & told him cooly what I thought of him, & his actions, & why I had put things in the shape they were in; he appeared to wish to do better, & I hope he will. I shall never do, or say aught against him except in the line of my duty as an Officer, & in that I shall do my duty, as near as with Gods help I am able to regardless of aught else. I believe God will & does assist those who try to do his will, & I feel perfectly secure in my efforts, for I ask his blessing on every good thing I undertake, & his forgiveness through the merits of the blessed Christ for all my sins. This may all be new to you, as I believe I have never before spoken, or written on the subject to you, but ever since I saw Louisa, & Lyman on their knees in prayer I have been humbled & have tried to increase my faith, & to improve my ways.

> *The Lord is my sheppard, no want shall I know*
> *I feed in green pastures; safe folded I rest;*
> *He leadeth my soul where the still waters flow,*
> *Restores me when wandring; redeems when opprest.*

. . . I have in my tent Sergeant Major Price, a young man from NY City (a clerk there last spring) & a member of the famous N York Seventh Regt, the second that reached Washington last spring after the war was declared by the bombardment of Fort Sumpter. He has the Camp Fever, & as the hospital tents are crowded, or rather uncomfortable I took him in with me; he is a very pleasant young man, attentive to his duties when well, & patient in his sickness. He is on my cot sleeping under the influence of a powerful opiate. My orderly Johnny Davison (also a young men, bright, quick, & attentive) is sleeping on a hand litter, & I shall soon go to sleep on another that Johnny brot in for me. I have plenty of blankets, & when tented we are perfectly comfortable so far as warmth, & shelter are

concerned. We eat out in the open air, & cook there. At supper tonight we had Ham, desiccated potatoes, tea, coffee, pickled onions,
green gage plums, preserved in airtight jar, dried peaches. How do
you like the list? A tolerable good bill of fare for the woods I think
I hear you say. I have just been out to close the "bonnet" of my tent,
& have secured the entrance, it is raining (having commenced since
I began to write). The "bonnet" of the tent is a conical cap covering the top, & secured by three guy ropes attached to it, & fastened
to pins in the ground, & acting as additional stays to the centre pole.

We have a hard storm, with thunder & lightning. I was out to
see (a few days since) one of our men who was knocked off his horse
by Lightning he was insensible for nearly a day, & now able to be
about. The lightning is very vivid, & the rain fairly strikes through
the canvas so that I have to hold my head over the paper to keep it
from being sprinkled . . .

[*On the other side of the river and in the real "zone of activity," General Henry*
W. Halleck was moving slowly toward Corinth, Mississippi.]

Many of our wise men think that but a short time will elapse till
the war is closed. Present indications are favorable to such a thought.
You were right about Island No. 10, we took that and six thousand
prisoners with large amounts of property without the loss of a single
man, but the loss at Corinth was fearful on both sides with the difference largely in our favor.[15] That battle will probably have to be
fought over soon. Whether our part of the army is engaged or not
is matter of doubt, though we have our share of the work to perform.
May we do it well is my prayer.

It is now about after midnight & I will leave this till morning.
Sweet sleep to my loved ones. Good night dearest.

Your affectionate husband, Charles Brackett

---

15. Dr. Brackett was hearing rumors from the front east of the Mississippi. Halleck,
moving as slow as Curtis, was in Mississippi pitted against Beauregard and the army
commanded at Shiloh by the slain A. S. Johnston (Army of the Mississippi). General
Curtis had been frozen in place west of the Mississippi by orders from Halleck; Curtis
and Steele would not be part of the main events east of the river, such as the first Battle of
Corinth, in June of 1862, where Beauregard successfully withdrew his men and equipment in the face of Halleck's vastly superior force.

UNKNOWN TO DR. BRACKETT, other Union troops were assembling in the area. Concerned about the raiding activities of the two cavalry brigades of Missouri "partisan" M. Jeff Thompson, Curtis's three-brigade division under Brigadier General Frederick Steele, called the "District of Arkansas" within the Army and Department of the Southwest, was assigned to hold Northern Arkansas for the Union against possible attacks from Thompson. However, after April 6–7, Shiloh, all of Thompson's Missouri brigade of state troops and half of his Arkansas brigade of state troops traveled east of the river with the "Swamp Fox" himself. Jeff Thompson's mission was to kill or mutilate as many Yanks as possible, wherever they might be, but he has left Steele's immediate territory. That half of Thompson's Arkansas brigade that remained behind was commanded by Major J. A. Johnson, an Arkansas Rebel state trooper.

★ ★ ★

THE FOLLOWING JOURNAL ENTRIES ARE TELLING; the one of April 20 speaks of the insanity of army life during what was loosely called the 1862 Arkansas Guerrilla War. On April 22 Dr. Brackett moves finally to join the rest of the regiment in Arkansas.

From the Journal:

Frid April 18th—Rain, clouds, rain. Slept very little during the night. wrote till 2 AM, & laid awake till daylight most of the time. Wrote wife long letter, eight pages, Send $20.00. Prescriptions yesterday, & to day not made up as directed by order, as boy dispensing says, of the Surgeon Jas W Brackett. have written him on subject; he gives me verbal answer that I may let the sick alone, & he will prescribe; that the whiskey or alcohol need not be used; that there is some "tincture of BloodRoot somewhere" that may be used—Take a jaunt into the country to get milk, Buttermilk, & Butter got a canteen part full of sweet milk. woods bright with beautiful flowers. Blue Bell, Red flowering Buckeye &c.

Saty April 19th—Clouds & rain. Cold—Slept well all last night. Took after retiring two swallows of Bourbon. Go out to Jas A Hammons to see John Cummings Private Co E. Bronchitis Diarrhoea, & Geo Olmstead Sergeant Co K. Took mumps Ironton March 1st not well since, Diarrhoea at the same time—Our camp S of Little Black is in Ripley Co. Try to have ambulance train take the lead through swamps on acct of ruts. Ordered to move tomor-

row, get place for sick men with Dr Holland. The Doctor is moving them, leaves at 4 PM. [*Fear of Thompson is like a cancer in the
Army of the Southwest.*]

    Sund April 20th—Rain, rain, all rain, water, & thin mud. very
pleasant, warm & dry in my tent. Slept well last night; got Tick in
my left shoulder very painful. Corporal O G May Co B goes to
private house to recruit. waters rising rapidly. Barrel of whiskey reported south one mile on road Boys scattering out rapidly in that
direction; no move yet of the Regt. Send Hugh Kirk Co H to
Vandeveres by order of Colonel. Doctor not yet in; reported to be
taken prisoner. 9 Oclock PM Doctor returned all safe; had bad luck
getting men in people generally unwilling to keep them. The whiskey seller sold out all his liquor; some of the boys stole thirty-five
dollars of his money, & he entered complaint to the Colonel who
fined him fifty & had him drummed out of camp so that with
fine, & loss his profits were small: he got about $120 for the whis-
key. Many of the boys got very drunk, & had some fights. Mr.
Whiskey Seller was pelted with mud, & stones till he was beyond
the pickets . . .

    Tues April 22—Arrive at 4 PM, & Camp on Hardees old
camping ground Burn Old Hospital building to rid camp of con-
tagion & offensive effluvia.

    Wed 23—Clear Pleasant. Spent a pleasant night this my first
in Arkansas. Day very hot: [We] have to put up Hospital Tent, but
ordered over the river, so will wait tent pitching till we get over.
Capt Gifford lost horse yesterday which vomited before dying
freely of undigested food, water &c. Capt says the Colonel saw
him vomit. Had an onion top; something they called coffee, & a
hard biscuit for breakfast; for dinner more coffee hard biscuit, &
chicken soup, or Salt soup I can't say which; if we had the Devil for
cook we could not fare worse.

    Thurs 24th—Cloudy, & pleasant. Regt crossing Current River.
Rain toward noon & pouring down; have not struck my tent; get
dinner at Kellys where Lieut Harrington is sick; had milk; good
corn bread, & biscuit. 33 Illinois joins us, with Artillery. One man
of 5th Cav shot mile, & half above on River day before yesterday;
not yet found; supposed from signs, body thrown in River. Forage
plenty for horses but men on short allowance. Officers not allowed
to get provision from Quartermaster. Take supper & lodge with
Q M Sergeant, my blankets being all over the River. Rains yet 9

PM hard. Am writing to Old Mr Johnson.

Frid 25th—Cloudy, cold, Cross River. Visit Old Grave Yard on River Bank on Jas Kelly's place: here is buried Jas Kelly, the spot marked by a beautiful marble slab. Nearby Private S A Dodd Co A Deshas Bat Arkan volunteers—marked by smooth pine slab. Also "Wm D Burns 1st Regt Ark Mtd Vol Hardees Brigade."[16] Also W F Skillian [?] Clark Co Light Artillery on smooth pine board with crossed cannon at top very neat. "Capt G A Ross 2nd Ark Regt" marked by plain board. Dr G H Carpenter from Dayton Ohio settled in Mo 2 yrs since. Died Sept 10th '61. Beside these are scores of unnoted dead of Hardees Brigade who must have suffered terribly during the last summer & fall; This place of burial is enclosed by no fence, & appears to have been a burial place for many years. One old man showed me an oak tree Blk Oak at least two feet in Diameter which he said grew on a grave; it must be sixty years old . . .

★ ★ ★

ON MONDAY, APRIL 28, one-third of Steele's force was formed into a single brigade under newly promoted Brigadier General William P. Benton, who had been the colonel of the Eighth Indiana Infantry at Pea Ridge. Colonel Albert Brackett's Ninth Illinois was detached to Benton's brigade. This brigade was deployed all over Northeast Arkansas, protecting the district from the feared Thompson. The Missouri partisan would, however, remain east of the Mississippi until the fall. As the result of a lack of information concerning the guerrilla chieftain's whereabouts, Curtis would keep Steele immobilized in Northeast Arkansas.

★ ★ ★

Mond April 28th—Clear, with detached clouds. Golburn H Way Co A had pre[scription] this morn at 7 O'clock for Qui zi five parts, four hours, & simple Cerate to eyes & at one O'clock it is not ready for him. On a par with the way things generally go about our Hospital. Dr. Jas W Brackett without seeing it said—You al-

---

16. This is Charles's first encounter with regular Confederates, even though they are dead. The deceased are from the First Arkansas Cavalry Mounted Rifles of Colonel Matlock, formerly of Hardee's brigade, at that time one of Churchill's six regiments, defending Confederate Arkansas. Matlock was in Jackson County in April of 1862 raising a new regiment which would become the 32nd Arkansas Infantry. [Lady Elizabeth Watson, *Fight and Survive*, Jackson County Historical Society, p. 53]

ways make such dmnd complicated prescriptions no one can put them up. This when I first gave it to Way. Dr Miner puts it up this time. New just in that Axtell with one of the Ambulances is a mile & half from camp; horse lost. Axtell has been missing since 25th at night after leaving Pitmans Ferry: his horse was hardly able to travel then. At 6 PM has reached Pochohontas. Regt camps one mile out. Stop ambulance train in town & canton there — sleep at St Charles Hotel with our Sutler Clark. Slept badly dreaming Unpleasantly. Feather bed too warm May be a cause.

Tuesd April 29th—Pleasant; with Clouds—Recd of Capt Bishop Colt 118423. Occupy residence of Dr Kibler as Hospital; Dr has left & his fine property has been somewhat abused in his absence—write wife.

★ ★ ★

CURTIS'S TINY ARMY, never less than Steele's three brigades but never more than six brigades, remained in Arkansas, frozen in place by Halleck's order to "hold" Missouri and Northern Arkansas. It was a non-campaign, totally ignored by modern historians, who report about the major activities taking place on the Virginia Peninsula, and the war in Mississippi (Corinth, Iuka) that followed on the heels of Grant's success at Shiloh. Note that the inept Van Dorn, stalled in Mississippi with his Army of the West, refused to move north to assist Beauregard's Army of the Mississippi or to move west to assist Hindman's Department of the Trans-Mississippi. Steele's troops were moving about slowly and without much purpose, because of his orders. Federal officers, like Major Charles Brackett here, are growing tired of this "phony war."

★ ★ ★

Headquarters Hospital of 9th Illinois Cavalry
Pochohontas Randolph Co Arkansas
April 29th 1862

Dearest Margeret

On acct of frequent moves since my last letter to you of the 18th inst in answer to yours of the 11th (the last I have recd) I have not had opportunity to write; we have had a series of moves since coming into this state. All attended with pleasant results thus far. Secesh here being fewer in number by far than in Missouri, the people better informed as a class (so far as I have become acquainted) & having a stronger Union feeling.

This town is nearly deserted by its residents, or citizens the idea having been prevalent that we would burn, pillage, & destroy as we advanced. One merchant who left wrote in large letters over his door "Yankees you may burn Pochohontas, & be damned, but I wont stay to see it!" There are some very pleasant, & convenient residences here; we are occupying one as a hospital that was owned by an MD (who has gone south on acct of the fear his wife entertained, that they would be murdered if they remained): they did not take time to remove all their goods most of which were ruthlessly destroyed by the soldiers who first entered the town. Nothing has been destroyed of people who remained to watch their property, & nothing of the kind done except through the agency of the soldiers without the knowledge or consent of the Officers. A part of our Regt is on the way to Jacksonsport sixty miles below on White River. The rest will follow if we meet with no reverses. Forage is plenty as we can wish, but through careless Officers the supply for man & beast is irregular. The health is generally very good. Our Hospital management is very bad, could indeed hardly be worse, & if there was last fall something to complain of, there is now incomparably more, in fact I never could have even supposed so much incompetence carelessness, & inattention possible in any man who possessed ordinary capability, but by enduring a great deal of extra labor, & worry we get along in a tolerable fashion.

Sugar was selling here when we first came at seven cents pr lb, & salt at ten cents pr lb. Cotton cards (for carding cotton by hand similar to, but finer than woolen cards) were selling at twentyfive dollars pr pair. Brandy sells at two & a half dollars pr bottle (holding something over a pint) & at this price the soldiers are anxious to get it (I believe they would freely pay one dollar pr drink) One of my greatest difficulties now is to get rid of applicants for "Orders" as they term it, for Liquor, none being allowed to be sold except on the certificate of an Army Surgeon that it is needed by the buyer for medicinal purposes. It is laughable, & also humiliating to see, & hear the multiform excuses, & pleas (made by both Officers, & soldiers) for the absolute necessity for whiskey, or Brandy.

Government furnishes Alcoholic liquors, wines, &c for the use of the sick soldier, but through mismanagement these things are lost to the sick, so that when needed the men must buy them at exhorbitant rates of sutlers, & others. It looks a good deal like stealing to me, & the meanest kind of theft. Yet practiced by those wear-

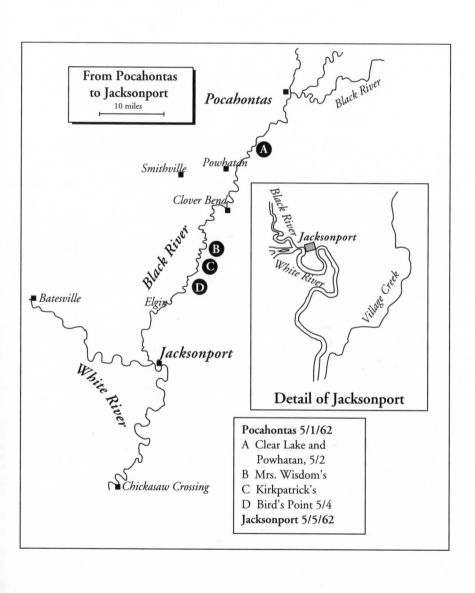

From Pocahontas
to Jacksonport
10 miles

Pocahontas

Black River

A

Smithville Powhatan

Clover Bend

Black River

B

C

D

Batesville Elgin

Jacksonport

White River

Chickasaw Crossing

Black River Jacksonport

White River Village Creek

Detail of Jacksonport

Pocahontas 5/1/62
A Clear Lake and
     Powhatan, 5/2
B Mrs. Wisdom's
C Kirkpatrick's
D Bird's Point 5/4
Jacksonport 5/5/62

ing shoulder straps it is thought to be all right, & unless a man is willing to make strong battle against him he must remain mute on the subject.

But I suppose you may be tired of hearing the dark side of the story, & I am tired of thinking, or writing about it where it['s] useless & I will let the matter drop, with a request to you to keep the matter to yourself . . .

You would like this country very much. It is a region ahead of any I have seen except northern Indiana. The season is now as far advanced, as with us on the first of June. Streams clear, cold; soil first rate, country gently undulating, free from high mountains, or perfect flats. A very much better country than south-eastern Missouri.

Do not neglect to write often though (unless we get possession of the River soon) mails transported overland will be few, & far between. We have some deserters caught, one or two of whom I am afraid will be shot. I had hoped that there never would be a case of this kind in the Division to which I was attached. It seems an awful thing . . .

Charles

Pochohontas Arkansas May 1st 1862.

Dearest Wife

. . . I was to see Genl Steele today first, then on business connected with the Dept at Washington; he recollected me, though I did not him by his looks. Our Brigade Surgeon Burke is a very good man in most respects, & he reposes sufficient confidence in me to send for me to see with him the members of the General Staff who only are under his immediate control.

I would like to send you the money I have if I dared, but I hope you will get along well untill I can.

This country is infested & overrun with "ticks" as are called of all sorts & sizes; they burrow in the skin making troublesome sores. They trouble me less than most others. I will try send you one of our Army Papers by times we publish two in our Brigade.

Dr Gregg is wounded & a prisoner at Pittsburgh[17] battle half his

---

17. The Battle of Shiloh, April 6–7, sometimes called Pittsburg Landing. Neither the First Indiana Cavalry nor the Ninth Illinois Cavalry was engaged in a major battle until Vicksburg, spring of 1863. During the Vicksburg campaign of 1863 the First Indiana Cavalry and the Ninth Illinois Cavalry served in separate detachments of the XVI Corps, Union Army of the Tennessee, commanded by General William T. Sherman.

Co was wounded; it was an awful fight, & a great victory for us. Now it is all quiet here, & I am momentarily expecting orders to move forward, but it is all uncertainty, & I do not allow myself to become excited, but take everything easy, execute my orders promptly, & then rest till the next come; *finish* what I begin when possible. So I have more leisure, less hurry, & a better reputation than those who play when business remains undone. My duties are not difficult under such circumstances. Jas is just in with a lot of papers returned on acct of informality Not his fault however.

I will close now by wishing love & sending kisses to Louisa, Lyman Rosa & Mary, & much & many to my dearest Margeret

Chs Brackett

Mrs M Brackett

I send some leaves of cypress tree. we are now in the Cypress swamps close to Powhatan Ark No secesh army yet—May 2nd Friday.

From the Journal:

Friday May 2nd—Clear Pleasant. Dr May leaves with effects [of] John Selvey Co B [William Selvey, Co. M] who died at Reeves Station April 28th Cash 50.00 with 3.50 with Layton Clothing left with Dr Bocker Asst Surgeon 13 Illinois. Waddle, & Storts of Pochohontas were anxious to get some few things of & exchange for what we needed; we let them have some camphor a lb & ¾ & a bot of turpentine for which he gave three lbs sulphur. At one dollar per lb. We also gave him some bottles, & vials which he begged I mean Storts, not Waddle.

Reached Clear Lake Lawrence Co five (5) miles from Powhattan, & fifteen miles from Pocha. Lake one mile long, & one hundred yds wide. About 12 feet deep in lowest stage. Sleep on ground in Capt Blakemores tent; prescribed for six men.

Sat May 3rd 1862—Cloudy, warm. Slept well last night. Travel eighteen miles, & stop at 2 PM. Adjt Stephenson gets a cot. Hear that 1st Ind had a fight below Jacksonport. No particulars except five killed & secesh driven.

Sund May 4th—Clouds, cold rain. Found at Mrs Wisdoms that one man of Co B has stolen ham offering bad money in pay.

Wisdoms house is twenty-three miles from Jacksonport. Get dinner at Reeves here they say that Wisdom is out "hunting horses" & another says he has been trying to raise Compy to "kill the Yankees" as they pass along singley, or in small squads. Stop at Kirkpatricks to dine sixteen miles from Jacksonport. Here see first cotton baled, of any great quantity; worth now 8 cts per lb. Quite wet when I reached here. See more pretty girls than I have before seen for some time past. Camp at Birds Point fifteen miles from Jacksonport by short cut, & seventeen by Riv Road. Prescribe for six men.

JACKSONPORT, ARKANSAS
Ninth Illinois Cavalry

★ ★ ★

From the Journal:

Mond May 5ᵗʰ—Beautiful, & bright Slept in deserted house. Visited patients at John Box, Samuel W Rude F 38 Ill. & Layton, of Co E 9ᵗʰ Cavalry. Get overcoat to give to soldier. Give it to him on road an hour after getting it. Layton better be discharged. Negro Jim Dickison—Daught Julia Jim belonged to Dr Dickerson. Daught is at Dr Vaugh[n]s. Julia over twenty. Dr Vaughn not at home. Reach Jacksonsport afternoon; find houses, & stores mostly closed; Two men of 1ˢᵗ Ind wounded, one head, & other hip. both serious wounds. Travel today fifteen (15) miles Corporal from Co D who took Lieut Knox up to Ironton, brot down two sick from P Knob to Patterson, of Co I charging 1.50 each It was reported to be Lawson but not him. Prescribe for six (6). Dr takes Residence private for Hospital.

[Dr. Brackett's letter of May 1, 1862, continues]

Mond May 5ᵗʰ—In Jacksonville [Jacksonport], all safe except two of First Cavalry Indiana badly wounded.[1] An awful time for the secesh, feelings hurt that the "Mudsills" occupy the town of the

---

1. Wounded by the Arkansas State troops, not Confederate regulars.

Chivalry. The women have more spunk than the men. A very pretty town is this & secesh say we shall not hold it one week they will die first

ALL OF THIS PEACE AND CALM would soon be over; Confederate Colonel Charles Matlock of General Churchill's brigade would be in the area soon. The job of Colonel Matlock's First Arkansas Cavalry Mounted Rifles was to keep Steele's division confused about enemy intentions. The regiment operated out of Helena in Central Arkansas on the Mississippi; the Second Arkansas Cavalry Mounted Rifles operated out of Little Rock, west of Helena. In other words, there were only two regular Confederate regiments in the northern half of the state, with the four Texas regiments posted in the southern half of the state. Curtis and Steele, of course, weren't aware of this.

From the Journal:

Tuesday May 6ᵗʰ—Bright, clear, cool. Took Hospital blankets for bed last night. Now Dr. Jas makes a fuss over it although he took a bale of finest white blankets for a stranger who came to see him. Am more than ever tired of his abuse; for it is nothing else, although by times he is more than good. Watson who married a Caldwell occupied the house we use. Miss Mary T. Caldwell was over & showed us what rooms to occupy.

"MAY 6, 1862. The Ninth Illinois Cavalry arrived at Jacksonport, Ark., after a long, but on the whole not unpleasant, march from Pilot Knob, Mo., of just two months' duration.

The town has been one of considerable importance, is pleasantly situated on the north bank of the Black River, near where it forks with the clear and appropriately named White River, sixty miles from Pocahontas, and about one hundred miles equidistant from Memphis and Little Rock, and some twenty-five miles from Batesville, Ark., where General Curtis had a large army. The First Indiana Cavalry, being in the advance, had a sharp skirmish with Hooker's men in the town, killing three and capturing a number of prisoners. In this vicinity we found Colonel Matlock in command of the larger part of the Guerilla bands ready to pick off our soldiers on all occasions, and

Captain Hooker, his trusted Lieutenant and Boss Guerilla, had about one hundred and forty men; Independent Cavalry, he calls them; Guerrillas, bushwhackers, and murderers, we found them to be." [Davenport, p. 27]

★ ★ ★

THE NINTH ILLINOIS CAVALRY remained at Jacksonport until the end of June and then moved south along the White River through Augusta and Clarendon to Helena, arriving July 14. The move to the Mississippi River was made necessary by the lack of adequate forage and subsistence inland. It was a difficult passage over swampy ground with little food or water to be found. Many of the regiment were sick upon arrival at Helena.

Charles, not well himself, tended the sick at Helena until September 12, when he obtained a leave of absence to return home to Rochester. He had been planning this trip for some time, because Margaret was pregnant and "ready to be confined."

★ ★ ★

Jacksonport, Jackson Co Missouri
Tuesday May 6ᵗʰ 1862

Dearest Wife

Since writing at Pochohontas I have had no chance of sending a letter off. A Courier with an escort will leave day after tomorrow, & by him I will send this unless accident prevents.

I am occupying a very comfortable residence deserted by its former occupants except three slaves (two females & one male): they with the house & grounds are owned by a Miss Mary T Caldwell[2] who resides a few doors below. She is a very ultra secessionist, though quite an engaging young lady in most respects. She gave up the house with a tolerable good grace leaving the slaves whom she directed to keep my room clean & to do as I ordered.

She said to me today with tears in her eyes that when she first saw our troops coming in town she wished someone would cut off her head, or shoot her: she glories in being a Rebel & told me that she wished she had power to kill every Officer in our Army, & Old Abe especially: said that she would do it with more pleasure than she

---

2. Miss Mary Tom Caldwell is described in Lady Elizabeth Watson's book *Fight and Survive* as having presented the colors for Captain A. C. Pickett's Guards with the hope that "our own noble state may be added to the constellation of the South."

could express; her greatest indignation is however devoted to her own people who ran off without firing a gun except a few in ambush who wounded (perhaps mortally) a couple of my old Regt (the First Indiana).

It is now late, so I will retire, & fill out this as near the time of departure as possible to give you the latest news . . .

Wed May 7th . . . Good news of glorious victories at Corinth, Memphis, Yorktown, New Orleans, & Mobile have reached us both from the north & from the south. Yet the Rebels here with their usual love of falsifying history tell the people that the French have occupied New Orleans to protect the people from the Government troops, & they are willing to accept French protection (the braggarts who only wanted to meet the Northern troops two, or five to one to teach us a lesson of Southern valor, & of Yankee cowardice).

Many say to us with woe stricken looks we know you can conquer us, but the next thing "to make us love you that cant be done." We tell them that we only came to whip them back to their allegiance that we do not come for their love; yet I believe they will hereafter both fear, & love us, a thousand times more than in times past.

Their King Cotton has served them worse than the King sent the frogs by Jupiter; they wanted a king with more life than the log on which they rested, & which was too tame for them when the Stork was sent & began eating them they repented too late. Common calico is selling for from seventy-five cents to a dollar pr Yd. Yarn they cant get except what they spin. While cotton in bales & in cribs huge as our barn & plenty on almost every plantation. Sugar is worth 3 cts pr lb by the Hogshead & many hogsheads lying on the street. They shipped it from Memphis here so as to have it out of the way of the Yankees. A smart chance of wisdom in Secessia. Many, many, families fled before us taking what they could with them. I thought that it was in their cases as with others true that the "wicked flee when no man pursueth." We have just had an excellent dinner. Our cook, an Englishman of long experience in the business having now everything needful to make good dinners: we only have six sick ones, & some seventeen Hospital Attaches, Ambulance, & mule drivers, nurse stewards, wardmasters, & orderlies; quite a retinue for the Dr to look after as he is acting the part of Quartermaster running the Hospital train, & providing for it making to himself continual trouble, & probably much expense.

Curtis advance force is crossing to us & he is about twenty-five miles back.[3] Sigel is also on another track further still to the south making with us a long arm of cannon & bayonets to stop any retreat westward of the Grand Army of Beauregard. Our Batteries in this Brigade are in splendid condition, Guns bright, & horses sleek & well trained with drivers & gunners in best trim for service. Our Cavalry are continually moving in scouting parties in all directions picking up guns, & contraband articles where-ever found . . .

Your affectionate husband

Chs

From the Journal:

Wed May 7ᵗʰ—Clear, bright, warm. Dr Jas treats me to another series of curses about the blankets Recd news (through secesh) of McLellans defeat at Yorktown, probably such a victory as they won at Pittsburgh Landing. Bands out serenading this evening. Cool, pleasant. Send two letters to wife, & paper & letter to son. Make out monthly report to Brigade Surgeon, imperfect for lack of regularity, & preciseness in our bookkeeping.

Enclose to wf $20.00.

Thursd May 8ᵗʰ—Morn cool, clear. Van Dorn reported to be in force near us.[4] McLellans defeat turns out to be a great victory!

Jacksonport, Jackson Co.,

Ark, Thursday, May 8, '62

To the Editor of the *Chronicle*

Dear Sir: I received the *Rochester Chronicle* at Pochahontas, Ark., a few days since. I am much pleased with the general appearance of the paper. It gives many items of news which I could get from no other source. Send it regularly as long as I remain from home, living.

---

3. Major General Samuel Curtis of Iowa commands the Army of the Southwest; that is, one division in Missouri, one division in Arkansas. This refers to the main body (other three brigades) of Curtis's small army. Rebel General Churchill is posted from Helena to Arkansas Post with a single brigade (District of Arkansas).

4. General Earl Van Dorn was never in force anywhere near Brackett. Dr. Brackett and the occupiers of Arkansas believe Van Dorn is near them; actually, he is east of the Mississippi.

We occupied this town peaceably, almost. A few of Van Dorn's rear guard[5] ambushed, shot a couple of my old Regt., (the Indiana 1st Cavalry). We captured most of the ambushing party, though some escaped; whether any were killed we could not find out. One of their wagons captured by our boys was literally covered with blood, showing that somebody was hurt, but as the rebels have a way of being silent on the subject of their dead and wounded, we could ascertain nothing more.

This is a fine town, situated on the left bank of the White River, not far below the junction of the Black and Current rivers, and about 100 miles West of Memphis. Day before yesterday, early, we hear cannonading in the direction of Memphis, and presume that place is probably ours . . .

I have seen just *one* school in operation in this State, a few miles North of this in a strong Union settlement. Sugar is very plenty; hogsheads of it by the score lying on the streets. It was selling at 3 and 4 cents per lb. when we came; now selling at 8 cents. Flour is $15 per barrel, and none to be had at that till we came—Calico from 50 to 75 cents per yard—Cotton cards are enormously high, in some instances selling as high as as $15 per pair. We captured a box of them coming down from St. Louis, and our Quartermaster was offered in gold, $5 per pair for the whole lot; they generally sell I believe at 40 and 50 cents.

It is all ruin and desolation, and they feel it, but how long they can stand it I do not know. I am satisfied we can bear it easily as long as they can bear it with suffering intense, and ruin on every hand. We cannot be too thankful that war keeps from our Northern homes. May God in his infinite goodness avert such a calamity from us!

There are many things to which Northerners are strangers. Among the birds especially I admire the paroquets with their beautiful plumage; there is not so much, however, to admire in their voices, which are harsh and discordant.

The weather is all one could desire; the days and nights of just the right temperature to invigorate and give sound repose. Mosquitoes and flies are strangers here yet, though in the swamps they are said to be very troublesome. To guard against them I brought with me a mosquito net, but as yet have had no use for it.

---

5. Actually, Churchill's.

I am hoping that before long we may make a junction with some of the Indiana troops. Curtis is close to us, and I believe some of our men are with him. Sigel[6] also is not far off, and the Hoosier, Jeff. C. Davis, near at hand. The cavalry force here is immense, numbering many thousands. One can have very little conception of the amount of forage consumed by one regiment. Our regiment of twelve hundred horses and two hundred draft mules consumes at a feed one hundred and forty bushels of corn, or two hundred and eighty bushels per day, and about ten tons of hay.

I must close—good-by.

C.BRACKETT

From the Journal:

Friday May 9th—Cool, clear. Took supper yesterday at Pattersons. Best coffee & cold corned beef Yankee style & Bread I have had for a long time. China trees in blossom at my window. Recd letter from T B Butter. Send his final statement E S Williams Attorney at Law Chicago Ill. Letters to Chicag Trib, Rochester Chronicle.

Saty May 10th—Clear Cool—very warm at m. Had a pleasant interview yesterday with old Mr. Tonsall Gfather to Miss Mary T. Caldwell. Our Regt with Indiana 1st started yesterday on a Scout I suppose to Des Ark forty miles hence. They return about M unable to make way through swamps. Secesh feeling less bitter than when we came in. This place subject to overflow. River very tortuous being eighteen miles by river to make a half mile linear travel. Soil Clay, with sand—bakes readily. Summers very hot, & unhealthy though Mr Tonsall tells me he has never paid a dollar to a Doctor during a residence here of years; moves family during hot season to highlands. Got whiskey, & wine on requisition 3 PM Wis 11th Ill 33rd & Manters Battery just coming in. Make quite a sensation among the citizens. Sent to Dr. Casselberry for Field Case.

Sund May 11th—Clear, cool. Read some Secesh letters. All desire chance to "Kill some Yankees." Removed a thorn of Honey Locust from forefinger of Capt Blakemore been in some weeks & healed over . . .

---

6. Major General Franz Sigel, who had his finest hour at Pea Ridge, was now in the East. As a result of all these false rumors, six Union brigades have opted not to pursue aggressively six Confederate regiments.

Jacksonport Jackson Co Arkansas
May 11th 1862

Dearest Wife

. . . Our wards are pretty well filled with sick, the diseases being mostly Dysentery Diarrhoea, & remittent. What it will be after the sickly season sets in I almost dread to contemplate, though I am sure we can bear the climate *as* well at least as they. Our habits of temperance, good diet, & clothing go far to give our troops a superiority; yet with all these some must suffer. Our Regt,[7] & the 1st Indiana compare very favorably with others in the Brigade numbering generally not more than a third of the sickness. As to mortality I suppose the ratio is about the same. Many southern Regts have lost fully one half since last fall. Two Texan Regts that were here have lost just one half, & this without a battle. Widows in this town are more plenty than married women showing the mortality of those who have gone from here. Many have (of these troops) been killed in the battles of Pea Ridge, Fredericktown, & Pittsburgh Landing . . .

From the Journal:

Monday May 12—Clear, cool. Have vist sick chld in Jail. Six poor ones are confined here. A sad sight. Lend Dr Jas W B 5.00 to send to his wife, & owe—two seventy-five to make change—Ordered back to Birds Point. Very hot, but health of Command good.

Tuesd May 13th—Clear cool. Get pass for discharge of Henry Brown Co K. Tuberculosis. Chronic Diarrhoea; Leave Jcksnsport at 8 AM. Reach Birds Pt at M. find Jas F Layton Co E failing rapidly must try & get him discharged. Had Dysenteria Acuta at PKnob, & directed by his Commander to come on when I had ordered him to stay; Consequence Chronic Diarrhoea & tuberculosis. Very hot till noon, then sharp shower with thunder, then sun again: Pleasant PM. Dr Watkins resides near.

Wed May 14th—Clear cool. First night I have been troubled by mosquitoes. Stayed in Lieut Blackburns tent on Riv Bank. Lieut B

---

7. Dr. Brackett mentions "his" brigade, presumably Benton's, but again doesn't identify it. He may not know all the regiments. It is a big regiment in a big brigade. Benton's brigade is one-third of Steele's division and one-sixth of Curtis's army: the First Indiana Cavalry, Ninth Illinois Cavalry, Eleventh Wisconsin Infantry, Eighth Indiana Infantry, Eighteenth Indiana Infantry. Infantry plus Cavalry—a Roman Legion!

Thomas Todd Tunstall (*left*)
bought the land and platted the
original town of Jacksonport,
Arkansas, in the 1830s. His
granddaughter, Mary Tom
Caldwell (*below*), was an avid
Jacksonport Southern sympa-
thizer who presented the flag to
the Jackson Guards in 1861.
(Photographs courtesy of the
Jackson County Historical
Society)

off to arrest parties near Powhattan who have threatened life of a Union man. Visited with Col Sickles, Mrs Green. Fine farm; twentyfive negroes. return after night. Liquor sent up by the Dr all gone except three bottles. One of them I take half to Capt Gifford & half to Layton Co E.

Birds Point Co Arkansas
Wed May 14th 1862

Dearest Margeret

I found at Mr Box's this morning a rose different from any I have before seen, & send you one full blossom, & a bud. It is yellow, & the bush resembles that of the Button Rose on a small scale. I arrived here at noon yesterday, having ridden seventeen miles in four hours including stops. There was an escort of ten men besides my Orderly, one of the Hospital Stewards (Dr Minor) & two men who came through with dispatches relating to the battle at Corinth, &c. I ride my mule yet, & like him better with each days travel Yesterday we walked our horses all the way, & my little "Burro" took & kept the lead, so that I had several stops to wait the coming of the escort. There has been no shooting of pickets or of straggling soldiers in this part of Arkansas, & only one instance in the state that I know of. All this business has stopped since we left Missouri. We sent out, last night, to Powhattan to arrest some men who have threatened a neighbor with death on acct of his Union sentiments. The Lieut is not yet in; the distance there is about eighteen miles so that he has had not time yet to return.

We are camped on the banks of Black River the left bank opposite is a large canebrake reaching out a number of miles. Lyman could get such nice fish poles here. I am staying for the present in Blackburns tent which [some text missing here]

A large cotton warehouse is being rigged for a Hospital. I caught last night some fine silver Catfish which we are expecting to have for breakfast. That is if our mulatto cook (Felix) lives to finish the job which he has been at for the past three hours. You may judge how amiable I feel over it, as I have been up since daylight. Mosquitoes troubled me first last night. I have a nice new mosquito net in my trunk, but there it did me no perceptible good.

To return to the subject of fish, we get plenty here; mine I caught from the door of my tent, which is just at the edge of the bluff bank some eight feet above the water. The silver Cat, Blk Cat, Drum (a sort of white Perch), Buffalo, Bass, & Sunfish are plenty, & furnish a very considerable portion of the diet of the detatchment here.

The command is very healthy though we have some cases of chronic Diarrhoea, & Dysentery (two) that should be sent home. Dr. James is perfectly mulish on the subject of discharging men for disability, & senseless in his ideas about it; men in several instances that I have begged to have sent home, he would remand to duty, saying they were "malingerers" that is feigning sickness, & are now lying in soldiers graves far from friends & home. It is hard to see men failing day by day with no prospect of ever returning health unless by a change of diet, & climate, & to see them kept pertinaciously with the command, driven back to their companies as soon as strength to sit up is restored to them—but so it goes: soldiers will often fall under command of brutal, ignorant officers, & then surely it is worse than death in many instances. Now, 8 ½ AM, Lieut Col Sickles & I have just eaten the breakfast, so long preparing, & it was really very good. Fish, Ham, & eggs, coffee, milk & sugar, & very nice biscuit with preserved fruits, pickles, &c. I speculate a good deal as I sit in my tent on what good shots I could make if secesh would appear on the other bank of the river: it is about thirtyfive rods across, & with my Rifle standing at convenient reach I feel quite confident of making every time a telling shot. I know every tree & bush in sight from the tent, & sight them frequently so that anything new there I would notice at a glance. There is no[t] much danger from a squirrel gun of serious wound at that distance unless a perfectly centre shot is made. With my Colt & Conical bullets I can do better shooting than can be done with an ordinary rifle. It is singular, but the more one thinks on this subject, the more eager for a chance for this kind of trial. Tell me if you receive the yellow Roses I send if they retain either color or fragrance.

We still have hopes of being at home by July 4th, so you may get your dinner on that day if you live, & I will try be with you. Kisses for the babies All—Love to Grandma, & for yourself the best wishes & love of yours ever

Charles

From the Journal:

Thursd May 15th—Cool, clear. Chs Barton Co L left at Pocha reported dead. Go out with Capt Gifford to capture secesh flags; get none; find two men at Dowels sick. Dr Boice attending them

Friday May 16ᵗʰ—Clear Warm—if possible find Saml L Box Capt Antonys Pattersons Regt 8ᵗʰ Arkan Vol. His Mother makes me promise to see him if a prisoner or wounded & care for him. Jacob D Rosencrants [Rosecranz] Co I, & Smith Wixon Co, & Arthur Gorman sick at H J Dowels one mile from Birds Point Jackson Co—Will try take them to Jacksonport. Capt Hooker of Birds Point Commanded Rebels. Got dish of strawberries at H J Dowels. Dinner at J H Fosels, Capt Knight. Arrived at Jacksonport about 4 PM. Recd two letters from wf yesterday with commission from Govr Morton to 29ᵗʰ Regt Ind Vol at Corinth. Officers come to Hospital; make disturbance at 11 PM. Whiskey works much disturbance. Parties arrested near Powhattan released. Much secesh testimony nullifying that brot against them. 11 Wisc, & 33 Illinois[8] with General Steele, & staff crossed River on way south.

May 18ᵗʰ—Sund Cloudy, cool. One of boys of Co C brot in dead. Shot below in a skirmish one of Ind 1ˢᵗ also killed one more of ours wounded through shoulder. Brot in some prisoners among others Capt Wm Griggs. Who brags he has "killed more 'dammed Yankees' than any other man in Ark." Very possible.

Mond May 19ᵗʰ—Cloudy cool Wm Y Shaw gives Recipe for Rheumat

Rx Nit Pot Ziii	Tablespoonfull two every
Water Zviii	hour during day. from
Honey Zii	Dr J L Scott one of Camp Jack Prisoners.

Take dinner with Dr Wm Y Shaw Recd sick from Hospital of 1st Ind. Case of Variola

Tues May 20ᵗʰ—Rain severe all night. removed variola patient to pest house. Got some coffee yesterday five lbs; plenty hidden about town Tollifer found sack of it at one place. I make distance to Pilot Knob one hundred, & seventy-seven (177) miles. Rain continuous. All sorts gloomy weather. Have to put up notice for soldiers not engaged in Hospital to leave us it is getting to be a perfect runway for all the loafers & whiskey suckers in camp. Wrote

---

8. The Thirty-third Illinois Infantry was added to Benton's brigade. They would stay with him through the whole war, along with the Eleventh Wisconsin, the Eighth Indiana, and the Eighteenth Indiana.

to Wm E Earle in relation to his discharge papers. Geo F Walker Co D shot in shoulder May 15th near Augusta down the river . . .

Jacksonport Jackson Co Ark
Saty May 24th 1862

Dearest Margeret

A mail leaves this morning early. Now at 5 AM I am writing this. Health is very good, Regt except two companies over the River. All other troops gone but a section of Artillery assigned to us, that is planted between the two rivers on the point commanding the town. We have been expecting an attack for the last two days. Pike's Indians & other white cutthroats are about us. They occasionally kill one of our men especially if alone. One was shot yesterday, & one day before this one with all the barbarism Indians[9] are capable of. I am very busy all the time a few hours with the sick, a few to reading, & regular hours for sleeping & eating consume my time. We get no news, & can only *guess* what is going on about us. Only the cannon threatening this town saves us who are in it. I stay at the Hospital & the Artillery is so arranged as to sweep each side of it . . .

Write often dearest & believe me yours affectionately

CBrackett

Camp on White River below Jacksonsville [Jacksonport]
Jackson Co Ark May 26th 1862

Dearest Margeret

Your very interesting letter of May 10th reached me last night. We moved from town yesterday on to this side of the River that we may be all together as the Rebels seem determined that we shall all be destroyed or that we shall destroy them, & they are likely to get what they need. Our cannon are bearing on the place, & we are ready for business; they have murdered some of our men with such

---

9. Brigadier General Albert Pike's Confederate Indian Cavalry Brigade of three regiments, consisting of the First and Second Cherokee and the First Creek are referred to here. Pike was a politician. The general's senior colonel was Stand Watie, a full Cherokee, who later commanded the brigade. Though they had participated at Pea Ridge, Pike and Watie were not in Arkansas at this time. The Indian Brigade was back in Indian Territory (Oklahoma). The "barbarism" had all come from a single battalion of white men from Arkansas.

HEADQUARTERS JACKSONPORT, ARK.,
May 24, 1862.

Brig. Gen. FRED. STEELE,
Commanding Division, Batesville, Ark.:

GENERAL: On the 21st instant Private Philander W. Pringle, of Company G, Ninth Regiment Illinois Cavalry, was murdered in cold blood and his body left lying in the swamp until yesterday, when it was buried by a party of soldiers, under command of Lieut. Arza F. Brown. Eight companies of my regiment will be on the west side of Black River this evening. The section of the Ohio battery is stationed near the junction of the White and Black Rivers. Two companies of my regiment will be left here to guard the stores, hospital, &c., in this place. This force is too small to perform the duty required of it.

My object in writing this letter to you is to say that an example must be made in some way here, or our soldiers and expressmen will be assassinated on every occasion. A most bitter and malignant spirit is manifested by some ruffians in the southern portion of Jackson County, which spirit I believe is fostered and upheld by the citizens of Jacksonport, or by a portion of them at least.

This morning a small party was seen in the timber having arms in their hands. These people will conceal their weapons and appear as good Union men. I wish to know what course to pursue with regard to the guerrillas in this county, and hope you will issue a proclamation telling the people hereabouts what they may expect in case they continue to commit murders as heretofore. Two Indiana soldiers and two soldiers of the Ninth Illinois Cavalry have been murdered already in this country and one soldier of the Ninth Illinois Cavalry wounded. I believe that no secession or rebel blood has been shed by our troops.

I am, sir, very respectfully, your obedient servant,
ALBERT G. BRACKETT,
Colonel Ninth Illinois Cavalry, Commanding.

P. S.—The people here believe that our army is retreating, and on this account they are becoming bold and clamorous. Moving the troops out of this place has had a very bad effect. I hope you will recommend to Major-General Curtis the reoccupation of Jacksonport.

barbarities as put Indian massacres all in the shade.[10] The Colonel commands here now & his blood is up, & the citizens have had fair notice. They have only as yet attacked lone men or small squads of two or three; they kill after their prisoners deliver up their arms. Day before yesterday at Birds Point they chopped the head from one & left him in the road. At another place took a Lieut prisoner & blew his brains out with his own pistol. Private Pringle below town on Cache bottom they killed by shooting with small shot, after a prisoner he had delivered up his weapons he was left in the road; these are the sort of men we have to deal with, & we are under restraint as to our mode of dealing with them. Sick & well receive the same treatment at their hands. We do not know anything about how soon the ball will open in earnest, but it will not be long. Our men are getting exasperated to such a degree that it is with much difficulty they can be restrained. We have four wounded men in hospital. Two were ambushed by seven secesh who fired at them shooting one (Geo F. Walker Co D) through the shoulder the boys fired back running their horses towards camp. Secesh followed taking short cuts till they had three shots at our boys their last fire killed one of the horses so both took to the bush afoot, & the secesh gave it up being afraid of being ambushed themselves & our two got safely into camp . . .

Your letter with Govr Mortons came to me I have written the Govr. The great battle at Corinth I would like to have seen, & had it been possible I would have gone across I thought some of changing clothes & going across above Memphis as a secesh but probably better counsels prevailed. The Col has just ordered over three companies to the town with only ammunition & no extra luggage. Our guns rifled twelves are shotted & things look like a storm was brewing. Pike's Indians[11] are on the Little Rock road where Curtis & the balance of our Brigade are working them. The citizens are in a great terror, & they well may be Death by torture has been practiced by them & they are suffering the tortures of a guilty conscience. They put one man in a dry goods box (alive) & threw the box in White River; how chivalrous? I do not want to think of it; but I hope some

---

10. Dr. Brackett, like other Federals, did not understand that he was part of an invading army. The notion that Arkansas civilians, moreover, were murdering Federal troops in cold blood is mistaken. Interestingly, Dr. Brackett seems unaware that there is a war going on around him. He mentions nothing about the campaigns of Curtis and Steele in the fall of 1861 or the spring of 1862.

11. Pike's Brigade was not doing any of this. It was all the work of Johnson's battalion.

man feeling as I do may be let loose with a squad of ten from each Co (volunteers). It would end their jayhawking. Yet I believe "vengeance is mine saith the Lord & I will repay" so believing (except when angered) am satisfied to let things work out their own results.[12]

I had some most excellent London Porter sent to me by a secesh last Sunday. I wanted it worse than I ever wanted anything before & it did me much good. We live very well, & are suffering for nothing except to see peace, & union restored, & again to be in peace with our dearest ones at home Kiss the children for Pa & for yourself accept the best wishes & love of your affectionate

Charles Brackett

Camp Tucker Forks of White River [Jacksonport]
Independence Co Ark Tuesday May 27th

Dearest Wife

. . . We are full of excitement here. Guns popping, companies moving, & messengers riding furiously back, & forth. I do not [know] what force is about us whether Pike's men white, black, & Red, or Hookers from the direction of Memphis. They are burning cotton by wholesale wherever it can be found unguarded by our troops. Citizens dare not say aught against it, but the storm is gathering for the Confederates to be used up by their own people. The farmers are highly indignant that their property must be destroyed by their own soldiers, who (when they have a chance) are committing the same barbarities which they told the people we would do. Now they know who their friends are, & are fearful to let us leave them: the Citizens of Jacksonport are praying us to return to save their town from their own marauders. They have sown the wind, & are reaping the whirlwind . . .

Dearest ever Yours C Brackett

★ ★ ★

THIS DISPATCH FROM THE *Official Records of the Union and Confederate Armies* (on the facing page) describes a May 27, 1862, skirmish at the Cache River Bridge near Jacksonport, Arkansas. Colonel Brackett names the wounded men who would be tended by his brother. When Colonel Albert

---

12. With accurate reports at his disposal, Curtis could have taken Little Rock and Helena in a week.

CAPTAIN: I have the honor to report to you that on the morning of the 26th instant I sent out portions of Companies G, L, and I, Ninth Illinois Cavalry, on a scout in the direction of Augusta. On the evening of the same day I received General Steele's orders to cause to be made a reconnaissance in force toward Des Arc as far as Cotton Plant, if possible.

Accordingly yesterday morning (27th) I sent Lieut. Col. Hiram F. Sickles, with Companies B, D, G, H, and M, out to carry into effect the orders I had received. I am thus left here with Companies A, L, and a section of the Ohio battery, with the teamsters, sick, &c. This morning Lieutenant-Colonel Sickles had a skirmish with a considerable force of the enemy at Cache River Bridge. This bridge has been partially broken down by the rebels, and it is yet uncertain whether he will be able to cross on it at all. He expects another fight to-night or to-morrow morning, and in the mean time will repair the bridge if possible.

On our side Adjt. William O. Blackburn, commanding Company H, and Private Frank R. Tift, of Company B, Ninth Regiment Illinois Cavalry, are wounded. One rebel soldier was killed and two taken prisoners, the latter belonging to Hooker's company. The rebels say that a gunboat passed up Red River yesterday and that another will pass up White River to-night or to-morrow. Lieutenant-Colonel Sickles does not credit these tales.

The general may rest assured that the telegraphic dispatches at the Cotton Plant office will be taken or my men will die trying.

I am, sir, very respectfully, your obedient servant,
ALBERT G. BRACKETT,
Colonel, Ninth Illinois Cavalry.

Capt. J. W. PADDOCK,
Assistant Adjutant-General, Steele's Division.

Brackett sent Lieutenant Colonel Sickles to cut the telegraph lines at Cotton Plant, Sickles had a skirmish at Cache River Bridge with Confederates under Hooker's command. Sickles, a friend of Charles, is Albert's second in command. It is not clear if Captain Hooker's company was at that moment part of Major Johnson's state troops, or Colonel Matlock's Confederate Cavalry soon (August 6) to be reorganized as the Thirty-second Arkansas Infantry. However, according to Watson's *Fight and Survive*, Hooker's company of Arkansas Mounted Volunteers served in the vicinity of Jacksonport in February 1862.

From the Journal:

Wed 28th—Cool, clear. Frank R Tifft [Tift] Co B Shot yesterday at mouth of Cache removed bullet from tend of little finger Right hand. ball entered inside palm through flex muscle of thumb. Sharp fighting at Cache Hookers Men & ours Two hundred to their three hundred & fifty

Thursd 29th—Warm men returned from Cache River, eleven prisoners, Four killed. We had two wounded none killed

Friday 30th—Cool, cloudy. Go to see Capt Braffett sick at Kleinards. one & a half miles from Camp. Make good shots with revolver.

Saty May 31st—Warm Clear. Slept for past two nights in open air. One of our men, & four mules drowned from the Ferry boat at 8 ½ AM. For last three nights we have been expecting Rebel Gun boat up with transports. Our troops except videttes, & Patrols for the town all taken west of Blk River on the point. Sect of Manters Baty Ohio 16th with us guns bearing on town. Find & Cleaned Arms yesterday.

Quinine gone—Dr. Jas has been nearly all the time in town—difficult to get him in Camp. Comes in about noon, Order to strike tents, & remove to Tonsalls three miles above on White River. People mostly gone from town: expect to be shelled. Wharf boat pretty well cleaned out by both Citizens & Soldiers. Receivd wfs letter of 10th inst this afternoon. It makes me more anxious to have war ended that I may return home. Blossoming of Peach at home forty days later than on Blk River at Reeves Station. Moved Hospital three miles above camp, one mile from White, & half mile from Blk. Stay overnight with Mr. Tonsall.

Sund June 1ˢᵗ—Clear, cool. I had good rest. Heavy cannonading down the River from 9 till 2 AM. Made out Certfcts of Disability for H Brown Genl Dibility, & Clinton Atkins Bronchitis. All of Co G Capt Buel.

Mond June 2ⁿᵈ—Left Carl Yinnike [?] Co H, Louis Boncher [Lewis Bunchner] Co A at Mannings three miles from Jacksonport. Gunboat came up & shelled our Camp, but as we had got out of it two hours previous nobody hurt. We fell back to Galloways Plantation, & Bivouacked. The 8ᵗʰ Indiana, & Manters Battery came down to reinforce us about 11 PM. 11ᵗʰ Wisconsin & another Bat go down opposite side of White River.

Tuesd June 3ʳᵈ—Cloudy Cool—Spy reports cotton, sugar, & molasses destroyed. I go down as far as Tonsalls: find Louis Bonchis [Bunchner] dead: Dr Shaw, & Judge _____ come along with a flag of truce, return to camp with them; they confer with the Colonel to save town from Bombardment. Gunboat drops four miles below town, when a few of our men run to the shore & fire on Cavalry on other side: this throws the whole population in grand fright & they run madly crying through the streets—Andrew J Sellers is name of Driver of Co M drownd Saty May 21ˢᵗ his body is buried today: found yesterday, but we were shelled out by Gunboat while attempting to bury him. Troops with two Batterys now at the point. Some expectations of An Attack on our camp.

Wed June 4ᵗʰ—Cloudy, cool. Slept in open air where we have Hospital—Report says that Major Humphreys Command are all taken. A third Battery of heavy field Pieces came in. I believe it is Klauss Battery (Indiana) Van Dorn reported in state with heavy force & Jeff Thompson on Crowley's Ridge with ten Regts.[13] Vanvalkenberg [W Van Valkenburgh] Co G died today of Inflammatory Fever, Brain & Lungs. Spend part of the evening at Galloways has very good new Corn Whiskey

Thursd June 5ᵗʰ—Cloudy, & cool. Our Hospital Locat by Galloways Gin, in which many of the boys sleep on the newly ginned

---

13. The Confederate enemy was neither Van Dorn nor Thompson with ten regiments. It was J. A. Johnson's four elusive companies. Once again, neither Van Dorn nor Thompson were west of the Mississippi. The enemy was the First Arkansas Cavalry Battalion, state troops. M. Jeff Thompson commanded a brigade of Missouri cavalry "partisans," or "irregulars." Thompson, the former mayor of St. Joseph, was a brigadier general in the Missouri State Guard. Since he did not trust the central government in Richmond, his brigade was never officially transferred to the Provisional Army of the Confederate States. Thus, he operated on his own.

Cotton. People here rampant at idea of having Cotton burned. Move again back to junction opposite Jacksonsport. At Galloways the idea struck me from seeing a boy whittling a conical Ball that to cast it with spiral twists would do away with rifling the Gun. This will I think be a useful invention. Write Colfax Caveat

Friday June 6th—Clear Cool Had sick headache last night. Went to point. Tree Twenty steps from my tent cut off by Sixtyfour lb shot from the Gunboat. Right smart shock of earthquake at our Hospital. Not attended with noise, simply billowy motion of earth rocking the log houses.[14] Citizens leaving Jacksonsport in toto, Gun boats short distance below. 8th Indiana, & Artillery returned & on road to Tonsalls east to Blk River. Gen Rains said to be advancing. Scouts (native) tells me five hundred (only) below Town

Saty June 7th—Clear Cool. Send for Salt & Brandy; Soldiers & Citizens destroyed a doz barrels liquor day before yesterday, & yesterday Indianians found barrel good Brandy which Dr Pain with one of our Sergeants poured out. Recd news of evacuation of Corinth Recd Paper (*Rochester Chronicle*) One of our horses shot in Skirmish with Hookers men. Paymaster here

Saty [Sunday] June 8th—Cool, clear: Write letter to wife. Send $10.00. Gen Benton[15] has sword presented by his Regt the 8th Indiana; makes a very eloquent speech on the occasion. Commencing earthworks at Point. I cannot think that we will have fight of much consequence.

14. Prof. Charles Ammon of St. Louis University has said, "It's likely that Dr. Brackett felt an earthquake in the region not reported in Dr. Nuttli's database. In the central Mississippi Valley a magnitude 3.5–4.0 earthquake occurs about every one to two years, and although these are not severe enough to cause much damage (most don't cause any), they may be widely felt . . . It was probably a small-to-moderate event that would be felt in the region, but not widely reported." [private communication, April 11, 1998]

15. William Plummer Benton, age thirty-three, of Richmond, Indiana, a veteran of the Mexican War and a lawyer, was the colonel of the Eighth Indiana Infantry at Pea Ridge. On April 28, 1862, he was promoted brigadier general of volunteers and given command of a new brigade formed from the Eighth Indiana Infantry, the Eleventh Wisconsin Infantry, the Ninth Illinois Cavalry and two batteries of artillery. Benton's brigade of Steele's division of Curtis's Army of Southwest Missouri, stationed in Arkansas, saw only light action throughout 1862, not participating in a major battle. Being one of two cavalry regiments in the brigade, Colonel Albert Brackett's troopers were nearly always on detached service, which often, de facto, made the colonel an independent commander.

THUS BEGAN A PROCESS of about five weeks in which General Curtis shifted his three Arkansas brigades under Steele south from Northeast Arkansas, also shifting his three Missouri brigades under Carr south from Southeast Missouri for the purpose of ousting the Confederates from Helena and Little Rock, Arkansas. He did not wish, however, to commit to a seige unless General Halleck reinforced him with two other divisions.

Camp Three Miles from Jacksonport
Sunday June 8th 1862

Dearest Wife

. . . We have withdrawn from Jacksonport on the 25th ult (two weeks today) camped on point, then for fear of the Rebel Gunboats on the 31st moved our sick to a house three miles off up in the woods, & with some fighting of Pickets employed the time two days when the Rebel GunBoat came up She was armed with heavy sixty fours, & as she rounded the point her first shot with a sixtyfour pound solid shot cut off a large tree eighteen inches from the ground twenty steps from my tent; the second cut off a Sycamore directly back of the Hospital tent twenty feet from the ground; the next two shots raked the line of the tents of Capt Bishops, & Capt Giffords (of Logansport) companies, & if the Colonel had not two hours before taken the men & horses out in the woods away from the camp, would have killed & wounded a vast number of men; then they threw shell with a vengeance most of them bursting over the camp about twenty or thirty feet in air, yet with all only one man recd harm & that only a slight scratch from a piece of shell on the cheekbone. They had our range perfectly, the citizens male, & female cheering them & telling them where the Hospital & Company tents were. The Colonel would not allow our Artillery to answer, as he was unwilling that the lives of women, & children should be endangered, however guilty they might be, & I know he did right. All the City was out cheering & waving flags, & handkerchiefs, the men directing the gunners where to fire to reach our tents. They report having killed fifty of our Regt. We had one man drowned whose body was lying on the beach, & one of the mule teams went down to get him for burial but when they stopped a shell bursted near the team & they ran off throwing the wagon over & breaking things; this was about our only loss. While this was being these Gunboatmen went ashore, burned about a thousand bales of cotton, rolled off in the river all the sugar & molasses they could roll then & stove in the rest. The town now is perfectly sour with the stench of commingled Sugar, Cotton, & Molasses. More of each was destroyed than you ever saw; this was a part of the programme the citizens had not bargained for, & when it was completed the Gunboat with Hookers men left on the double quick; then the wail of Sorrow, Anguish, Fear, and Anger went up in one Grand Chorus mixed, flags of truce were flying, & dilapidated F. F. Vs.were crying for the mountains to cover them. They expected we would burn the town, Artillery, & Infantry come pouring down from Batesville, & they expected nothing but swift destruction; we however only laughed at them for their treachery, & took a few who directed the Shot & Shell in our camp & sent them off as prisoners; the town is most entirely deserted, only negroes, & few poor whites remaining: Goods of all kinds are cheap: to be had for picking up; the town soaked with Whiskey, Brandy & other liquors thrown out to prevent the soldiers from becoming mad with drink. This mingled with half burnt cotton, Sugar, & molasses makes the atmosphere sickening & nauseous with its mingled odors . . .

Our Hospital is on Mr Tonsalls place three miles from the Point. This Mr Tonsall is an old soldier was at the battle of Tippecanoe, & the Thames was wounded on the Mississinnewa, & is a perfect Union man. He was at the point when the Gunboat came up & was a special target for one of their Shots which cut off a large limb over his head. His negro the old Ferryman was much frightened, but the old Gentleman took it coolly & brought a bit of a splinter (which hit him) home.

A Mr Manning, wife, & one child occupied the house before we came, & yet have one room. They have rented the place of Tonsall. I am boarding with Manning on account of the crowded condition of our tables. We are sending home such sick, & wounded as are able to travel. General Benton is now here with a force of Hoosiers the 8th & Klausses Battery the 16th. All have seen service in Missouri, & this state. Benton was Col at the Pea Ridge fight, & promoted for his bravery. Dr. Ford of Wabashtown is Surgeon of the 8th Indiana. Today a splendid sword is to be presented to him (the General) by the members of his Regt.

Our wounded get along wonderfully well as do our sick. No supperating wounds from bullets, all do well; this is a source of great satisfaction to me, & I hope that if perfect attention to my duty will do it our good fortune may continue. We have one man shot through the scapula the bullet coming out under the scapular end of the clavicle, & one shot in the thigh high up & coming out at the knee, one shot in the popliteal space (back of the kneejoint) & coming out through the tibia who have neither of them lost a meal, or nights sleep from their wounds now about well.

We have just heard of the evacuation of Corinth.

Day before Yesterday we had two shocks of an earthquake not severe but enough to rock the houses very perceptibly. We are close to the sunken lands as they are called. Sunk by an earthquake during the present century. This that we felt was only a rocking of the houses not accompanied by noise or explosions . . .[16]

Chs Brackett

AT ABOUT THIS TIME (June 1862), Churchill's northernmost regiment clashed with various companies of Colonel Brackett's regiment. The Rebels were troopers of Matlock's First Arkansas Cavalry Mounted Rifles.

From the Journal:

Mond June 9th—Very cool, & Clear. Mornings are wonderfully cool, even cold. Very hot at M—Paymaster in—I do not receive my pay. Will reserve it till I can make use of it in paying debts. Cannonading heard about sundown.

Tuesd June 10th—Clear cold, almost a frost; had severe headache last night. Took Opium gr 1, feel well this morn. slept well: receive letter from wife. Wrote yesterday. Major Humphreys command in from Mo soon after noon. Two cases of Rupture, & one bruise from falling horse. Co B Sund had one horse killed by Secesh.

Wed June 11th—Cold Clear. Dealt out rations of whiskey to sick last [night]—all improved by it. One of the ways of cheating soldiers is to pay them off only in bills none less than five, then retaining any surplus less than five. Then selling the silver to sutlers who buy bills at a discount of twenty percent. So at least the sutlers clerk said to day that he bot of PMaster at twenty prct—then Dr

16. See Footnote 14, Journal entry of June 6, 1862.

directs Suts Clerk to buy poor Laytons Claim of ten, to pay him only five. May God pity & protect me from such frauds. Moon eclipsed commencing about ten Oclock & passing off after two AM; Semi transparent, yet darkening moon completely. Moon of Blood Red, or mahogany Color changing slightly with coruscations similar to the Aurora Boreal . . .

Camp Tucker near Jacksonport
Arkansas June 12th 1862

Dear Wife,

I have an opportunity this morn to send a letter home by Johnny Smith, our Hospital Steward who goes home on a sick furlough. I enclose a ten dollar bill for you.

Last night about ten OClock the moon began to be obscured by a circular body passing over its face, partly transparent showing perfectly the form but obscuring its light making it of dull mahogony color. Seemed to pass on from the East to the West, both in coming on, & going off Showing that the body obscuring it was globular in its shape. Nothing new since writing last. We are discharging many of our sick, & wounded sending them home. Major Humphreys & his command came in day before yesterday all safe. We had heard they were all prisoners. Your letter of the 22nd ult is recd. I wish I could get some of the asparagus. We do not have many vegetables; have had a few messes DewBerries very nice; had no wheat bread for a long time, corn altogether. It luckily agrees with me very well. I pity the many of whom suffer terribly from it. In some instances nothing but meal without salt has been had for four days together.

Brackett

FOLLOWING IS A REPORT of the first real standup battle for Colonel Brackett and his Northern Illinois troopers. Apparently, Major Johnson could not resist the temptation of plundering thirty-six Yankee wagons, using at least two of his companies under Captains Hooker and Shuttlesworth. Since the train was saved, Albert reports a small but satisfying victory in the Official Records, recorded as the "Skirmish at Waddell's Farm."

JUNE 12, 1862.—Skirmish at Waddell's Farm, near Village Creek, Ark.

Report of Col. Albert G. Brackett, Ninth Illinois Cavalry

HEADQUARTERS NINTH ILLINOIS CAVALRY,

*Camp Tucker, near Junction of Black and White Rivers,
June 12, 1862.*

GENERAL: It gives me great pleasure to report to you that I have this afternoon had a most successful fight with the rebels. This morning I sent out a train of 36 wagons for the purpose of getting corn and bacon at the Waddell farm, near Village Creek, Jackson County, Arkansas. I sent as an escort parts of four companies of the Ninth Regiment of Illinois Cavalry, under Major Humphrey.

The farm is about 5 miles from Jacksonport, and when the train was within about half a mile of it my men were suddenly attacked by a large force of the enemy. Major Humphrey, seeing his command was too weak to cope with the rebels, sent word to me to join him as soon as possible with re-enforcements. I started with two companies of Bowen's battalion, with two small howitzers. I found the train halted in the road about half a mile from the farm, and the enemy in strong force in front, shooting at my men and occasionally exchanging shots. I removed the fence on the right and unlimbered the howitzers in the road, and then formed Companies A, M, K, and C, Ninth Illinois Cavalry, under Captains Burgh, Knight, Cameron, and Blakemore, on the right in a cotton field, with orders to charge the enemy as soon as Lieutenant Madison, of Bowen's Battalion, should fire the howitzers, which were supported and defended by Captain Williams and Lieutenant Ballou, of Bowen's cavalry battalion. I fired two shots directly into the enemy, when the four companies of the Ninth Illinois Cavalry rode forward with drawn sabers, and made the finest cavalry charge I ever witnessed. The enemy was scattered in every direction, being completely routed and broken up. I continued to fire several rounds into Waddell's building and then advanced upon it with Captain Blakemore's company. I then filled my 36 wagons with corn and bacon, and returned to this post, arriving after dark.

Captain Cameron behaved with the greatest gallantry, as did his company, K, Ninth Regiment Illinois Cavalry. I must particularly recommend to your notice the conduct of Major Humphrey,

Captains Burgh, Knight, Cameron, Cowen, Blakemore, and Perkins, Lieutenants Benton, Hillier, Shear, Conn, Butler, and Smith, and First Sergeant Clark, of the Ninth Illinois Cavalry, and Captain Williams, Lieutenants Madison and Ballou, and First Sergeant Miller, of Bowen's cavalry battalion. My thanks are due to Surg. James W. Brackett for his care of the wounded, and to Battalion Adjutant Blackburn, Quartermaster Price, and Sergt. Maj. George A. Price, Ninth Illinois Cavalry.

The enemy lost 28 in killed, wounded, and prisoners. Private Hutsell, of Hooker's company, one of the prisoners, is mortally wounded. Captain Shuttlesworth, in command of Hooker's company, is also wounded. My loss was 1 taken prisoner by the enemy and 12 wounded, all of Company K, Ninth Illinois Cavalry.

I am, sir, very respectfully, your obedient servant,

ALBERT G. BRACKETT,
Colonel Ninth Illinois Cavalry, Commanding.
General SAMUEL R. CURTIS.

ALL OF THIS MEDICAL ATTENTION which is described in the following journal entries comes from the action of June 12, Waddell's Farm.

From the Journal

Frid June 13th—Clear, Cool. Matt Futrell Co Hookers (Secesh) wounded. Ball entered left side lodged under skin right side below point of scapula. Extract Bullet. F M Shuttlesworth commands the Hooker Company. Two companies of Jeff Thompsons* Men joined Hookers yesterday. Jos B Chamberlain Co K shot in left side on eighth rib.

Wm Luce Co K shot left side in at point scapula, out Pectoral Maj muscle.

Oscar D. Herrick Co K shot in thumb muscular part—Edward Young Co I shot through phalangeal bones of toes, next to little toe. Shot self with buck shot, wound powder burned. J R Wilder, Co K Scalp wound Rifle ball strikes over S_____. Coming out through left of median line. Kept horse all day after shot. Am-

---

*but Jeff himself is not present in Arkansas.

putate toes for Edward Young Co I. Gunshot wound.

Saty June 14th—Warm, clear. Regt move to Tonsalls; men in Hospital doing well; wounded suffering very little only two remaining in Hospt.

Sund June 15th—Clear warm. Yesterday very hot. Private H Strong Co K reported to have been killed by Hookers men after being taken shot with fifteen balls.

> Camp on Tonsalls Plantation, Independence Co Ark
> Mond June 15th 1862

Dearest Wife

. . . Our Hospital is pretty well filled & takes pretty much all my time. We have one wounded secesh named "Matt Futrell" shot through the body a bad wound. Our wounded are mostly about none confined to bed except one for whom I amputated part of a foot.

Our medicines are nearly gone & we hear nothing of our new supply sent from St Louis. There are no mds in this country, & if ours does not soon get in we will loose many men. My pen plagues me much, but I am forced to be patient with it. My mind is trained to bear petty evils better. I do not think I would even grumble about sour bread, or muddy coffee at home . . .

> Charles.

> Camp near Jacksonport
> Arkansas Sunday June 22nd 1862

Dearest Wife

. . . We have over fifty patients in Hospital wounded, & sick. We have one wounded Secesh shot directly through the body; I have hopes he will get well; we had thirteen wounded one day last week, & some few during this week.

This has been a very busy day as most of my help has been out in the Country. The Arkansas men in the three counties, & more perhaps are rallying to the standard of the Union in great numbers. Also from below they come in our lines in squads of from four to a dozen thoroughly armed flying from the conscription; there are horrid scenes being enacted hereabout in the way of murders &C.

To day troops by Regiments have been passing our Camp from above going South, some new move on foot. What or when I cant say.[17]

We hear little news, know nothing of the operations of the eastern armies. only hope all is well with them. The Gunboat that gave us such a hearty greeting is still below us, & I hope before long to know that she is ours. Jacksonport is about gone up. About as desolate as a town can well be; its Citizens mostly fled. Since the violation of their Oaths, by taking part against us when their Gunboat was up they have made themselves scarce.

It is now long time since I have seen Miss Caldwell. She skedaddled with the rest after the Gunboat left.

. . . There is now a probability that we shall have Texas to whip in after Arkansas is finished, & it will of course be no childs play, but however it may be the time will soon pass, & time spent in defence of ones country is not lost, & I have the faith that everything at home is right with your good management. However things may go I am well satisfied if only health & peace remain with my family. If by any mischance this war is protracted I hope to be able to visit home sometime during the summer, but it is time enough to talk of this when the time comes.

We lost another man yesterday by drowning in Black River. He leaves a young wife & two children. We have bad luck with Black River Ferries. Our pontoon train passed to day & will be put in the River tomorrow; then we will have no more ferrying.

I was out hunting one day last week. The Colonel gave me permission to try my new projectiles & I improved it by shooting a mess of squirrels. I had an Arkansas man with me, & we kept a bright lookout for larger game than squirrels. We were careful not to unload both our guns at the same time . . .

Charles

From the Journal:

Mond June 23rd 1862—clear cool. Got Qui & morph from Dr Chs [?] S Whitaker of Blk River __ Ind Co. A needed supply. Get

---

17. These troops are the other two brigades of Steele's division.

also morph & Qui from Batesville[18] by Capt Bishop & Brigade Surgeon Burke. Recd order to purchase for 174 sick from Batesville. Get order two hours before sick arrive. Send on to Jacksonport. Write to Chronicle.

[*Continuation of June 22 letter to Margaret*]

Monday June 23rd 5 AM

We have just got news that Co F is cut off by Hookers men & we are all going out to relieve them. I have an idea now we will get them all, but they are a hard set to deal with, good horsemen, well armed, mostly descendants of Merrills men, a sort of half horse, half alligator breed. They will ride to the bluff bank ten feet above the water, & make a spring off with their horses in the water, & get away like so many turtles. Yankees will however soon entrap them. They have got to be afraid of our men unless they have five to one, but now knowing their haunts we will soon have them. They are better men than Jeff Davis & his Richmond crew. In our last skirmish Private Strong was fallen on by his horse & crippled, one of our men tried to get him on with him on horseback, but Strong could not get up & told his comrade to leave him. After the Rebels came up the Rebel leader Shuttleworth commenced abusing him, when Strong seizing a pistol shot him through the body it so pleased the Rebels that they have treated him well ever since . . .

Charles

The following letter was published in the *Rochester Chronicle*:

Camp near Jacksonport, Ark.,
Tonsall's Plantation, June 23, 1862

Friend Fuller:

. . . Buckshot and balls from secesh rifles and shot-guns do but a trifling amount of damage. They fired over our boys, as they

---

18. Batesville was the headquarters of the Union high command (Curtis, Steele). Steele's other two brigade commanders, Grenville Dodge and Thomas Vandever, both brigadiers, had been reassigned, leaving Benton as one of only three Union generals in Arkansas, ranked by only Curtis and Steele. Steele was about to head for Helena, Arkansas on the Mississippi, where Confederate District Commander Churchill was located.

generally do. Matt. Futrell, our wounded secesh, will get well, I hope and believe. He was hit in the left side, over the spleen, and the ball came out at the right side, lodging under the right shoulder blade, whence I removed it next morning.

Futrell is one of the nigger equality men having no wife, but a number of female slaves. Whenever you hear one of these chaps calling out, "Nigger equality, nigger equality," you will find him with less brain than belongs to an average negro of pure African blood, and a reputation for fair dealing tolerably low. It is a sign to me when a white man with staring eyes is portraying the horrors of "nigger equality," that he feels himself below average negroes, and wishes on that account that those with black skins should be enslaved and deprived of all rights which a white man is bound to respect; that is my private opinion publicly expressed, if you choose to make it public, as I desire.

Troops are pouring south in a perfect stream, some new movement being on foot. When we move from this delectable canebrake, I do not know, and do not much care, so long as we are of service to the United States, and the glorious constitution which we are sworn to defend . . .

CHARLES BRACKETT

JUNE 23, 1862.—Reconnaissance toward Augusta, Ark.

Report of Col. Albert G. Brackett, Ninth Illinois Cavalry.

HDQRS NINTH REGIMENT, ILLINOIS CAVALRY,

Camp Tucker, Ark. June 23, 1862.

GENERAL: Captain Perkins, of Company F, Ninth Regiment Illinois Cavalry, has returned. The result of his reconnaissance may be summed up as follows:

He went down on the right bank of White River to within about 5 miles of Augusta, he being on the opposite side. There is a considerable rebel force at Augusta, and the rebel gunboat is still there. They are awaiting an attack from our forces. Our gunboats were reported at Saint Charles, about 200 miles below Jacksonport; possibly they may be this side of that place. Quite a large rebel force is at Grey's Bridge, on the Cache River, where they are fortifying.

Captain Perkins had two skirmishes, in which one man of Hooker's rebel company was killed. Captain Perkins had one horse killed and two wounded by the enemy. Please forward this letter to Major-General Curtis, commanding, if you think the information is of sufficient importance.

I am, sir, very respectfully, your obedient servant,

ALBERTY G. BRACKETT,
Colonel Ninth Illinois Cavalry.
Brig. Gen. FRED. STEELE, Commanding Division

★ ★ ★

SLOWLY THE REBELS ADVANCED. These were Major Johnson's guerrillas; Colonel Matlock's regulars had returned to Helena with General Churchill. Aware now that Steele was moving against him, Churchill notified Hindman of a possible Yankee advance in strength. Johnson's task was to steal or destroy Union Army supplies and equipment.

Hd Qrs 9th Regt Ill Cav
Camp Tucker
June 23rd 1862

Dr. James W. Brackett Surgeon 9th Regt. Ill. Cavalry will turn over to S. H. Price Regtl Quarter Master all ambulances, horses mules & other means of transportation in his possession.

Albert G. Brackett Col. 9th Ill. Cav.

Hospital of 9th Ill Cav, Tonsalls
plantation Independence Co Ark June 24th

Col A G Brackett:

Dear Sir: There is almost a continual call on me to assist in repairing ambulances, shoeing horses, & divers other work belonging in the QMaster Dept. I do not feel disposed to do this business thus forced upon me, & Dr James, who has assumed the business does not attend to it; & when he tries to do anything at it he only meets continual difficulties.

If the ambulance train, & its immediate appendages were in its proper place (the QuarterMasters care) there would be no such difficulty as it is in the line of his duty; Dr James has other duties which ought to take his undivided attention, & I wish to lay the matter before you; for you to advise him as to the better course.

If the Hospital transportation is with the QM a simple order from either of us will bring it up all ready; & when we stop we will be rid of all trouble of Drivers Horses, &C.

All of which is Respectfully
Submitted—C Brackett Asst
Surg 9ᵗʰ Ill Cav

P.S. Dr James is in town fitting up for the Batesville sick; they came (one hundred & fifty of them) two hours after I recd the notice. I sent to town & had houses ready for them. Dr Jas was there & immediately furnished the requisite room.

From the Journal:

Thursd June 26ᵗʰ—warm clear—Asa W. Wilson Co M died at ½ past 12 PM Fev Typhoidis, with Tetanus Regt moves today. Chaplain Briggs cash at Mannings to pay his board 5.00 Paid Manning for 22 days board 15.75

June 27ᵗʰ—Frid warm clear with some clouds. Moved to Jacksonport last night visited Gens Curtis, & Steele, & all the surgeons of this division have four hundred sick to move—Vst Dr Paine Col Baker of Ind 1ˢᵗ there-Stop at Jas L Robinsons eight miles from Jacksonport. Very hot. Camp on grounds just occupied by secesh fifteen hundred in number Get no dinner except a bite with teamsters. Iowa 4ᵗʰ forage train attacked; three killed, two wounded; Col goes with Regt has a fight till dark, brot back some twenty wounded, one missing, men brot in after dark, & I am too tired to count the no correctly—Col saved by steel vest.

1—Mat Abbott [Mather] Co M wounded by buckshot over right eye died night

2—Peter Zerbey [Zerbe] Co E Through lower lobe left lung ball lodged, & cut out

3—John Lyons Co L through left shoulder near neck two balls

4—George Vaness [Van Wess] Co M through right illiac region buckshot & ball through right arm

5—Frank Blakely Co M Ball through left leg

6—Chs Paddock Co K through foot rifle ball

7—Thomas G Robinson Co M thru left axilla, & right shoulder.

8—Corporal Francis M Herrick Co K. Through neck Rifle ball, cutting trachea low down entered left of third dorsal verteb out in front.

9—Jesse Hawes Co I through calf right leg Rifle ball

10—Frederick Saindon [Sindon] Co M. through left arm, & side severe flesh wounds minnie musket

11—John Craig Co M Ball in right leg above knee.

12—John Racus Co E. Ball from rifled musket in left wrist removed

13—William J Teas Co I in left breast Rifle ball

14—Edward Nicholson Iowa teamster. contused wound right side.

15—Chs Nugent Co L. Through right shoulder

16—Cornelius Vermule Co M shot in occiput ball lodged in bone removed this morn no symptoms of compression.

17—Captain E R Knight Co M Left Hypochond Rifle ball

18—Lieut Wm B [C] Blackburn Co A Left arm rifle ball flesh wound

19—Major Wallace Flesh wound buckshot leg.

20—Col A G Brackett struck in left side below heart with heavy minnie ball; saved by steel vest. Concussion severe—Ball deflected passing out through Coat carrying handkerchief two thirds through ball hole[19]

Videttes report all confeds departed none at Grand Glace [Glaise?]. Enemy had many killed, & wounded. We buried three of their dead. Capt Knight killed two, & probably five—his wound probably not fatal. Ind 1st arrive; have had a hard scout in S W Missouri Casselberry, & Patterson both look jaded—say they had good time with Kansas troops in Missouri.

Afterwards ascertained Twelve killed, & thirteen mortally wounded

---

19. Charles treated the wound of Albert, at the early stages of the Federal advance from the northeast to northeast central Arkansas, as the fighting heated up between the vanguard of General Benton and the retreating Colonel Matlock.

Report of Col. Albert G. Brackett, Ninth Illinois Cavalry.

HDQRS. NINTH REGIMENT ILLINOIS CAVALRY,
Camp on Village Creek, Jackson County, Ark., June 28, 1862.

CAPTAIN: Yesterday afternoon I received orders from General Steele to send a force down White River to re-enforce the third battalion of my regiment, which I had sent out under Major Wallis on a foraging expedition, the train of the post quartermaster having been attacked by the enemy. Accordingly, I started with the second battalion of my regiment, and shortly after overtook my train, which was returning without corn. I caused the train to go back, and joined both of my battalions together. At Stewart's farm I learned that the enemy was near by, and I determined to attack him.

When a mile beyond Stewart's farm, which is about 6 miles from this place, my advance guard, under Captain Knight, came suddenly upon the enemy, and the fight commenced in earnest. I sent my companies forward one after another amid a continuous blaze of fire from the enemy, who were strongly posted among the trees and on the edge of the swamp. I tried several times to charge them, but they were so well posted and the underbrush was so thick that I was unable to do so, notwithstanding my men were close upon them, some of them being within 50 yards. I fought them in this way for at least half an hour, when seeing that I could not force them from their position, as they outnumbered me greatly, and it being nearly dark, I gave orders to move back to a large corn field, where I knew if they followed me I could cripple them, as they would not then have the advantage of their cover. I got my men out in fine order, and upon reaching the turn in the main road halted a short time; but the enemy had been so severely handled that he made no attempt to follow. It was now dark, when seeing that nothing further could be done I returned to this camp. On my way in I met an artillery and infantry force going out, under Brigadier-General Benton; it was too dark for him to travel, and he halted.

My officers and men are entitled to great praise, and fought with the most perfect coolness and determination. I had with me Majors Humphrey and Wallis (wounded), Captains Gifford, Chidester, Knight (wounded), Buell, Cameron, Blakemore, and Booth, Adjutant Stevenson, Battalion Adjutant Blackburn (wounded), Lieutenants Harrington, Shear, Ellsworth, Warner, Bayley, and Shattuck, all of the Ninth Illinois Cavalry. My guide, William McCulloch, Sergeant-Major Price, Battalion Sergeant-Majors Knight and Roberts, and Chief Bugler Fritson also behaved admirably. I was struck with a ball, which sickened me for a time, but I soon recovered from its effects. My wounded men were well cared for by Surg. James W. Brackett and Asst. Surg. Charles Brackett, for which they have my thanks. My loss was 3 officers wounded, 1 man killed, and 28 wounded; 7 horses killed, 24 wounded. I send list herewith. The loss to the enemy was severe; 5 of their men were seen dead on the field.

I am, sir, very respectfully, your obedient servant,

ALBERT G. BRACKETT,
Colonel Ninth Illinois Cavalry.
Capt. J. W. Paddock, A. A. G. Steele's Division.

From the Journal:

Sund June 29ᵗʰ . . .Peter Zerbey [Zerbe] Co E died at M—Pulmonary Hemmorhage—bore his wound, & consequent sickness with great fortitude. Buried at 4 PM

Mond June 30ᵗʰ—Cool clear. Col unwell yesterday-has been since he was shot. Recd order to move at 6 AM tomorrow.

From the Journal:

Tuesd July 1ˢᵗ . . . Cloudy, cool. Start South. Stop at Dr. Picketts ten miles from Robinsons; Eighty negroes, Pickets away with Hooker, obstructing road south; cotton gin burned, & Press, Steele mad, & offers $100 reward for incendiary.

Wed July 2ⁿᵈ—Clear cool—best soil [?] Slept in open air, good sleep: Moore of Wabash calls to see me—no meds as we need—18ᵗʰ Ind in; look well bands playing. Very hot.

Thursd July 3ʳᵈ—Clear cool Move at 6 AM. Leave Matt Futrell secesh Prisoner at Picketts Travel 17 miles to Augusta; road blockaded, by felled trees many miles Overtake secesh[20] kill six, wound

---

20. From this point on, the Rebels were the Arkansas Confederate cavalry regulars of General Churchill's brigade.

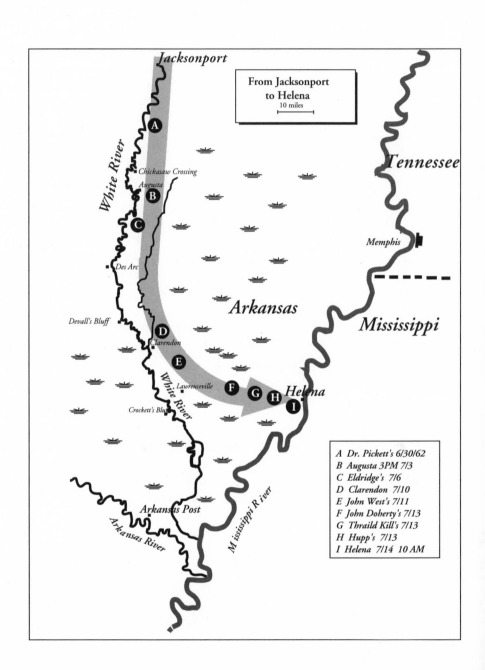

From Jacksonport
to Helena
10 miles

Jacksonport

Tennessee

White River

Chickasaw Crossing

Augusta

Memphis

Des Arc

Arkansas

Devall's Bluff

Mississippi

Clarendon

White River

Lawrenceville

Helena

Crockett's Bluff

Arkansas Post

Arkansas River

Mississippi River

A Dr. Pickett's 6/30/62
B Augusta 3PM 7/3
C Eldridge's 7/6
D Clarendon 7/10
E John West's 7/11
F John Doherty's 7/13
G Thraild Kill's 7/13
H Hupp's 7/13
I Helena 7/14 10 AM

fifteen with shell: reach Augusta 3 PM take row of offices for Hospital; Dr Bland, & Wm P Campbell have offices use one as dispensing room Dr.____ take fine trunk for sf. Very hot. Secesh[21] crossed White River this morning.

Frid July 4th—Cool, clear. Have grand parade 15 regts Cav, & twelve Infantry beside Batteries of 100 guns & Squadrons very hot

Saty July 5—Cool clear. Roberts Co L died had cash 1.25. Returned to Mrs Mary Patterson letters of Wm Campbell to Miss Davis. Private letters, also miniatures of his sister & _____ Mr Bland killed yesterday by one of 8th Indiana—Firing yesterday & today down river.

Sund July 6th—Clear, warm, Move this morn Transport sixty sick & wounded. Eight wanting places to ride: Gen Steele gave up to Twitchell his Carriage which we wanted for the purpose. Twitchell was at fight at Stewarts Plantation, & probably shot some of our men.

Stop at Eldriges for dinner 10 miles from Augusta. Intensely hot, & dusty, Eldriges very pleasant people. Road obstructed three miles below. Kill a few secesh. One Iowan & one of 9th Co A wounded by bushwhackers. Shell the woods all around.

Mond July 7—Clear, pleasant. Bivouacked in cane brake in Cache River bottom . . . Go over Cache after night and stop at _____ till morn . . .

Tuesd July 8th—Clear, cool; had good rest Sutler Clark, Jos W B, John Davison and I stayed at ____ Went to Mills & helped with wounded there. We buried one hundred & thirteen secesh, & six of ours & had about forty wounded; get good water at Dr Chunns. Camp two miles beyond in secesh camp whence we shelled the Texans. They had been cozily chatting of how they would thrash the "dmnd Yankees" when a shell started them in such a hurry that they left their pistols—forage—At Col Hills they tied to a tree & shot one of the Wis boys—I helped bury him he was filled with shot. Rear guard burning all the fine houses on road. Doctor Chunns beautiful place in ashes -Awful condition of things.

Wed July 9th—Warm cool Start south; get off noon: travel fast; fighting in advance, & in rear; wells filled no water; Curtis stops

---

21. Colonel Matlock's command; Major Johnson was back north fighting pro-Union Arkansas guerrillas.

our train at 5 min of four to get his in middle of train Arkansans[22] in fast to join us. Stop in beautiful pine woods resting while Curtis train passes. Stop to feed at 7 PM. Start at 9 & reach Clarendon County at daybreak next morn

Thurs July 10th—Clear cool Has been pleasant nights travel. All wells filled. No water but that from a slough where we supped last night. Get Hospital building at sunrise Drug store opened & stripped Get very few things we need. A poor business this of allowing stores to be broken into & pillaged Thus we loose those things we need, & get the name of common robbers. Boats left this place Tuesday morn 8th inst. No Hospital stores, or mds.

Frid July 11th Clear, cool. Osterhauses[23] Brigade moves this morn. Go out with music at 4 AM; two hours passing. Clarendon almost entirely evacuated or deserted; have seen but two houses occupied Start at 10 AM, travel 17 miles on Helena road to John Wests place. Stop the night with west, Capt Braffit also

Saty July 12th—Cloudy cool—Rained hard yesterday. John Wests crop destroyed fully Resides in Monroe Co. Clarendon County town—water scarce none except rain water in hollows. Fortyfive miles to Helena from Wests, made thirtytwo miles from Clarendon Stop at 10 PM Sandy roads.

Sund July 13th—Clear warm Road yesterday on sandy ridges except first four miles. Houses deserted. Had four hours good sleep the night past, horses had nothing but thick muddy water passed no running streams since leaving Clarendon. Well water on ridge good. Stop at John Doherty twenty two miles from Helena One of Iowa 3rd, Bell, Co I died here, detained to bury him. See Memphis Appeal of 27th ult with news of McClellans defeat? Stopped last night near Spring Creek. 26 miles from Helena[24] according to Dohertys measurement. Ten miles hence to Lick Creek good water there. Pass Thraild Kills plantation nineteen miles

---

22. The newly organized Second Arkansas Cavalry, United States Volunteers.

23. Steele's First Brigade was commanded by the recently promoted (a few days earlier) Brigadier General Peter Joseph Osterhaus, a superb Prussian-born officer, who would prove to be the best of the German-born Union generals. At this point, there had been a confusing change of command structure. Colonel Julius White commanded the Second Brigade, with Brigadier General William P. Benton continuing to command the Third Brigade.

24. General Hindman sent the Third, Fourth, Sixth, and Eleventh Texas cavalry regiments to reinforce Churchill at Helena, uniting all six Confederate regiments. Hindman remained with the state government at Little Rock.

from Helena Cotton gin burning Planters in great fear, & pray for guards- get supper at Hupps with S Major Rice Q M Brackett Get to camp late. Best alluvial land, & Finest plantations. Bivouac

*Mond July 14*th—Clear, warm Sick all as well as could be expected, but some failing fast. Hope keeps up spirits. Reach Helena at 10 AM; Cut my hand on way

*Tuesd July 15*th—Clear Warm Wollensack died last from congestion coffee, & crackers only for breakfast no requisitions yet made out; plenty in Quartermasters hands—wrote wf & Chronicle.

HELENA, ARKANSAS
Ninth Illinois Cavalry

AS THE FEDERALS ADVANCED toward Helena, there was some initial fighting between Steele and Churchill; Hindman, however, fearing that he was fighting Curtis's "army," ordered Churchill to evacuate the town without a major fight as the Yankees, including Brackett's unit, approached.

★ ★ ★

Helena Arkansas Tuesday
July 15th 1862

Dearest Wife

We arrived here yesterday & today at 11 OClock the boat goes north with our mail. We have had to fight our way through since I wrote my last letter, but got along without serious loss. At one fight we had thirty one men wounded, & two killed. The Colonels life was saved by a steel vest. The heavy ball struck the vest denting it, but [not] going through. The last letter I had from you was dated May 22nd.

My letters sent north I suppose have been mostly lost.

We were two days without water except that standing in pools covered with thick green scum. We brot here eighty sick & wounded of our own Regt, & about four hundred of the Division. We killed in one fight (with Texan Rangers) one hundred & thirty & wounded one hundred who will mostly die.

I have stood the march well, never in better health. Will try to go north with the sick & wounded whom we will send by boat to St Louis. We are now one hundred & eighty miles (by river) below

Memphis. Fitch Regt (46th Indiana) is in White River with some gunboats & transports with stores for us; they were at Clarendon on White River last Tuesday, & hearing that we were all cut off they dropped back. We got to Clarendon next day, & finding boats had left struck immediately across to this place.

We were compelled to get to the boats for Provisions & medicine. Our supplies were cut off from above by the land route & we were two months without medicines except such as we could Jayhawk & that was but precious little. A boat arrived here last night with stores, but I have had no time to go down to it yet. I want a drink of something cool, but will finish my letter first. When I have time you shall hear some particulars of our march (one of the hardest on record perhaps). Yet I suffered really very little probably because I can accommodate myself to circumstances better than most men. Some of our Officers cried like children for food, & drink. I rode my mule "little Burro" through, & he took it as I did without complaining, never tiring, or showing signs of fatigue. Some of the scenes, & incidents of our march were truly awful, & others ludicrous, embracing all the incidents peculiar to the march of a hungry maddened army through an enemy country where wells are filled, & provisions buried, & burned. Direct letters to the Regt here for the present. Ever yours

C Brackett

[*marginal note*] Tommy Howes was here in a boat looking for me yesterday, but I did not see him being busy getting our sick in comfortable quarters. We find many Baubles in secesh houses, & if I can I will bring some home to you & the children.

★　★　★

AS CHURCHILL PROCEEDED SOUTH away from the Yankees at Helena to hole up at Arkansas Post with his six regiments, Curtis occupied Helena with Steele's three brigades (including Dr. Brackett's). Because of the storm of protest from pro-Confederate Arkansas civilians following the evacuation, Hindman was forced to resign as department commander of the Rebel Trans-Mississippi. In an attempt to save face, Hindman later took field command away from Churchill before being reassigned.

Slowly but surely, Curtis pushed the Confederates out of all Missouri, all of northern Arkansas, and all of central Arkansas without having to fight a major battle, sustaining very few casualties. They simply melted away in the face of Yankee strength.

[*The following letter was published in the* Rochester Chronicle]

Helena, Ark.,
Tuesday, July 15, 1862

Friend Fuller:—Since writing the foregoing, we have had no chance of sending off a letter with any expectation that it would reach its destination.

We have had almost one continual fight with bands of Arkansas and Texan Rangers[1] and Guerrillas, meeting with various success, but never turning back on our march. Provisions were buried and burned to keep them from us. Wells were filled up to keep us from water, yet, we got along well. At one place where attacked, we lost four killed, and killed one hundred and thirty Texans, whom we buried. I was present at the burial, and saw one man, of the 11th Wisconsin, who had been taken prisoner, and tied hand and foot, and shot, and one who had been taken wounded, and re-taken, who said the butternut suit he had on, saved his life; they thinking from his suit, that he was one of their men . . .

Yours truly,

CHARLES BRACKETT

HINDMAN WAS SOON TO BE REPLACED as Trans-Mississippi commander by Major General Theophilus Hunter Holmes, a fifty-seven-year-old North Carolinian from the Old Army, who had not seen field service since the Mexican War. Holmes would hole up in Shreveport, Louisiana, with Churchill continuing to command the District of Arkansas for the remainder of 1862.

★ ★ ★

---

1. Throughout the "slow but sure" campaign in Arkansas, "The Texas Brigade" did the bulk of the fighting for the Rebels. The Texans despised Hindman but respected Churchill. The commander of this Texas brigade in Arkansas was the distinguished Colonel James Deshler of Alabama, West Point Class of '54. The small, red-headed Deshler and his Texans would be the only Confederates to do any real fighting at Arkansas Post. In 1863, Deshler was commissioned a brigadier general and given command of the Texas Brigade of Major General Patrick R. Cleburne's division, the Army of Tennessee. At the Battle of Chickamauga, September 20, 1863, Deshler was killed in action by a Federal shell.

Helena Arkansas July 16th 1862

Dearest Wife

. . . I shall of course try to be at home at the time you speak of.[2] I cannot tell where I may be ordered, but time will make us know. We are sending off our sick up the River near one hundred sick, wounded, & disabled, & the day of course is a busy one for us all. There are about Twenty transports here, & about thirty thousand troops. Generally in best spirits.

My head is so confused I hardly know what I am writing. We are in a house owned by a secesh officer. Our General Curtis occupies Gen Hindmans residence[3] (the finest in the place). Hindman is rabid, & orders the people to burn their towns, fill up their wells, Bushwhack, & Rifle our men whenever, & wherever they have a chance; this last is for the boys, & old men who are not liable to be drawn as conscripts. The Conscript act takes all between the ages of 18 & 35. Jeff Thompson is over the River on the Mississippi side,[4] his pickets in sight with a small force, & Price further down trying to cross. Price has superseded Hindman in command of the Army of Arkansas,[5] & he opposes Hindman's policy of destroying their (Rebels) property.

I put in with the things I sent you an elegant duster for dusting fine furniture; it is made of feathers & very pretty. I forgot to put in some beautiful swans down, will send it by another opportunity. Over one hundred & fifty of our Regt are now (Frid July 18th) on their way north on Furlough, sick leaves & discharges. The colonel has gone home; since he was shot he has been very nervous; the concussion having affected his whole system . . .

ever your loving husband C Brackett

GENERAL CURTIS STILL COMMANDED the two remaining Northern divisions, which were officially called the Army of the Southwest. Because of recent events, army headquarters was transferred from Batesville to Helena. General Carr's division joined General Steele's division in Arkansas under

2. Margaret's delivery time.
3. Accurate. Hindman had joined Churchill at Helena.
4. The "Swamp Fox" had never really been on Dr. Brackett's side of the river.
5. Not true. Price was in Missouri, Churchill in Arkansas. The "Army of Arkansas" has been since March a single brigade. It is called the "District of Arkansas."

General Curtis, who continued to urge the war department to send him two more divisions for the purpose of driving the Rebs into Louisiana, reinforcements that he did not need, but would eventually get.

From the Journal:

> *Wed July 16ᵗʰ*—Cloudy, cool. Letters from wf of 24ᵗʰ May, & 7ᵗʰ June. Send some patients to Hospital Boat. Hard rain PM
> *Thursd July 17ᵗʰ*—Cloudy, cool Got off all our sick, except five, (about one hundred & thirty) very sick from fatigue, & exposure to wet last night, severe storm 3 PM. Sent Cape, & other things home by Dr Grovers trunk.
> *Frid July 18ᵗʰ*—Cloudy, cool. Quite unwell this morn, neuralgia head, & face; Sent letter to wf by Yenneke. Take dinner today & yester with Richardson Make acquaintance with Mrs Waite whose husband has been compelled to flee north Ride to Curtis Hquarters to assist in release of Powell of Mississippi arrested today, released. Sup with Capt Grover, & Dr Coleman of 46ᵗʰ Ind.
> *Saty July 19ᵗʰ*—Cloudy cool. Marshall left 17ᵗʰ. Have yet five sick in Hospital. Dine & sup at R

[*"R" is Richardson, but Dr. Brackett roomed next door at H. C. Rightor's house when in town.*]

> *Sund July 20ᵗʰ*—Cloudy warm Dine & sup at Richard Twenty-five down with fever since others left. Get Qui oz vi Morph Zii from Dr _____ of 11ᵗʰ Wisconsin & four Bots whiskey.

[*Now that the Yankees were secure at Helena, nothing much would be going on in Arkansas for the rest of the summer.*]

> *July 22ⁿᵈ*—Clear, warm. No wind oppressive. Jas W B sick. I have been unwell past three days not seriously. Mrs Rightors warehouse pillaged last night wine, sugar, &c—write Dr Gould, & requisitions on St Louis for mds &c
> *Wed July 23ʳᵈ*—Clear pleasant. sick today & yester Jas W also sick not seriously. Dine & sup at R's
> *Thurs July 24ᵗʰ*—Clear cool. Has been quite pleasant since the rains. Breakfast at R's, & dine. Move to camp. Many boats passing loaded with troops going down. Troops went out last night four thousand, supposed after Jeff Thompson.⁶ All still—quiet no loud

---

6. Another wild goose chase. Thompson would not cross the river until the fall.

word spoken. Tent on high bank. Read Burns this evening a copy
one of the boys brot to office.

Frid July 25—Clear cool. Troops in from Jeff Thompson hunt;
Of course they did not go near him, & would not answer to catch
him; safer hunting such game when it is gone.[7] Send three to Hospital. Back to town at noon Dine Sup at R's. Wait long time for
Capt Grover of 46th Ind. See Walter McCarron [McCaron] Co D
Shot by accident last night in town; stops at Private house will pay
his own board. Sleep at Rightors

Saty July 26th—Clear, warm. Payday yester & today. I have not
yet recd mine—Breakfast at R's Recd of Paymaster on the 24th inst
Pay for the following Hospital Attaches

F Holliday	15.25	Pd 15.00
McCassion	15.25	Pd 15
King	15.25	Pd 15
Woodward	15.00	Pd 15
Ayers	10.75	Pd 10
Bowdoin	10.75	Pd 10
Dobbins	12.00	Pd 10
H Adams	15.00	Decr 2.00
Burns	5.50	Pd 5
McMahon	5.50	Pd 5
Layton	*15.00*	
	135.25	

Have been using Ellis, & Co (Philadelphia) Confection Sen-
nac—very good. Hiram Latson Co L shot sf through second phalangeal bone of fore finger amputate at second joint. Conclude to
send Ambulance to Hospital at 9 AM & 4 PM. Sup with Q M
Price.

Sund July 27th—cool, clear. Move patients, in part, to camp.
Lawrence Cherry Co C shot sf through left hand __th inst. Sick sf
since the rain only able to be about when under the influence of
med: come to the conclusion that the majority of Regt are thieves,
Trunk has been opened & ransacked, & articles abstracted. Drink
bottle catawba wine to put me in better spirits, does not work well.
Three boats down this PM one with US Flag flying at peak & bars
& stripes at half mast. Fires a gun when opposite. Fig trees in town

---

7. They didn't go near him, because he wasn't there.

During part of the time he was in Helena, Charles roomed at the residence of H. C. Rightor, shown above in 1897. (Photograph courtesy of the Helena Library and Museum Association)

no[w] full bearing Peaches, nectarines, & other fruits plenty. Slept last night in tent Miner with me. Read Burns till midnight. Negroes kept up singing music till near morn. Some of African birth here . . .

Mond July 28—Cloudy, cool. Rained hard after daylight with heavy thunder; got bonnet fast & all secure & went to sleep again. Clear at noon Q M Morrison, & Private Hall get back today, both hearty. Meds arrive by boat Read Moore today & yester. "The Loves of the Angels", & the "Sacred Songs" full of beauty.

Camp near Helena Arkansas
Monday July 28th 1862

Dearest Wife

It is a week the day since I wrote you last (making two letters since I have been here) in my last of the 21st I enclosed $20.00.

Time flies very fast though I have been under the weather for a few days past. We have not a half doz officers in the Regt fit for duty. I have not been excused from duty till yesterday, & today I have done nothing but lie in my tent & read, & eat at meal times, & I feel the benefit of the rest. Our march from Jacksonport was a harder one than I had even thought it at the time; you may have seen some acct of it in the papers. It was really a fearful march (made so in great measure either by knavish or foolish leaders; this entre nous) you need not repeat it only in the family . . .

We have as I told you but few Officers fit for duty. Some have gone home who I presume will not return, having borrowed money & run in debt to all who would trust them. Some such have returned to Indiana. None of them owe me I have been careful on this score. My pay due now is sufficient to pay off Albert.[8] I have not drawn it; had I a sure way of sending it to you I would do so, & let you pay off the judgment, but two months will soon roll on, when if alive I hope to see my Dearest Maggie, & my children.

A bit of gossip. Albert is about getting a divorce from his wife as Joseph tells me. He drew up the papers. I do not know as anyone else here knows anything of it. Cut this off & throw it in the fire I wish you to say nothing of it. You are the only one I have spoken it

---

8. Dr. Charles continued to owe money to Colonel Albert, because his patients wouldn't pay Margaret.

to since Joseph told it me. I felt bad about as I always have done to
see difficulties of this nature arising. It need not be so if parties will
try have it otherwise. But we are all imperfect & err most when we
expect, & demand perfection in those with whom we associate. Only
by commencing with ones self can we expect to approach that con-
tentment, & happiness that may be had here

    This life shines or lowers

    Just as we weak mortals use it

Charles Brackett

From the Journal:

Thurs July 31ˢᵗ—Cloudy cool Took supper last night, with a
Mr Jackson a Tennesseean. Steady cool rain with no wind AM—Dr
Jas Yester, & day before stays at Camp. Lieut McMahon sick at private house next door to Sutler Clark. Staying with Maj Humphreys at Mrs Rightors. Have good bed, a pleasant, airy room. Get
fresh figs—insipid fruit! Trees bear wonderfully, each new leaf having a fig at its base—fruit ripens in succession. Ripe & green on
trees till frost. Breakfast, dine & sup at R's Taken twenty-one 21
meals at Richardsons.

Hospital of 9ᵗʰ Ill Cavalry at
Helena, Ark July 31ˢᵗ 1862

My Dearest Margeret

    I wrote you a letter night before last from camp near town which
letter is yet in my trunk there. I have not been well for some days
past, in fact since we got here. I was up all the first night with my
boots full of water; this through necessity. I have kept [to] the house
one day of the time taking medicine, & have taken med nearly every day since though keeping at business.[9]

    The Lieut Col Sickles[10] told me to quit business for a few days,
& remain in town till restored I am taking his advice; feel very well
yesterday & today. My trunk is at my tent so I write this letter which
may go out to night—will send the other when I go back to
camp . . .

---

9. Unsanitary conditions in camp, hospital, and on the road took their toll on weak
constitutions.

10. The regimental No. 2 officer was mentioned often.

The seige of Vicksburgh has been abandoned for the present. How this will operate on us at this point I do not know, & I should not be surprised at any hour to see the *Arkansas* (that so successfully ran our blockade of Gunboats, & Mortar vessels). At this point when the stampede of Jacksonport would be re-enacted with (in all probability) not so successful results as to ourselves.

She is a powerful boat in truth, yet it seems (to look at such formidable boats as the *Carondelet*, & *Essex*[11] impossible that she could have passed their death dealing thirteen inch guns with anything else than certain, & swift destruction . . .

Write as often as possible to yours ever, Charles

Hospital of 9th Ill Cavalry at Helena
Ark Friday August 1st 1862

Dearest Margeret
. . . Tell the children that Pa does not need a shield other than that he has in the wish to do his whole duty whatever, & wherever it may be. The Breastplate of Righteousness is about the best a man can wear. I have not been exposed except to the fire of bushwhackers, & they have as yet done little harm. But it is all right enough to protect oneself by any means recognised that does not include poltroonry.

I have known but one instance of a steel vest saving life, & that was in Albert's case when had it not been for his steel vest, a two ounce ball would have gone directly through him from the left, to the right side. Immediate death would have followed. He led in succession every company of his command into the heaviest fire. It is now ascertained that the enemy at that place had twenty-five killed, & mortally wounded. Those slightly wounded we had no account of. Young Kitt had his horse killed at the first fire.[12] This is a nephew of Widow Kitt of Rochester. That Co went in first, & in the charge their horses heads touched before they commenced firing. So near were they that his captain (E Knight) had his coat partly shot away & shirt set on fire from his enemys gun We had thirtyone men wounded (two fatally) & the negro guide killed.

In the next skirmish they acknowledge a loss of two hundred,

---

11. Comparing the Secesh ironclad with famous Union ironclads.
12. Dr. Brackett was treating the wounded still laid up after the initial fighting in front of Helena.

& thirty. We buried before I left one hundred, & thirteen & several more dead yet lying there.[13] I was with the burial party part of the time. We buried six of our own men & had about fifty wounded. Major Clendenning was shot directly through the right breast, will probably recover. He is the one you have heard me speak of so often. Poor Capt Sloan was killed by a buck shot that went into his mouth lodging in the spine. Most of the wounded & killed were of the 11th Wisconsin that bore the heaviest of the fray. Two Cos of that Regt held sixteen hundred Texan Cavalry at bay for a long time.[14] Only about eight companies of our advance did all the fighting. One of our men just died from Mania a Potu. The worst enemy we have is whiskey. My trunk is just arrived from camp so I will get the letter I wrote a few days since, & enclose with this.

From the Journal:

Saty Agst 2nd—Clear Cool. Attend at Hospital Breakfast & dine at Rs Sup at our guide Newcomb. Am called to see slave woman of Mrs Rightors in labor midnight. Child, female, born quarter before one AM. Forty-five minutes after Rupt membranes. Mrs. H. C. Rightor gone to Memphis to see husband

Sund Agst 3rd—Clear, Cool. Long discourse with Chaplain Briggs, & Major Humphreys on the evils of gossip. Breakfast, dine, & sup at Rs

Mond Agst 4th—Warm, clear. Six negroes hung as Dr L B Dunn says: he told Mr H B Murch so. On this street low down town. Cannot yet ascertain this to be true. Regts out to meet Hindman on Clarendon road. Receive invoice of meds from the Dept of the Ohio. Morrison from Camp to stay with us. Have bot of wine after dinner furnished in a sort of mysterious way by Humphreys. Dr Jas, Joseph partake. Feel better than for some days past. Hope to return to duty tomorrow. Dr has sent for his wife Mrs Capt Perkins arrived from Chicago Saty last. Capt Cameron

---

13. Apparently, this is the skirmish at Round Hill, July 15, at Helena, not Stewart's Plantation of June 27.

14. The Eleventh Wisconsin was engaged and did suffer some casualties. The sixteen hundred Texans present in the four regiments is close to accurate. The idea that two companies of the Eleventh Wisconsin "held" four regiments of Texas cavalry "at bay" is, of course, wishful thinking. The July 15 action at Helena was a minor skirmish prior to the evacuation.

sick. Prescribe for Richardsons Servant, & for Mr H. P. Murch

DR. BRACKETT WAS DESCRIBING nothing more than the aftermath of July 15. The skirmishing, such as it was, pitted the Federals bivouacked at Helena against the rear guard of Churchill's retreating twenty-five hundred officers and men.

Hospital of 9th Ill Cavalry at Helena
Arkansas. Tuesday August 5th 1862

Dearest Wife

. . . Our Chaplain who occupies a room at Mr H C Rightors with Major Humphreys, & me gets by nearly every mail a letter from his wife. She also is expecting to be confined about the same time with you, & the Chaplain expects to be with her at that time as do I with you.

Capt Perkins had the pleasure of receiving a visit from his wife from Chicago; they are newly married.[15] She came last Friday; but the Capt is so much engaged that he cannot be with her much of the time; he went out with the Regt day before yesterday with three days rations, they are not yet in; have had a series of skirmishes, & sent in last night for reinforcements. About eight thousand are already there, & more needed.[16] The rebels took of the Wisconsin 1st night before last one hundred prisoners; killed eleven, & two wounded since dead. They are in large force this side of Clarendon. I do not know what their loss was; the negroes with our regiment fought bravely using knives, bludgeons, & fire arms with telling effect. A few of them were killed; I am satisfied they will do well for soldiers, & expect to hear of most effective fighting from Jim Lanes Regts when they get in the field.

From what I have written above concerning the fighting of the negroes you are to understand that they were Officers Servants. Each Officer is allowed one or more servants, & they are most generally negroes who are employed, though I employ a white man. The servants of course are armed, & the negroes take especial delight to be

---

15. If the wives were allowed to visit, it was certain that Curtis had no intention of moving south anytime real soon. It also indicates that the guerrilla attacks have lessened.

16. These eight thousand are, of course, the men of the three brigades of Steele's division.

well armed. The hundreds of negroes who have been deserted by their masters are using all means to improve their condition, enquiring diligently after spelling books, &C. Volunteering is I hope put an end to after this month. All other troops necessary to be employed in the future will I hope be drafted, or taken by conscription giving authority to draft or conscript at pleasure from localities infected with traitors. We ought to recognise the idea promulgated here, that all who are not for us are against us, & treat them accordingly. Let those demi traitors feel the power of the government, & the most powerful among the nations.

You of course have heard that the seige of Vicksburgh has been raised: Com Farragut was needed at Richmond, & has gone thither with his Flotilla, & Com Davis has come to this place with his. The Arkansas a very strong rebel iron clad, went through our fleet without very serious damage, but her doom is sealed. She will go under at the next encounter I have no doubt. The commander of one of our best boats there is reported as a most dastardly coward[17] refusing to encounter the Arkansas when he was in perfect fighting order which was not the case with the others wholly. I would rather suppose him a traitor. I do not like to have any American considered a coward. It is not well (whatever betides) that foreign nations shall think or know that cowardice is an American trait. Let it not be said of either party.

For the past week I have been doing little else but rest, eat, & drink. I was pretty well used up in our trip from Jacksonport, & after our arrival here exposed to unusual fatigue, in the storm wet through for a number of hours, having not time even to get something to eat, not a cup of coffee for twentyfour hours. From the effects of this I have now as thoroughly recovered as could be expected, & have returned to duty this morn. Saty our Lieut Col (Sickles) was boasting his good health, saying that *he* kept perfectly well on account of his total abstinence from alcoholic stimulants. Sunday he was taken severely sick, & remains so yet, & altogether I think he has complained of ill health as much as the average at least. He had two attacks of Icterus at least since leaving Chicago. The Col has been a total abstinence man for a long time past, but after the fight at Stewarts he took some liquor, but not much, refusing it when pre-

---

17. Dr. Brackett is too hard on his own navy. It was not always possible for one gunboat to duel another. The commander in question may have been under orders from a superior officer, merely doing his job.

scribed, although he had a great desire to use it. I was rejoiced to know that he considered it his enemy, & had the courage to refrain wholly from it (the only safe way for one who loves it for its effects). All our best, & most generally respected Officers, & men are, & must of necessity be temperate, just, & true. This obtains as a general rule. It is a truth & as such the sooner men embrace it as a rule, the sooner they will be of necessity recognised as among the Princes of the land. None other are worthy of confidence, & none other receive confidence to retain it long.

This is among the most sickly places on the River. Yet the health of the men generally is very good. The only death we have had originating here was from Delirium Tremens, or rather Mania a Potu. We lost one man here whom we brot sick from Jacksonport.

Cotton comes in in abundance, for all that the Confederates supposed they had burned all in the country. One man here (with whom I have boarded) had thirty thousand dollars worth of it burned in town; he is an Union man, a native of New York, & on account of his being the only Boot, & Shoe manufacturer was allowed to remain. For the past year he has sold a pair of Boots for a bale of cotton. Boots are worth (over the River) from twenty to thirty dollars a pair. Cotton baled weighs on an average five hundred lbs to the bale, & averages ten cts pr lb, or fifty dollars pr bale. Cotton growing is a very profitable business, good land producing a bale to the acre. Our soldiers pay from two, to three dollars pr bot for whiskey, which the dealers manage by the connivance of the Officers to smuggle to market. Each Regt is supplied by the Government with enough (in ordinary cases) for medicinal purposes, & this is in hands of the surgeons in trust for the men; in too many instances this trust is betrayed, & the men have to buy when necessary. I have furnished to our Regt by foraging more than the government has, & this without charge. The ordinary three months supply for a Regt is whiskey, & Brandy each two dozen bottles, wine two dozen. It was six months after getting our first supplies before we got any more. This on account of bad management, & from our communication being cut off. Now we are well supplied, & I hope will not again want.

Wed August 6th

Yesterday I went to work visiting patients in Hospital, & at different quarters in town, & by the time I had finished was thoroughly used up. It was the hottest day of the season when even the acclimated citizens kept the house. I feel none the worse this morning, & have a hard days work before me preparing Report for the Doctor James. He keeps hearty having the Sense, or the faculty of keeping hard work away from him. Yet the Lieut Colonel keeps him in camp which is galling to him. The Regt must not be left without one of the Surgeons. Staying where I do I have forced on me some private practice, but of a character not to give me any more walking than I would have without it. The servants here where I room, & at Mr Richardsons where I board (the next door to Rightors) with the families & boarders are some of them sick all the time. At Rs two slaves (house servants) & two boarders (citizens) Judge Baker & Mr Murch, cotton dealers, are sick, & here one of Mrs Rightors female slaves has puerperal fever.

Medical practice is lucrative in this country, fees being more than double what they are with us.

Chaplain Briggs, Major Humphreys, & QMaster Morrison are all three staying here sick, but able to be about.

The Col has got some new arms for our Regt, & two field Howitzers which were much needed. You have no idea how the Butternuts make the brush fly when a shell or a charge of Grape Shot from one of these little persuaders is sent among them, it always sets them in motion when of course our Cavalry having a sight of them driven from their holes, & hiding places can lay them to the land.

The assistance, or rather reinforcement sent to the Wisconsin 1st has returned, after a bootless chase, could find no enemy; they were a lot of Col Mattocks[18] [Matlock] Rebels who attacked. The Wisconsin men had no guards out, the enemy surprised them by night & took the whole rear guard, & their teams wagons, & good store of Guns, Sabres, & Ammunition. A bad thing for us, though very good for them. So it goes all about this region. Thirty thousand, & perhaps forty thousand as we are could clear the states of Arkansas & Mississippi[19] in six weeks I believe, yet we lie still horses, & men dying for lack of healthy travel, & good feed.

The Surgeon of the 18th Ind goes home to day; at some risk however going only on a pass from his Col.

---

18. Charles Matlock continued to command the First Arkansas Cavalry Mounted Rifles under Churchill. He was sending scouts out from Fort Hindman to observe the Federals.

19. The state of Mississippi was a tougher nut to crack.

When I get ready I hope to have full Authority; though it is much trouble to get it. From present appearances we are to remain here for an indefinite time; I have hopes as there are other troops out that Mattock & his men may be taken. Write often to yours ever

Chas Brackett

BRIGADIER GENERAL EUGENE CARR'S division of three brigades was the other half of General Curtis's Army of the Southwest. Elements of Carr's division now have been ordered by Curtis to join Steele in Arkansas.

From the Journal:

Wed Agst 13—Cloudy warm. Very hot. Go afternoon to review of Carrs,[20] & Thayers Brigades. Take to Gen Thayer papers for Morrison, & Briggs Morrison improving Attend at Hospital patients doing well but Lieut Conn at private quarters. Miss Carr take sick yesterday chills. Write wf four pages

Helena Arkansas Wednesday
August 13th 1862

Dearest Margeret
. . . I have to day been out riding. We had a review of two Brigades in one of which the 2nd Brigade of the 1st Division of the Army of the Southwest.[21] The 1st Nebraska is now in our Brigade, & its Colonel (Col Thayer) is our Brigadier.

---

20. Carr commands a division, not a brigade. Thayer would soon command Benton's brigade when Benton replaced Carr. The command structure within the Army of the Southwest, also called the Department of Missouri and Arkansas, was changing. The First Division (District of Missouri) under Brigadier General Eugene Carr and the Third Division (District of Arkansas) under Brigadier General Frederick Steele were now (August 1862) both in Arkansas under Major General Samuel Curtis, whose mission called for a movement against the Confederate command in Southern Arkansas for the purpose of clearing the enemy from the state. Brigadier General William Benton, commanding Steele's Third Brigade, was promoted to command the First Division as Carr was transferred out. Benton, in turn, was replaced by John Milton Thayer, the former Colonel of the First Nebraska Infantry, also of Steele's division.

21. Carr's division now appeared in force. At this moment Curtis, the army commander, was a major general; Steele and Benton, the two division commanders, are brigadier generals; all six brigade commanders are colonels.

HOSPITAL OF 9TH ILL CAVALRY

Helena Arkansas August 11th 1862

To All Whom it May Concern Greeting
I Thomas E. Morrison 2nd Lieut Co E & Acting Quartermaster of 2nd Battalion 9th Regt Ill Cavalry, on account of sickness which threatens my life, beg leave to resign my commission, & be honorably discharged from service. I make this resignation solely on account of ill health, & from no other cause.

T. E. Morrison 2nd Lieut
Co. E. 9th Ill Cavy

This is to certify that the above named Thos E Morrison has been for some time seriously sick with remittent fever, with extreme gastric irritability, & his condition is such that I believe a change of climate is necessary to restore his health, & probably to save his life, & I recommend that his resignation be accepted or a leave of absence granted.

Charles Brackett Asst
Surgeon 9th Ill Cavalry

Helena Arkansas
August 11th 1862

[The note below was written in pencil by CB sometime later:]

Disapproved same day by Sickles. New ones made out then sent off. Disappointment threw Morrison into a demented condition from which he never recovered. Died of Red Tape.

We are expecting our Col every day; he has been North since the first week after we got here. We have now two new Howitzers with our Regt; this will help us materially in Bushwhacking, & save a good many men if we have as much service yet in store as we have already passed. The Butternuts cannot endure shelling; it is wonderful how soon shells will start them from their coverts. Part of the Regt has been over the river in Mississippi hunting for a few days past. The Guerillas killed four Wisconsin men, & took two Indianians Prisoners.[22] This was close to the River, & then on their way back they cut the throat of one of the prisoners leaving him in the road. This was on Sunday. Our boys got after them the same day killed some, chased a lot of them back into a bend of the river just below our Camp, & I believe killed them all; they followed on the next day, & yesterday breaking them up completely, & I believe took no prisoners; this looks tolerably hard yet it may be right, for they who are bushwhacking are declared outlaws, & it is esteemed worse than useless to take them prisoners, swear them, & turn them loose to renew the work the next chance they get.

. . . I have not been out much since we came here (I told you about getting so wet after our long tramp). Since then I got all right as I supposed, & walked about too much during the midday, & received a "coup de soleil" "Ictus Solis" or sunstroke from which I think I have now perfectly recovered. I was out to Col Thayers quarters this afternoon,[23] & enjoyed the ride very much, besides feeling much strengthened by it. Our Chaplain is going home on sick leave; he also was sunstruck on our march hither from Jacksonport, & has not been able to endure the direct rays of the sun since. After recovering somewhat he was deranged so that he gave his horse away & everything else he had about him; he said since that he knew what he was doing but thought it all right, & if his money had not been in his trunk in a baggage wagon he would have given it all away. I think he will not return to the Regiment. I have not heard him

---

22. The guerrillas were probably Confederate regulars from Col. Matlock's Thirty-second Arkansas.

23. Thayer's new brigade was Benton's old brigade; that is, the Third Brigade of Steele's Third Division. The First Indiana Cavalry and the Ninth Illinois Cavalry remain in this brigade—for a while. The infantry regiments continue to be the Eighth and Eighteenth Indiana; the Eleventh Wisconsin; and the Thirty-third Illinois. The Federals within the Army of the Southwest were learning that brigading cavalry and infantry together is not practical for deployment purposes. Soon the First Indiana Cavalry and the Ninth Illinois Cavalry would be detached.

say much only that if he "learned some things at home that he had no means of knowing here" he would resign. I suppose he meant something in regard to what I mentioned of Albert's difficulty with his wife.[24]

I have heard nothing more of it since I wrote to you, but I hope it may be settled amicably. I find the chaplain to be rather too much disposed to gossip, never speaking well of any man & fond of retailing scandal. He has in some instances informed the wives of Officers of scandalous reports concerning their husbands, & thereby created a good deal of bickering, & ill will. It is a common thing for him to say of an officer, "I will write to his wife about [it]" or "I will tell his wife." But enough of this. The evil are often the first to think evil of others, & probably this is one of the modes of punishment decreed to evil doers.

Quartermaster Morrison who resides in Lake Co Inda[25] is also here sick, & intending to return home soon having resigned on account of ill health. He, Mr Briggs, Major Humphreys, & I are staying at a Mr Rightors near the Hospital. Mr Rightor ran off (a few days before we occupied this place) to escape conscription; his wife supposed he had gone to St Louis, but he returned home last Saturday direct from Richmond where he got from the Rebel authorities an exemption from the conscript law. Yet he passes here for a Union Man, & is so looked upon by his own brothers who with others were preparing to burn his house, & (can I tell it?) hang his wife.

At any rate she & her neighbors think it would have been done had it not been for the opportune arrival of our forces (who took the town by surprise). Rightors is one of the finest residences in town. Mrs Rightor is a woman about twenty years of age, & looks very much like Patience Parmalee. She has seven slaves, & offers to give them their freedom, but they say they will never leave her; seeming to covet her as if she were one of their own blood. Our soldiers broke into the store house, & stole nine hogsheads of sugar, & thirty boxes

---

24. Probably these are veiled references to infidelity.

25. Charles was in the First Indiana Cavalry from August to December of 1861; he had been with the Ninth Illinois Cavalry since February of 1862; the history of these two mounted regiments continued together. In the fall of 1862 the First Indiana Cavalry and the Ninth Illinois Cavalry were transferred out of Brigadier General John Milton Thayer's infantry brigade into Brigadier General Willis A. Gorman's cavalry brigade. Gorman then became Steele's cavalry commander, District of Arkansas, Third Division under Curtis.

of wine. On this account she sent for us to occupy the house while staying here.

Rightor's secesh brother told the soldiers that a secesh lived here, & where they could find the sugar, & wine, but he has paid pretty well for it the boys having (after they found out the facts) taken nearly everything he has in the world, & his property was worth thousands. his fine store house was burned, though this was supposed to have been accidental I think it was purposely done by some of the citizens. You cannot imagine anything about Civil War, & its real horrors. If I live to get home I can tell you some things concerning it which even then will hardly seem to be real . . .

From the Journal:

Thurs August 14ᵗʰ—Clear, cool Mr Rightor sick Congestion stomach see him & prescribe before family Physician Dr McAlpine comes. write wf again letter not sent off: go Saturday

Frid Agst 15ᵗʰ—Cloudy cool. Rain last night—Morrison moves to Newcombes. Mrs Rightor charges 50 cts pr night for lodging Dr Jas, & 40 Cts pr night for Morrison.

Saty 16ᵗʰ—To Qui—Cold Clear. North Wind.

Sund Agst 17ᵗʰ—Cool Clear. D. Hoover in Yesterday from Fulton Inda

Mond Agst 18ᵗʰ 1862—Cloudy, cool. Morrison much worse this morn. Take his pocket book containing eight Dollars, a Recpt, & postage stamp. Morrison worse from mental disturbance frm not getting his discharge. Dr Jas wf arrives evening.

Hospital of 9ᵗʰ Ill Cavalry at
Helena Arkansas Agst 19ᵗʰ 1862

Dearest Wife

Your very welcome letter of the 6ᵗʰ reached me this morn, & relieved me of much anxiety. I wrote you day before yesterday. David Hoover leaves this afternoon I sent by him a violin, & a few trinkets. There were some tooth cleaning instruments. Let the Children be careful not get hurt by them; perhaps they better not play with them. With the rest is a nice bit of swans down that will do for winter use. The violin lay by in a dry place till I return.

I sent also a sort of Porte Monnaie with a ten dollar bill in it. This was directed to Lyman to be applied by you as you thought best.

Mr. Briggs now has his leave of absence & will leave tomorrow for home. I think I told you he had a sunstroke. The Doctor's wife came in last night.[26] I have not seen her. She comes I understand to remain till we leave. Capt wife left this afternoon for her home (Chicago). She has been here over a week. There are several other wives of Officers here. I understand that this place will be permanently garrisoned which will give the Officers of the Regiments a chance to remove their families hither; after next month this would be very pleasant. This is a pleasant town, with many fine residences in, & about it. I lodge in one of the best as I believe I wrote you. Here grow Figs, Pecans, China trees, Pomegranites, the flowering myrtle, Oleander, magnolias &C all different from anything we grow.

. . . The sick improve with cool weather fastest; with each day of such weather the strength of the Regts increases. Instead of turning out in Skeletons now each Regt shows almost, a full rank. Yet strength to bear exposure cannot come with a few days of convalescence.

. . . They grow beautiful Quinces here, & if we remain here till they are ripe I shall try send or take a box home. This is a perfect country for fruit. All the sorts that grow with us do well here except currants Gooseberries and hawthorn it is too dry. Peaches are plenty but none good; this is the fault of the people not of climate . . .

From the Journal:

Tuesd Agst 19ᵗʰ—Clear warm. Morrison better. Letter from Wf, & from Manning.

Wed Agst 20ᵗʰ—Cloudy, cool: Geo H Keeler in Hospt one month Dysent. now Diarrhoea maximus John Hall in Hosp two weeks in camp two weeks Dysentery Chron Diarrhoea Cornelius Cunningham Two weeks in Hosp Two wks in quarters- Fever Diarrhoea.

26. The Chicago wives continued to visit; Colonel Matlock's Rebels weren't much of a threat, and the majority of Arkansas Confederates had already been sent to the Army of the West, or the Army of the Mississippi.

Thursd Agst 21ˢᵗ—Cool cloudy. Sarah & Doctor stayed at Rightors last night, & Capt Bishop slept with me Boarded four weeks at Richardsons.

Thursday Agst 21ˢᵗ

As the mail has not yet gone out I will fill out a few more sheets for you

Mr Briggs left yesterday thoroughly disgusted with the service with Our Regt as he says. Sarah & the Doctor have taken my room & I shall return to camp. Sarah says she will return home perfectly contented so long as an invading army keeps away from her home. She went with me this morning to see Lieut Harrington of ours who is sick, & staying with a widow King near the Levee. There were several Officers & soldiers there, & some citizens. A son in law of the widow, & her daughters. They were afraid to sing & play a secesh song that Sarah asked for, as a few days before some soldiers had raised a row on account of it. To think of having her (Sarah) house occupied by invading armies from the South she thinks the most severe, & unendurable of calamities. The secesh however take it with good grace, & in truth seem rather to like it, especially our money which they almost beg, & will do most anything desired to get. Still they pretend that it is hard to do such a "low down" thing as to keep boarders. They are poor, & proud, out at elbows, & many out of everything decent.

. . . How well I should love to practice medicine among a people who were willing to pay their debts: My practice amounts generally to over two thousand a year, yet scarce five hundred is paid voluntarily. On that account much less in the army paid promptly is better. Yet to [be] exiled from home with all the additional deprivations incident to the operations of an army in the field is really nothing desirable, & I would not remain an hour were it not for the consideration that the country needs the services of each & all her sons. You read in the papers of how much Curtis is doing in the way of war, & I see it copied from paper to paper yet it is all fudge. Cotton buying is about the briskest trade driven here. You may get an idea of it by the doggerel verse I send which takes in the truth of the matter as near as it can be expressed in so many words. Sutlers too make money by thousands you can form but little idea of it. We are sending out recruiting Officers to fill up our Regiment. Two

Lieutenants & twelve Sergeants leave tomorrow for the purpose. We need about five hundred men to fill up the Regt. There is a great waste of human life in this business; when we take the numbers or figures for it we can appreciate it best.

. . . One of the Colonels died here last night I did not learn his name. Sickness here is uncommonly mild this season so the citizens say. They have been hoping to see our men swept off by the score by disease yet they are disappointed. There seems to be a blessing with us so far for we have been put at the sickliest point at the most sickly season, & suffer less than the acclimated citizens.

Hindman brags, & blusters like a vain fellow as he is, & threatens us with dire destruction, but from most reliable accounts from his army it takes one half of it to keep the other half from running off. Our men are generally contented, & cheerful, only fretting at our inaction probably this now will continue till cool weather; then I hope to see a speedy end to the rebellion. The Government is getting on the right track, & going at it full handed. Armies may however be too large, but properly divided with the new force called out we can overcome all obstacles.

Woe be then to the nations or nation that has, or will treat us with disrespect. This is the army feeling, for my own part I want home when the war is closed.

Pa sends many many kisses to his dearest children, & to his dearest Margeret best love & a hope soon to be with her. Do not neglect to write often to your ever loving

Charles

Camp of 9th Ill Cavalry
on the banks of the Mississippi two
Miles from Helena Ark Sun:
day August 24th 1862.

Dearest Wife

. . . I have had on no day so many vexations as I have had to day. Nothing of any magnitude yet a score of petty annoyances, & allowing myself to be annoyed by the first, the others, as they came, were adding fuel to the fire. We are deluged with "Orders" nearly every day, one countermanding the other till even the simplest duty is now so complicated with contradictory orders, that no two understand it alike & the opinion on a subject of today is tomorrow reversed,

& for all blunders of a negligent superior I have to be the victim whose duty it is to restore order from the chaos, so that my patience is continually tried in righting the tangled threads. If our army had only secession, & its advocates to deal with in open field it would be but a short job; but instead we have an unseen foe who with perfect cunning annoys our army, our navy our Congress, Senate, President, & Judges even almost to the death.

I hope the authorities will take all cowardly sneaks, & send them south of our lines, & if they sent all sympathisers with the rebellion south it would be a good job done. Every boat up takes some She seceshers to the north; they go for safety, & to foment rebellion, & discord among the Loyal ones north. The dregs of society from the sinks of iniquity, & the abodes of ignorance are the active secesh in this country. If you were to hear the whole truth in regard to these people you would not credit it; you would think the picture, or relation distorted by prejudice. Truly truth is stranger than fiction.

We hear now frequent discharges of muskets, & Rifles. The guards are mostly drawn off from Rebels houses, & property, & they have the supreme pleasure of taking care of themselves, & watching their own property.

. . . I paid one dollar for a watermelon to day for dinner. I send some of the seeds. You can save them for next spring. They are from an orange melon a very good one; from the price of this you may judge all other vegetables. Onions are seven & a half dollars pr barrel.

It makes me gag this muddy River water. The men have dug wells, & found springs in the River banks, from which they get clearer, & somewhat colder water yet not much better as to taste. I board with QMaster Brackett. He sets a good table. We have Fish, Potatoes, Tomatoes &C, & so on. In town I boarded with a Mr Richardson; his wife was drowned a few days since from a boat that snagged a few miles above our camp. She had ten thousand dollars in gold with her which was also lost. There were about forty persons drowned, among whom were seven women, & two children. One of our wounded men caught a plank, & helped a woman onto it (the wife of one of our Captains) they floated down together about a mile when the plank struck a snag, & both were knocked off. The soldier had only one hand that he could use. While struggling in the water a cabin or stateroom door floating down hit him on the head, & in his struggle he caught the door handle with his sound hand, & after floating with it seven miles further he was saved. The woman he did not see after she was washed off the plank; he told me that she did nothing but scream the whole time! Probably if she had not had so great fear of death she might have stuck to the plank.

. . . I of course shall not again trade a bird in the hand for any number in the bush, yet I hope the Governor will give me a place in one of the new Regiments. I wrote to K S Schryock that if he would go to see Govr Morton I would pay his expenses, or if he could not go I would like to have Keith to & see the Govr personally. He has not written me yet; there is not much time to spare, if I do not go home on that account I will soon have to go on yours.

I have been hoping that about the time I would want to go home to see you that I would receive a new Commission from him.

. . . My tent is immediately on the River Bank with its large door fronting the water. My bed in the centre gives me a fair view of the steamers passing. It is pleasant at night. They can be heard a half hour before they come in sight blowing & puffing like horses; & then they come in sight round the bend with their red & blue lights aloft, & the bright lights from the deck shining cheerily over the water on they come nearing us slowly now to this side, now to that to avoid the bars of sand that abound in the river. It seems wonderful how the Pilots know where to take the boat. The river looks all alike to a stranger & that a boat might take the centre & go straight along, but they must take the channel or woe betide the boat, & passengers; the lives of all are in the hands of the Pilot; how necessary he should be a man sober, upright, & educated to his business; there is a good deal that seems mysterious in the operations here especially on the River at night. Boats constantly on the move now going in now coming out of some heretofore hidden bayou, or Cutoff. Boats stopping at the shores loading, & unloading something I know not what . . . these operations I see every night, & of course they afford me much food for thought.

The negroes here are a study in themselves. Of all characters, & grades from the petted house servant, to the roughest field hand, we have them all. Many with eyes as light as mine, & some with skins as white you would wonder why & how can these be slaves! The Answer is the *mother* was a slave; all those born of slave mothers are bond forever.

After supper. I find that my letter is so made up of disjointed sentences that it is difficult for "Myself" to understand its drift, but you will excuse me on the ground that when I sat down I was much irritated. Now I feel better, but the mosquitoes bite terribly; there is not much comfort here after night except under my mosquito bar. Once there I am safe. It is so nicely fitted, round my cot, hanging from the top of the tent. I may bring one home.

. . . Monday Agst 25th—We have a beautiful morning It is just sunrise. The old negro Cyrus is putting things "to rights" in the tent, sweeping in front with a few twigs tied together with a string, & with this he makes things look neat. I said to him "Uncle, how old are you?" "Oh I spect I am somewhere between eighty, & eighty-two, when was it the battle was fout at Hampden Roads?" I told him it was about fifty years, says he "well den when dat battle was fout, I was a smart chunk of a niggah; old enough to plow corn; as well as I can now. I spect I was den as much as twenty or twenty-five year ole." This would make him from seventy to seventy five years old! He appears about fortyfive, keeps everything neat about my tent. He gave me a good washing this morning before sunrise. I feel better than I have for a month past. Cyrus is very anxious to get north where he can be his own man. Only think this man as smart by nature as his master, & as smart anyhow as any of our whites who cannot read & write has worked for seventy years under the lash; his children all sold away from him, & alone in his old age he has now nothing but the rags with which the chivalry have clothed him.

Adieu

Charles

From the Journal:

Mond Agst 25th—Clear, cool. Take Randall Kitt into my tent. Mrs Sarah Brackett comes to camp on horseback Finish & send letter to wf in answer to hers of the 17th inst. Mond Agst 25th 62 Geo W Carlisle Co I shot Sf right foot through metatarsal bone of little toe.

26 & 27th—Clear hot. Sickness same as for few days past.

Thursd Agst 28th—Cloudy cool. Ordrs recd to send all sick north to Hospitals. Rebel Boat Captured at mouth of Yazoo over five thousand stand arms for rebels of Arkansas on board. One Regt Tena troops aboard Wold Co L had ring finger left hand torn off at first joint by rope halter amputate & make clean stump. Discharge Geo F Walker who was shot through right shoulder at Cotton plant.

Cool cloudy this morn at sunrise: Recd letter frm wf. Answered this evening. Boys shooting at each other for amusement. Whiskey starts them. L C Johnson [Lucien S. Johnson] Co C Congest Brain Qui & Op as necessary to relieve head.

Helena Friday Evening Agst 28th

I neglected to send the letter to day so will write some more to bring it up to the time. You may give it (that I wrote last night) to the printer if you please.

. . . Genl Curtis[27] left to day (I understand for St Louis). Our Genl Steele now commands the Army of the Southwest. I have liked Curtis very much in many respects though there has been much complaint of him. My horse has just got loose. I have two now a fine black large & a good traveler, & a medium sized bay four years old one of the best saddle horses we have. I have not yet found Burro— I think some of our boys have stolen him. I am so sorry that Dave did not come with me; he would have made ten times as much as at home, besides being worth hundreds of dollars to me. It is to be hoped he will be caught, though I do not think it probable [the burro]. Young Kitt who joined us at Pocohontas is staying with me now; he is not well though about all of the time. He has improved wonderfully since entering the army, before he could write scarcely a legible hand, now he writes a beautiful hand, excelled by very few. Soldiers have a great deal of leisure time, & those of the right training, & with good companions have all chances of improvement. Kitt keeps my tent in my absence, spends the time in reading, & writing taking no part with the vicious, & unprincipled . . .

From the Journal:

Friday Agst 29th—Clear, warm. L C Johnson died at 11 AM

---

27. Army of the Southwest commander Curtis, evidently considering that not much of a war was going on (in actuality due to his own inactivity), took a month's leave to iron out some railroad business back home in Iowa. He was replaced by Steele. Both of Curtis's divisions, then under Steele, continued stalled in East Arkansas; when Curtis returned, he still refused to move unless he was given two other divisions.

Congestion. I should have given more Qui spend evening with Col, Jos, & Yates.

Saty Agst 30th—Clear, warm: Had part of fine Buffalo for breakfast brot down from mouth of St Francis by Scouts. No enemy seen . . .

Tuesday Sept 2nd—1862 Cool, cloudy. Signed discharge papers for Private Co D Furlough Geo Price Serjiant Major, wrote letter to Stailey 1st inst. Certificate of Disability for Jas W Tracy Co L. Christoph [Christoff] Paul Co D recent injury to abdomen bent [?] hernia near umbilicus, & other internal injuries. John Campbell Co L Genl Debility Diarrhoea Chronic.

Wed Sept 3rd—Cool Clear. Send off Hiram Higgs [Hicks] Co F with Descrip Roll Incipient Phthises, Splenitis &c Cert Disability Lorenzo W King Angina Pectoris

Rightors Helena Ark. Thursday Sept 4th/62

Dearest Margeret

I moved back to town to day, the Doctor [his brother] having returned to camp. His wife got on the boat yesterday (the Planet) expecting to start at 4 PM but she did not go, & the Doctor wanted me to see her when I came down; I went aboard the boat, & found the Passengers were all put off, the Planet having been stopped by Genl Steele,[28] who is now in command here. So I went to the "Knickerbocker" I think & there found her. She is very impatient & fretted a good deal.

I promised to go aboard again before she started, & in the meantime will fill out a letter for you, & take aboard with me.

Sickness in our Camp is not as bad by any means as one would suppose for this climate at this season, but I find the Fevers more serious than during the summer. There is a greater degree of suffering in each case. More inflammatory symptoms attending. The men suffer without complaining however. It is wonderful how much men can suffer, & it is a disgrace to Officers some where, that so much suffering exists for I am sure there is no need of it, but every thing is bound with "Red Tape" & woe to the luckless wight who presumes to cut it, though life depends. Yet the forms must be all observed. To save life one of our lieuts deserted a few days since; he although

---

28. Steele had, in fact, been commanding at Helena since July 15.

suffering from fever, & his wife very sick could not get his papers for Furlough signed by all the Officers whose names are necessary (by the red tape rule) to be appended. So he left without leave thus running the risk of being followed, apprehended, & shot as a deserter . . .

Charles Brackett

From the Journal:

Friday Sept 5ᵗʰ—Cloudy, cool: Mrs Jas Brackett left yesterday in Steamer Gladiator. Sent letter to wife by her. Prescribe in Hospital for Patients. Brigade Surgeon Burke returns Certif of Disability of Joseph Helmer Co K with following endorsement on its back. "Surgeon will give date, & station of this certificate, & order the soldier to report in person. Th Burke Medl Drctr A.S.W." I keep certificates, & direct him to get new ones. Sign certif Disability for Corp W. S. Thorne. Debility from _____ Feb. Bronchitis, & lax fastenings to shoulder joints.

Saty Sept 6ᵗʰ—Cool Cloudy Write H. Manning Princeton Inda Sign Certificate Disability for Jos Helmer Co K. Furlough for Michael Maloney [Mahoney] Co D.

Sunday Sept 7ᵗʰ—Cloudy, warm. Sign Certf Disability for Wm Withrow debilitas & complctn diseases. Write wf.

Helena Ark Sunday Sept 7ᵗʰ 62

Dearest Wife

Two days since I wrote you a letter & sent it by Sarah who went up Thursday on the Steamer *Gladiator*. She had been here nearly two weeks, but thought she was not appreciated & left much dissatisfied with matters, & things generally hereabout. She went up to Camp, & at the Colonels tent got mad because the Col, & Major Humphreys said to her that all women were not angels of light, & purity. After her return she said she would not stay where men were so immoral, there were none among the Officers that were what they should be except her husband, & Capt Chidister.

I never saw anyone more eager to dispraise others, & to laud self than Sarah. Her righteousness is the main theme of her discourse . . .

The wind is now rising with tokens of a storm of rain which we need much. The streets are deep with fine dust, & the air before noon hot, burning, & still . . .

There is a great fear among the surgeons about granting Certificates of Disability, as an order was issued that the Med Directors should examine all carefully, & if any were issued to those not entitled, the Officers issuing should be reported to the Surgeon General, who would then dismiss such offending Officer from the service.

Thus putting it in the power of the Med Director of each Division to oust any med Officer whom he wished out of the way. The order does not affect my conduct in the matter, as I grant certificates whenever I think the service will be benefitted by it, as I have always heretofore done. I never intend through fear or favor to be turned from the path that I consider the right one, though of course I will do all I can to know the right Course, & to this end will get all the information possible on the subject.

A man may become too much of an egotist, & may render himself ridiculous by setting his opinion above others. Yet I cannot see but that one's own conscience should be his own monitor, & if, unhappily for him, his education and associations have been of such character that he judges that right, which his neighbors have been taught to think wrong, & vice versa, he is then looked upon by community as one out of the church, & must bear the odium of eccentricity, or something worse. The good God is the final Judge & at the longest it is but a short time till the matter is before him for arbitratment. Knowing this it may be well to remember the precept to "judge not lest ye be judged, & with [w]hatever measure you mete to others, so shall it be measured to you in return." . . .

Rochester Sept 7th/62

My dear Charles

Although it is but a few days since I wrote to you and several since hearing from you yet as it is one of those Sabbath mornings in which the rain & wind seem contending for the mastery & it is dark & gloomy indoors & out and is lonely for me "Bull and Ben" I thought I could not do better than to write to you.

The long looked for trunk came last night, & such a time as we had unpacking you seldom, if ever, have seen.

We found all safe except the cover of the little clock, Rosa's Lancer & a few Bottles: they were broken in many pieces.

I was sorry about the glass cover of the Clock but hope to get one to fit it.

Who were the Shawls, Pickle Plate, Salt Celler, Soap Dishes, Shells, gravat, Syringes &c intended for? I presume they are for Mrs Grover as you did not mention having sent them to *me*. Sept 12th I had written thus far on Sabbath morning when I was taken sick had a slight attack of Dysentery which left me suffering with Piles I have not been able to sit up more than five minutes at a time since Sunday until this afternoon—I have been using the Sugar Plums you sent & think they have done me much good and I feel as if I should soon be well again.

I sometimes think I have a little more than my share of suffering to endure but when I look around and see others who perhaps suffer more & have less of the comforts of life & complain less than I do I feel that it is wrong for me to complain at all and lie down contented.

Your good letter of Augt 28th came this morning & was gladly recd by all.

Lyman feels badly about the "mule" he had anticipated a good long ride on him—GranMa says "she is always glad to hear from you & know that you are well but she would rather see your face once more" she is some worried about me & gives herself trouble needlessly.

I sometimes feel as if I should not get along well if you do not come home soon—but hope silently whispers—"he will be here" & I drive "dull care away"—Dr Plank came home yesterday without leave or license from any one (as he says) & does not intend to return he told Vernon that he would rather be in the Penitentiary than in the Army only for the name of it—The little ones have cried & made such a noise since I began to write that I feel just now as if I shall never try to write another letter & will close this one with Mary's "Ma" & Rosa's cry of a sore toe ringing in my ears—With a hope of seeing you soon I am as ever yours

Margaret

From the Journal:

Mond Sept 8th—Cloudy warm

Tuesd Sept 9ʰ—Clear cool. Apply for furlough on acct of sickness Coup de Sol recd Agst 6ᵗʰ getting some better, but hemorrhoids with Diarrhoea [acuta?] worse.[29] Get letters from wf 1ˢᵗ & 2ⁿᵈ insts. Answer wife send five dols in one letter. verses from Louisa very pretty.

Hospital of 9ᵗʰ Ill Cav
Sept 9ᵗʰ 1862

Dearest Wife

Your two letters of the 3ʳᵈ inst came duly to hand this morn; they found me not very well & about applying for a leave which I have just done. I shall get [it] or resign—in either case if I live will be at home probably by the 25ᵗʰ, & as much sooner as possible. If I meet no delay I can be off by the 12ᵗʰ & home by the 18ᵗʰ but you need not look for me before the 25ᵗʰ. Care for my own health, & that of my family when the army is doing nothing is my first duty.

My application has just gone up to the Dr, & Col, thence it will go to the Med Director, & to Genl Steele Commanding[30] Dept. of A.S.W.

There is nothing doing here now except waiting on the sick, & drilling. News is rather discouraging, though I think every thing is working for most ultimate good for the Country . . .

THIS SERIES OF JOURNAL ENTRIES relates the events of Charles's departure from Helena by boat up the Mississippi River, stopping in Memphis, going on to Cairo, and then by train to his home in Rochester, Indiana. He was evidently quite sick during most of the trip. He arrived home on September 19, 1862, just ten hours before Margaret gave birth to their fifth child, Charles William Brackett.

---

29. Charles is too ill to do a surgeon's tasks; he wants to be relieved of duty. He is aware that it will take quite some time to get a leave. He is also motivated, of course, by the desire to be at home with Margaret when their baby is born.

30. Temporary command; Curtis did return.

From the Journal:

Wed Sept 10^(th)—Clear cool. Chester C. [Chamberlain] came up to Hospital with a fine melon Capt Grover has applied for a sick leave. Write him to wait, & go with me.

Thurs Sept 11—Clear pleasant Dr Hampton off on furlough Go to camp. leave Colonel to draw my pay. Henry Adams Geneseo Henry Co Illinois. Pay him amt due as nurse . . .

Saturday Sept 13^(th)—Cloudy Cool Chas B. Miner Kewanee Ill Send box magnet. Galvanic to above address. Slept at Hospital last night. Severe rheumatic pain in shoulder during night; feel better than for some time past. yesterday Cloudy & cool, as is this morn. My head has been much freer of dizziness. Quiet & cold relieve the vertigo. Paid board bill at Richardsons to date $20.00. John Campbell Co L growing worse make out furlough; has had discharge papers for month past; Md Drctr thinks cause not sufficient. Will die probably soon if not send home . . . Capt Grover brot to boat sick, has resigned because he could not get sick leave Ship on Gladiator to Memphis $5.00 Take stateroom with Capt Grover 46^(th) Ind. Leiter J. Have Gun to take home for the Doctor James W B. Give it to negro for safe keeping. Grover quite sick pulse 100 Boat "the Gladiator" ordered back to Helena. Start again at sundown. River low. Feel better for my ride on river. 10 ½ make ready for bed, Waked, or rather get up (I have not slept) at 1 AM to see cotton taken abord. One hundred bales on the Arkansas shore Busy & exciting scene Negroes & whites rolling the bales down the steep bank to the boat. Cloudy, pleasant air feels moist, clouds detached: this would be a good place for Guerillas to operate. 9AM warm Cloudy Stop long time to wood on east shore. 11 ½ AM pass sunken rebel gun boat below Memphis just above Beauregard sunk Typical of Confederacy Arrive at Memphis at noon 90 miles from Helena. Fare to Memphis $5.00. Liquor bill for Sf & sick soldiers 40 cts. Memphis a city of fine buildings as seen from the River. Too hot to go up to the town. No boat here for Cairo. One said to be coming up. Lieut Metcalf QM of 2^(nd) Wisconsin Cavalry tells me that the Surgeon, & Chaplain of 1^(st) Wisconsin Cav killed. Surgeon shot while watering his horse. Chaplain killed fighting.

Get good dinner on boat Fifty cts Get dinner for old Mr Howden. Several loads prisoners here; wonder why they keep them so long. Does the government loose anything by it? I wonder.

How tedious this waiting. Gun boats lying here very heavy. Fine thunderstorm, with rain. have hiccough quite hard; had it last night five hours. Came on to day after dinner. It fatigued me greatly yesterday, & now again begins to wear me. No boat up river to day Eugene leaves tomorrow at 1 AM for Cairo, then farewell to Dixie for a time.

Monday Sept 15th—Clear cool—Mrs Capt Buel 9th Ill Cav, & Mrs Col Cameron 34th Inda of Valparaiso came aboard last night on way to Helena. Col Cameron is of 34th Indiana. They then take passage to Helena on [boat not named] Start at 10 AM. Get aboard the Eugene which starts at 3 PM for Cairo. See Adjt De Hart on way to join Regt at Helena. Says Fitch has not left his house since return to Logan; Says he has an apptment in another Regt, but wished to go back to own Regt to clear up report that he was "absent without leave", bound to make that all straight. Porter & chg 75 cts. 2 PM Start for Cairo; had excellent dinner on Eugene Provost Marshall comes aboard to examine papers &c. Allright[31] Stop to Coal just at upper end of town. 7 ½ Stop to wood on Arkansas shore. Feel quite sick this eve. In sun too much, perhaps have eaten too heartily. Mrs Col Cameron told me she edited husband's paper during his absence. Wished me to write an article now & then. Promised I would. Euchre tables filled with earnest players. Paid Fare $6.00 to Cairo. Paid Barkeeper twenty cts for a cup of Lemonade for Mr Howden Co [?] a poor, sick soldier.

Tuesd Sept 16th—Cloudy, cool. Broke tiller rope at 7 AM. Stop at sand bank for repairs. My seats reserved for sf & Capt Grover taken by a couple of boors. Make no fuss about it, but feel very much like it. 11AM Wood on east shore Tennessee shore Capt G recovering very fast. voice strong as ever. Appetite good. Barkeeper charges Howden twenty cts for cup full of weak lemonade. Have a nice watermelon. 11 ½ AM Stop at mouth of Ohio to take aboard Tobacco, & passengers

Wed Sept 17th—Cloudy Cool Passed Belmont at 5 AM. Reach Cairo at 7 AM Leave 1 PM Fare to Lafayette 11.30 Supper at Centralia sf & servant .75. Arrive at Tolona at 1 AM

Thursday Sept 18—Cold, cloudy, Distance from Cairo 180 miles. To Logan 120. Arrive at Logan 8 AM Stop at Barnetts. Vst

---

31. Charles has not mentioned receiving approval of his sick leave or leave of absence, but presumably he did, since his papers were in order for the Provost Marshall.

Mrs. Capt Gifford with message from husband. Feel not so well more oppression about my head. Fare from Lafayette to Logan 1.35 Dine at Barnetts. No chance to get home yet today. Stage goes tomorrow. Get copy Robinson Crusoe 1.50 Cup & saucer 1.50 Papers, magazines &c 65 = 3.75 Copy Gen Rosencrantz 10

Have severe attack colic followed & preceded by prickling sensations through whole peritoneum, & pleura of left side. Saw Layton, Marshall, & several others of our Regt Discharged & furloughed men. All much improved, & anxious to return to the Regt. Overcoat has been very comfortable during the day & last night. Had no sleep during last night, & but a short nap in Barroom afternoon. Retire at ten PM Severe colic. Glass brandy makes all right.

Frid Sept 19th—Cloudy, cool. Started for & reach home at 2 PM Find wf sick with Dysenteria acuta as she thinks: male baby born 11:45 PM Labor short. Twenty minutes after Rupt membranes. All hands comfortable except sf. Wife took Opii grs X during evening before labor ended.

Saty Sept 20th—cool clear Capt Grover left yesterday Negro Philip stays with me till Capt returns. Dr Grover to cash fare frm Logan 2.50

Sund Sept 21st—Clear Cool Quite unwell the day

Mond Sept 22nd—Clear Cool. Remain at Home. Not well. Diarrhoea worse than yesterday, & have slept very little since getting home. Ernstberger Md chld pr sf .50 Jackson Crums S in law Md wf 50

★ ★ ★

Charles began his return trip to the Ninth Illinois Cavalry in Helena during the last week of October 1862. However, his illness forced a return home. The sequence of events is confusing because he evidently got the dates wrong. The notes fit if he left Rochester on Monday, October 28, and stayed at Perrysburgh; stopped at Peru on the way to Indianapolis on Tuesday, October 29, staying at the Palmer House; began his return trip on Wednesday, October 30, reaching Peru; continued to Perrysburgh on Thursday, October 31; and arrived home on Friday, November 1.

★ ★ ★

From the Journal:

Tuesd Oct 27th [29th]—Cloudy cool. Throat very sore, uvula swollen Stayed at Harris Perrysburgh [Monday night]. Very comfortable as to bed & board. Bill .62 ½ . . . Took Cars at noon for Indnpls Fare 2.50. Stop at Palmer House at 5 PM. Suffer from my throat Uvula swollen . . .

Peru Inda Tuesday Oct 27th [29th]

Dearest Margeret

At about 11 AM we arrived here; were forced to stop at Harris last night on account of the Doctor (Grover) who had a severe chill on the road. This morn I awoke with a sore throat, if it is no better tomorrow I shall return home. My palate is much swollen, yet I do not feel very sick from it.

I put some Strychnine in two small bottles in my desk, in the middle bed room. You better take it over to Holmans I am uneasy about having it in the house. Clouse wanted some to poison rats. Probably Arsenic will be cheaper. Let your cider be put in the dark cellar & closely bunged. Clouse will make more for which you will have to buy a new barrel. Buy a whiskey or alcohol barrel, & keep closely corked after the active fermentation has ceased. I payed old Mr Carr for killing the pig, & Sam Heffley for fixing the buckboard.

Dont pay any bills except such as you know are right.

The candy Lyman put in my trunk just suited my throat this morning . . .

Charles

From the Journal:

Wed Oct 29th [30th]—Clear, cool. Throat yet sore, worse than yesterday though my voice has returned in part. Write to Jas W B. for extension of furlough. Will return home if no better tomorrow. Pay Ferguson clean & repair watch 1.75 Bill at Palmer House 2.00 Leave at 6/30. PM Reach Peru at 10. Stay with Bearss.

Thursd Oct 30th [31st]—Clear pleasant. Go as far as Harris' (Perrysburgh) stay overnight

Frid Oct 31st [Nov 1st]—Clear, cool. Ride with Doc [?] to Greenoak then with Dr White home arrive at 11 AM. All well.

Smoke house burned. Careless piece of business; Clouse burned all his molasses, & mine with barrels &c.

A LETTER FROM MAJOR CHARLES BRACKETT to his brother, Colonel Albert Brackett. Charles still owed money to Albert. This continuing embarrassment could be a factor in what earlier seemed to be his desire to be transferred out of the Ninth Illinois Cavalry, perhaps back into the First Indiana Cavalry. Army rules, however, made this impossible.

> Rochester Fulton Co Inda
> Mond Novr 3rd 1862
> Col A G Brackett
> 9th Regt Ill Cavalry.

Dear Sir

On the expiration of my leave of absence I sent to you stating, on my own certificate of honor, the reasons for not returning to duty & asking further leave; This became, according to the regulations, necessary to be twice repeated; I started a week since to return & took a severe attack of sore throat, which is so prevalent, under the name of Diphtheria. It was followed by total loss of voice so that after reaching Indianapolis, by the advice of all who saw me I returned home. My voice returned yesterday, & by the first day I am able to travel I shall return to the Regt. James W. Brackett is quite unwell (as his wife writes) & in a great hurry for me to return. I wrote him at Indianapolis.

I shall take a most efficient recruit with me, who if allowed will supply any place which may become vacant in the Hospital. I wrote to Surgeon Jas W. in regard to it. I will probably return by way of Chicago if I have the papers returned to me so that I can draw one or two months pay. I wrote Fittsworth to see you if you had drawn my six mos pay, due when I left Helena, & get the amt of his Acct which I supposed that Wm had probably paid. I was mortified that it was not paid before, but as I have only drawn one mo pay our Debt, & his is perfectly safe if not already paid.

Write if possible by return mail; it may reach me here:

> Respectfully yours
>
> Chs Brackett Asst Surgeon

ON SEVERAL OCCASIONS in July and August, Dr. Brackett requested transfer out of the Ninth Illinois Cavalry to an Indiana outfit. Sometime between September 19 and November 22, he must have found out from Governor Morton that his request could not be granted. This event is not recorded.

From the Journal:

> *Saty Nov 22ⁿᵈ 1862*—Left home via Plymouth for Helena.
> *Sund Nov 23ʳᵈ*—Leave Plymouth at 6.47 AM Fare Chicago $1.70 Soldiers Ticket. Reach Chicago at about 10 AM. Do not feel able to ride the night to Cairo.
> *Mond Nov 24ᵗʰ*—Send Wf Lives of Ill Officers Slept tolerably well last night, Room 42 Fremont, Saw, yester, J Smith. learn quite number of our officers are in town. Forgot to tell Sheriff of Deserters at Rochester as desired by T Ralletin [?]. See Scammon, Stamposki, Wallace, &c.
> *Tuesd 25*—Cloudy. Start for Cairo at 8.45 AM Reach Cairo

Memphis Tenn Friday Novr 28ᵗʰ

Dearest Margeret

Now aboard the U.S. Transport "Adriatic" I am waiting to start down the River to Helena or probably below . . .

CHARLES RETURNED TO HELENA with the Ninth Illinois Cavalry to discover that Major General Samuel Curtis had also returned from his leave to once again, and for the last time, lead these two divisions of westerners referred to as the Army of the Southwest. Brigadier General Frederick Steele returned to command his division, and Brigadier General William Benton, Albert Brackett's former brigade commander, continued to command the other. Colonel John Milton Thayer, Albert's present brigade commander, had been promoted to the rank of brigadier general. Now the bad news: Jeff Thompson was back. In October, Thompson crossed the Mississippi at Memphis with his band of "Swamp Rats" to wage a guerrilla war against the immobilized Steele, holed up in Helena. There had been some skirmishes but no major battles, because the "Swamp Fox of the South" did not, of course, "fight fair." Actually, the hard-drinking partisans hadn't done much more than steal the army's whiskey supply, while scaring the wits out of the Yanks.

Helena 6 PM. We are safely here. The Regt is mostly, that is the active force, out on special business: what that is you will learn in a few days. I am yet aboard the boat, & shall remain till a carriage is sent from our Head Quarters to convey myself & trunk. The Doctor Jas is well, & our men greatly improved; our force being nearly equal to eight hundred men: this is a wonderful improvement, though a part is due to new enlistments.

Mr. Richardson, the one with whom I boarded when last here, has left so now I have no acquaintance here (except my Regt) with whom I am on terms of familiarity.

There have been great changes here since I left, & now although many troops are out, there are, apparently, more here than when I left. The 46th Ind is here all right. I have not seen Capt Grover, & probably will not before sending this out: a number of our Officers have been aboard to see me, & all give glowing accts of our improvement; this is so satisfactory to me, & I take it for granted that our whole army is in a similar good condition for a winters campaign. The troops left here are all under marching orders, if necessary to reinforce the troops now out; the Mississippi Shore is all dotted, as far as the eye can reach on both banks, with tents & barracks. The force here is immense. Greater by far than I had any idea of. You will get less news by the papers of what is going to be done, & more of what has been done. I hope it will continue thus; we have too many of the going to do sort, & too few of the have done. I believe we now have the force able to crush their Armies in the field, & I have strong hopes that we have the commanders willing to do it; If not, another year of war will follow. If we have them, as I hope, a few more months will elapse & then glorious peace, & an undivided country . . .

Camp of 9th Ill Cav near Helena
Ark Wed Decr 3rd 1862

Dearest Margeret

I have now been domiciled for a few days in the negro quarters of a cotton plantation, three miles south of Helena; cold cheerless quarters. Imagine to yourself a square in the center of a clearing of five hundred acres; the square about forty rods each way made up of twelve houses about like Josiah Hoovers for size—these standing on the N, S., & West & open to the River on the East; three occupied by the Q Master, Commissary, & the Doctors, & the balance by negroes who in addition have built some thirty huts, & number nearly three hundred of all shades of color & of all ages, & sizes. You may judge how pleasant it is. Our men occupy their tents on the River Bank a half mile distant.

These negro houses, & overseers house are built of plank neither ceiled, or plastered inside. Each one has two rooms of equal size about 16 by 20 ft, separated by a partition of boards, & brick chimney & fireplace to each room. The plantation belonged to a Mr Williams of Memphis He never resided here; leaving the Plantation to be managed by his Overseer. It is only one great cotton field on all sides of us. The cotton all picked now, & fences entirely destroyed having been used for fuel &c.

We live pretty well considering our facilities for cooking, but the sleeping is of the hardest. I do not enjoy my lone camp cot as well as I have in times past. The weather is too cold for one to sleep comfortably on such a narrow bed, & I roll & toss about with but little sleep the night long. Monday night I had the worst night, what little sleep having been disturbed by horrible dreams Everything seemed wrong at home, & everywhere else. Probably a few nights more will get me used to it.

I do not hear from the Paymaster, but hope he will be here during the month.

Our boys had a hard fight near Lagrange in this State. Our Regt, the 1st Kansas, & a Missouri Regt in all four hundred men were attacked by over one thousand Texans. We killed & wounded one hundred & forty Texans without the loss of a man on our side; here our little Howitzers saved our men & destroyed the enemy. After a few more lessons of this sort I guess they will let our Cavalry alone unless they know to a certainty we have our Howitzers away.[32]

---

32. "At the fight at La Grange, Arkansas, two companies of the [Ninth] Regiment, with soldiers of other regiments, under Captain Marland L. Perkins, with two howitzers just referred to, behaved very gallantly against a considerable force of the enemy; he losing over fifty men, while our loss was inconsiderable. This was on the 8th of November. The command also repulsed a charge of two regiments of Texans." [Adjutant General's Report] Charles, having just arrived back in Helena, was relating events of several weeks past. La Grange is about 10 miles northwest of Helena. Now in December, Curtis has been reinforced; his army consists of Benton's division, Steele's division, and the other two divisions of farm boys from Iowa, Kansas, and Nebraska.

The weather is just clearing up. Since I came here it has been cold, with high winds, & rain, & this evening is the first time I could write in the house with any comfort. We are the outlying Regt on the South. Our Fort on the Bluffs west of town commands all the roads which makes us safe from any serious attack.

The only thing we have to guard against is a night attack from a dash of Cavalry. We hear good accounts from our troops now out, & are prepared to reinforce them if necessary. When reinforcements go out I want to accompany them if possible. It is irksome to remain in camp when part of the command is off on a march. Yet the time during the day passes pleasantly, as we have plenty to do. Now is the time for making out returns, inventories, reports &c for the closing year so that we are not idle. I am glad Lyman did not come with me on account of our uncomfortable quarters. Bye&bye I hope it will be better. Our Regt has had no chance like the others to fix Barracks for winter. They have been continually on the go, only men enough left at camp to guard, & care for the property[33]. . . .

Camp near Helena Monday Decr 8th 1862

Dearest Margeret

Having finished my work at the Hospital which I have now all to myself I will write you a letter though I have as yet heard no word from home. I just recd a letter from you written Sept 12th when you were sick, it has lain here, & I did not get it till this morning.

We are having beautiful weather. Our boys returned yesterday from a ten days trip in the interior of the State of Mississippi; they went as far as Grenada[34] tearing up R R tracks & burning bridges on the way, besides doing some very good fighting with Price's forces driving them every time, with the loss of no one man killed during

---

33. After December, when Curtis assumed command of the District of Missouri, Steele was promoted to command the Union District of Arkansas. In 1863 Steele received the rank of Major General, and his four divisions were classified as the VII Corps. In the middle of December, Colonel A. Brackett's regiment was detached from General Thayer and assigned to the cavalry brigade of Brigadier General Willis A. Gorman of Minnesota. Gorman's brigade consisted of the First Indiana Cavalry, the Ninth Illinois Cavalry, and the Fifth Kansas Cavalry. Gorman's original command had a total of about two thousand officers and men.

34. Dr. Brackett is, of course, referring to action on the other side of the Mississippi— the buildup that will soon launch General U. S. Grant's first (and unsuccessful) campaign against the Confederate garrison at Vicksburg.

the time; we had of our Regt two men wounded. We took many horses, arms, & prisoners besides great booty on private account.

Our Regt saved the 1st Ind Cav (my old Regt) from total destruction; this was a great feat which I may detail more at length another time.

Our quarters are most miserable not as comfortable as if we were in the wild woods with tents for shelter, but I hope in a few days we will be moved to a more sheltered position.

Dr Witherwax (my old partner) is here, Asst Surgeon of the 24th Iowa Regt Infantry. He appears just as he did fifteen years ago . . .

I took a severe cold in my head fixing some instruments for James (you know how sensitive I am to a draught of air); yet with the Commissary (Joseph) I am as comfortable as can be with the shelter we have; we live well have every thing necessary to eat, & drink.

Till we have a better chance for good quarters I shall not want you to come here.

An old Scottsman, a drummer in the 24th Iowa[35] was to see me yesterday; he has been twenty-five years a soldier, has had his skull split at Palo Alto, struck on side with a spent cannon ball, & had many other lesser injuries; he is a complete Drummer, & is anxious to have Lyman here as a pupil; if we all live till spring I want Lyman here, even now he could sleep with me, & do tolerably well. Today the weather is beautifully pleasant—warm, clear, & dry . . .

6PM I was called off to pick a new camping ground which I have done two miles from the River in a beautiful Beech woods. After returning I found Capt Grover, & Sergeant Chester Chamberlain at my place; they returned yesterday from the scout into Mississippi; they only went as far as the Tallahatchie, the Cavalry only going as far as Grenada. Sergeant Cham[berlain] is very hearty having gained twenty lbs in the past four weeks. They both gained on the march, & are looking well. The Rochester boys are generally well.

I have ridden a new horse today, one captured from the Texan Rangers.[36] I believe I will buy her as I have ridden no such animal. I want her for you as well as myself. The best broke, most tractable, most enduring of fatigue that one would find in a year's travel. I hope

35. The Twenty-fourth Iowa is one of General Steele's infantry regiments.
36. Dr. Brackett has used the term "Texas Rangers" a few times; technically, this term applies to Texas State Troops. The Texas Brigade in Arkansas consisted of Confederate regulars, the Third, Fourth, Sixth, and Eleventh Texas Cavalry.

you will have her for your riding horse after the war. If Lyman comes on he must have her unless I get a Pony better for him.

All the men are gaining health, & spirits & at the prospect of active service rejoicing on all hands. Our new camp is well protected by hills & timber, has good water, & dry roads. All necessary to a good camping ground.

I am called to see a sick negro in a cabin near at hand, & will finish this after my return. I find it too dark so will wait till one of the boys comes to go with a lantern with me. There are so many muddy places, & the moon is not yet up; this is the first evening when the candle did not flare so as to prevent one from writing or reading with comfort . . .

Ever your Dearest Charles Brackett

From the Journal:

Tuesday Decr 9th—Clear, Cool. Moved part camp yester to Bluffs.

Wed Decr 10th—Clear, warm, Dry.

Thurs Decr 11th—Warm, Clear, Commenced moving hospital to Bluff camp. Had long talk with McCulloch our guide with History of scouts since I left. Lieut Butler of our Howitzer saved at two places our men from loss, & disgraceful retreat, once at Lagrange Ark where at two shots he killed & wounded eighty of Carters Texas Cavalry, & at Miss where he saved one gun of the 1st Ind Cav, even in face of a retreat of all the advance. Drs Jessup Div Surgeon, Irwin Med Inspector, & Dr _____ with rank as Lieut Col visited our Hospital & quarters yesterday (the 10th) I send order for digging sinks, & general sanitary rules for camp to Lieut Col Sickles, & returned to Quarters from camp late

[*Copy of Order*]

Camp of 9th Ill Cav near Helena
Ark Decr 11th 1862

Col Sickles Commanding
Dear Sir

You will please to give orders in regard to sinks for Officers of this Regt & men, that they are dug at proper distances from the lines as pr Regulations;[37] that at least every second day that the excrements are covered at least four inches in depth with fresh earth; & that the men & Officers use these sinks. Already the camp is offensive about its outskirts from a neglect of this matter, especially along the edge of the ravine whence we get water for drinking & culinary purposes.

Respectfully yours

Charles Brackett
Asst Surg 9ᵗʰ Ill Cav

★ ★ ★

[*Printed official order*]

HEADQUARTERS, ARMY DIST. EASTERN ARKANSAS

Medical Director's Office.
Helena, Ark., December 5th, 1862

CIRCULAR
No. 10

I . . . The Surgeons of the various regiments, battalions and batteries of this army, will immediately make out requisitions for medical supplies for the first quarter of the approaching year, and send the same to this office for approval. In making these requisitions, Medical Officers must be guided by the standard supply table, and if articles are required in excess, satisfactory reasons must be given. The requisitions will show the amount of supplies on hand, and the quantity necessary to complete three months supply, will be the amount required.

II . . . Officers will be particular in giving the strength of their force, for which they require supplies.

III . . . Such of the regiments as have already forwarded requisitions to Columbus, Ky., and St. Louis, Mo., will specify such fact. Requisitions will be made out in duplicate, and signed by the senior medical officer present.

B. J. D. IRWIN
Surgeon U.S. Army
Medical Director Army Dist. East. Arkansas

---

37. It was Dr. Brackett's duty to see that these regulations were enforced; he was concerned about the health of his men, a situation complicated by the fact that wounded men from Prairie Grove may have been part of his responsibility.

[*note by Charles Brackett*]
Requisitions made Decr 12th

Camp near Helena Ark Friday
Decr 12th 1862

Dearest Margeret

Nearly three weeks from home, & no single word from my dear ones! I hope none are sick yet I fear they are, or that some trouble befalls—though should this be the case I ought to know it. Possibly the care of the little ones gives you no time to write.

To day we have wet, murky weather though warm; I have been out till now noon looking after the sick, & the removal of our tents to the Bluffs where our Camp is now located two miles from the river. A pleasant spot in the Beech woods, well sheltered, & with good water. I wrote you that the expedition to Grenada had returned; they say they performed the mission (on which they were sent) with perfect success. Lieut Butler here again saved the whole concern from a disgraceful rout. Our General Washburn with his body guard was in the advance (where he should not have been) ahead of the Advance Guard proper; the Indiana 1st was the advance. Washburn ran into an ambuscade, & retreated pellmell through the Ind 1st throwing them in confusion so that the enemy rushed in & took two of their Howitzers by which time Butler with our two peices, hearing the firing rushed forward, & amid the retreating troops unlimbered his peices & threw shot & shell among the enemy so fast as to check, & finally to rout them; in retreating with the peices taken from the Inda Battery they were overtaken by one of Butlers shells which killed two horses hitched to one of the peices, & they were on this acct unable to get off with it. Butler had sixteen horses killed, but no men their shots from heavy rifles flew thick & fast among the horses. One ball was thrown into one of our Howitzers, almost preventing it from being loaded. It caught the shell so that it took two of our strongest men to drive it home. We got more horses than we lost besides a first rate lot of guns, & a number of prisoners among whom were one Colonel, & a Lieutenant.

One of our Lieutenants, Bailey of Co L with one of his men was taken prisoner Tuesday night. He had become acquainted with, & engaged to a young lady whose parents reside on a beautiful plantation below our lines, & spent all his leisure time there; was watched by the Confeds, & taken. The young lady from what I hear had been engaged to an Officer in the Confed service (on Van Dorn's Staff) & I suppose that he, having heard of Bailey's attentions there, was instrumental in his capture, & some even think the young miss herself was true to her secesh lover, & helped entrap our young man; it does not matter; he was not in the line of his duty, & but little sympathy is manifested for him. When last heard from he was tied to his horse & on the road to Little Rock with a safe escort. As Jeff Davis has ordered Gen Holmes to execute the first ten Officers caught on this side of the River, in retaliation for the execution of ten Guerillas in Missouri by Col McNeil, poor Bailey may possibly be among the number, & without doubt he will be if his rival for the girl's affections has any influence. Dr Jas, Joseph, Major Humphreys were also that night outside of our pickets just this side from where Bailey was taken. They were staying at Dr Deputy's plantation whither they had gone to fish & shoot ducks. It was a lucky thing that they were not also taken & had they been, as they were outside of our lines, they would have all been cashiered. But they returned all safe, & stand as well as if they had not been outside our lines . . .

. . . your affectionate husband Chs

My darling Daughter Louisa her first letter from her Decr 17th 1862, Ansd Decr 29th/62

Rochester Dec 17th 1862

My Dear Pa

I think you say I must write to you and I ought to obey as good a Pa as I have got but all the trouble is I dont know what to write that will interest you one thing you will be glad to hear is that Brother Willie is better he was a great deal worse after ma wrote to you a week ago and as Dr Hawes was drinking so hard ma thought best to send for Dr Heill he came right over and sead he had inflamation of [both?] Lungs but if he could live twenty four hours he might get well he got better soon after he took the medicine and is a great deal better but cough a little yet ma is not giving him any medicine today she thinks good care is all that is necessary to make him well again we have a little snow and clear cold wether Lyman is drawing wood on his little sleigh up to the Porch Susan is making a fire in the fireplace to iron minnie crying about a sore toe Rosa rocking Willie Ma is making a Cloak for me and I am writing my first letter to my dear Papa I have read all the Books you sent home except the one from Chicago that we did not get Iread yesterday an account of the Fight before Fredricksburg and was mch pleased with it Lyman sends a letter from the Chronicle there will be a Christmas Tree at the Church. I dont know whether we will go or not I want to mail this tonight and will close with a goodnight from your daughter

Louisa E Brackett

Camp 9th Ill Cavalry in woods
near Helena Saty Decr 20th 1862

Dearest Margeret

Your long looked for & very interesting letter of the 8th came today. I had almost been afraid to hear for fear of bad news you waited so long—but now I feel relieved. My books papers, & trunk are at the old camp nearer town so I cannot tell how many letters I have written to you. We are under marching orders, & to take nothing but the smallest quantum of baggage. I am writing in my tent, lying on the ground & my papers on a bit of pasteboard: have a fire in the tent which gives so much smoke I have to be down to be able to see: in one side of my tent an old Polish refugee of the Rebellion of 1830 has his bed. His name is "Felix Mondzoleski" an old soldier; his Father was killed at the battle of Waterloo; he was Colonel of the 23rd Cuirassiers under Napoleon. Felix is acting as my orderly. If I live I may bring him home with me. An old man, but as smart as most young ones; he owned in Poland eighteen thousand serfs, & a half dozen villages. Was able, & did fit out at his own expense a squadron of cavalry for the Revolution. All these he lost, & was banished. The Rebels in Missouri sacked, plundered, & burned his house, & he in his old age was driven again to arms. Being an old campaigner he knows how to make everything comfortable for camping. Nearly every evening, a countryman of his (also a refugee of the Revolution of '46) comes to the tent, & I have a pleasant time, & an instructive one listening to their tales of accidents by flood & field: Rotzike is the name of the other; he joined us on Little Black River Mo where he has his family, & a good farm. They speak Polish, Russian, Hungarish, & German as well as English.

My bed is on the ground, & I miss the comforts of home more than ever. You would find cold comfort here, but perhaps we may be stationed where you could be comfortable then I would like to see you come sailing in some pleasant evening, and not with "wings" yet. I could make Lyman comfortable here, & would like it were he here, but I think he would want Mother, & her warm suppers, & Breakfasts often, too often to enjoy himself right well. The Bugle sounds the "Retreat" & "out lights" It sounds beautifully through the still night air, & as I am writing to my wife minds me of one of Napoleons Captains who having kept his light burning (after the hour) to finish his letter, Napoleon came to his tent just as he was sealing it, & ordered him to open it, & add a postscript "Add I am to be shot tomorrow at 9 Oclock for disobeying orders" the poor fellow did as the stern General ordered, & was shot before his Regt next day; but we are not so strict, & (unless the secesh come on us) I am in no danger except from accident. We are too careless, & negligent in enforcing the rules of war. I cannot tell when we will move but all is astir, & everything necessary is being inspected so that we may start at any moment . . .

Charles

THE WASHINGTON WAR DEPARTMENT, over the objections of Major General U. S. Grant, has allowed Major General John C. McClernand to begin gathering a thirty-two-thousand-strong "Army of the Mississippi" for the purpose of sailing down the Mississippi River to the Arkansas River and capturing Fort Hindman. The Ninth Illinois Cavalry of Gorman's brigade of Steele's division would be a part of this expedition. Curtis had four divisions of about thirty-two thousand for use at Prairie Grove. McClernand also had four divisions of about thirty-two thousand for use in the expedition to Arkansas Post. However, only Steele's division—thus the Ninth Illinois—was with both Curtis and McClernand.

★ ★ ★

Camp 9th Ill Cav in woods near Helena
Ark Wed Decr 24th 1862

Dearest Margeret

It is but a few days since I sent you a letter & I have recd but one from you since leaving home, but now alone in my tent, I can but employ my leisure time in writing home. I have been thinking how this Christmas Eve would be, if I could be with my loved ones at home instead of being here in the heavy Beechwoods with the enemy harassing our Pickets, & for our Christmas eve supper Coffee, Sugar, Salt Pork, & Bread eaten alone: it needs this kind of a life (a little while only) to make one more than ever love his neat wife, & home comforts more than ever.

I have been imagining how at home this evening I would be preparing the Christmas tree on which to hang the presents for our loved little ones, & GrandMa, bought by my dear, loving, economical little wife. The next is for yourself only to read. I have just finished a good long look at her picture, & how more than ever I long to have her in my arms with my lips fast to hers in one long, loving kiss of love. I am not funning now—good sober earnest. You dear one may you ever be happy! What a pleasant Christmas Eve could we make of it; but mine will be on the cold ground, but even then I shall doubtless dream sweetly of thee unless indeed our secesh neighbors disturb us again. They killed & wounded fourteen of our men night before last, & one last night.

The 46th Indiana went out this evening beyond us on Picket duty, so we will be somewhat safer.

The most of our Regt is over the River on a scout: started today. I suppose to bear dispatches to Genl Grant seventy miles east of us. There is warring now in earnest, though with an increase of danger our men become more careless. I am not inclined however to relax my caution. My camp fire is constructed on the same principle as the light we use in fire hunting, & my experience in that business is now of such value to me as to make me feel secure here unless caught napping, or by accident.

Dr Jas is off with the Mississippi Scout: they have a long, & dangerous scout ahead, but I think will be successful, but the fortunes of war are fickle, & disaster often follows the best laid plans. You know "the best laid plans of mice, & men gang aft aglee"

I am just thinking how pleasant would be an evening with Annie, & Uncle Frank in their clean, warm, cozy sitting room, & how well we could enjoy a sup of home made wine, & a bit of Annies nice cake. How I would enjoy it to see Lyman take his big sup of wine, & Louisa her moderate one, & Rosa, & Minnie their frequent sups, & the sparkle of Maggie's eyes as she took her sup, & lastly I fancy my own palate would be hugely tickled by the sup that I would get: maybe we will be all together again, & then we will make up for lost time; & if not, may we all meet where partings shall be no more, to enjoy there the purer bliss when our souls shall be made perfect.

The Commissary invited me to dine with him tomorrow at the plantation (our old camp) I will go down if nothing happens to prevent. Capt Grover was at my tent to day. We dined together, & I went with him to his camp just in time to find his Regt on the move leaving their comfortable quarters on the River, to go back on the outpost beyond our Regt. The Captain just had time to buckle on his sword, & put off.[38] You can't guess how mad Chester was: he had just finished his neat little cabin. John Hoover took it more philosophically, & did not grumble. Doc Grover looked the picture of disappointment, but marched off with a proud step to the music of the fife, & drum; while I sitting on my Pony, enjoyed the sight of a fine Regt (as theirs is) "terrible with banners" muskets, & glittering bayonets.

I met Dr Witherwax of the 24th Iowa, on my return to my camp. The Dr looks well, & does not dislike a camp life. Now my Dear Margeret I hope you are just about kissing the little ones to bed, that your slumbers may be peaceful, & that you may wake to a Merry Christmas. I will leave this to be finished at another time while I smoke a pipe muse of home, wife, & children & turn in to my lone hard bed. I often sing now the Soldiers dream, & feel it too here is a part of it.

> "Then pledged me the wine cup, & fondly I swore
> From my wife & my little ones never to part.
> My little ones kissed me a thousand times o'er,
> and my wife sobbed aloud in the fullness of heart.
> Stay! Stay with us rest thou art weary, & worn,
> And fain was the war broken soldier to stay,
> But sorrow returned with the dawning of morn
> For the voice in my dreaming ear melted away."

Do you recollect it? I often feel it now. Good night dearest & joy be wi you

Charles

---

38. Steele was moving out to join McClernand. The men of the Ninth Illinois Cavalry were about to do a lot of riding.

Christmas Noon, Commissary Bracketts HeadQuarters
I am down here to dine with Joseph who is getting a Christmas dinner: he has just recd a letter from his wife: all well. Mrs Parmalee was quite sick, but has recovered. Our Chaplain returned today. I have not seen him; he lost his little boy while at home. The Col is yet at St Louis, is Chief of Cavalry[39] there retaining his regt which is in command of Lt Col Sickles. I spent a very comfortable night though somewhat disturbed during the forepart of the night by frequent firing: There was also quite a heavy cannonading over the River the particulars of which I have not learned, though I presume it was from our own forces shelling the woods in front. A large force is reported over there, if so our expedition will be repulsed. We are moving in our sick from the outposts; this looks like work ahead; it is however not possible for any ordinary force to take this place; though without close watching a force of Cavalry might make a dash in, & do some damage. This is not among the probabilities, though it has been done in other places, & might be here.

The soldiers last night were troublesome & did considerable injury to the negroes & their houses. They threw a pound of powder in one chimney blowing it, & the fire place all to pieces. There was a sick woman in the house who died shortly after from the effects of the fright. Miserable cowardly dogs only could commit such an outrage on poor defenceless people as these are; but the unwashed democracy think they have a special right to injure, & maltreat those a little lower in the scale than they, & who have not the means of defence. How Brave for an armed man to kill a helpless sick woman. Yet it is but the same spirit that breathes through the clamor of the villianous secession democracy, of which our County has a large share, & who may yet win us all though I believe they will be put down. Thomas, a slaveholder from Kentucky who was down here for a hundred negroes that he claimed, told me that he thought slavery would not be interfered with: that the Doughface Democracy of the north, even if the rebellion was put down, would unite with the south at the Ballot Box, & save the institution. Poor Godforsaken lickspittles: I would rather live in poverty, & do the lowest drudgery than to take my rank among the Doughface Democracy . . .

---

39. On July 17, 1862, Albert had been promoted to major in the First Regiment of U.S. Cavalry, and during the greater portion of 1863 he served as Chief of Cavalry of the Department of Missouri under command of Major General Curtis (per Albert's petition for promotion to brigadier general).

Till I write again farewell & believe me ever your affectionate husband

Chs Brackett

In tent 6 PM Thursday Decr 25ᵗʰ 62.

I am now back to my tent waiting my supper, to which will be added, to that I had last night, potatoes, & Sauer Kraut, & Cheese. This will be a glorious supper won't it, & I will eat alone too. This last not so pleasant, but it must be endured. I will try & imagine you are sitting by me pouring coffee, though I dont know how I can make that, expecially as I have "John" the Colonel's colored servant to wait upon me at table. I don't keep him long in tent. Send him out as soon as the things are ready & pour coffee for myself. So I can know that if you are not here your "worser half is". Did I write Capt Grover took breakfast with me this morning, he had had no supper; nor breakfast when he came to my tent while I was eating. John has the things ready so I will give up till after supper.

After supper 9 Oclock our scouting party is just in; they pretend they could not get along for mud, but I suspect they were driven back. A bad tale either way. We will get the particulars tomorrow when I will write again, but this letter will go out early tomorrow, & you will get the news if any by another letter. Every thing is uncertain but death here as elsewhere we see that exemplified every day, in most all kinds of business; especially that connected with the army.

How any one can like the life of a soldier is beyond my ken, except indeed in a time of great danger to the country like the present when every one should like it from motives of patriotism. But in a time of Peace it must be most irksome. I am getting more tired of it every day, though were we on the march I could be very well satisfied . . . A fleet of about one hundred & fifty boats has passed going down. Once more, good night dearest

Charles

Camp 9ᵗʰ Ill Cav in woods near Helena
Ark Saty Decr 27ᵗʰ 1862

Dearest Margeret

I wrote you last day before yesterday my letter covering a period of three or four days, written at leisure times generally in my tent at evening. I am now more comfortably fixed having a good field cot in my tent to sleep on, & which I use as a chair; holding my portfolio on my knees for a table. I did not fix these things because we were under marching orders, & I thought I should not need them long here. So I have slept every night on the ground, & had no furniture in my tent. Modzoleski keeps a good fire of logs near the tent, & frequent shovelfulls of fresh coals put in the centre of the tent keeps the ground dry, & is convenient for warming, & drying feet at bed time. We are having a lively time here with our Officers: they are divided, & abuse each other at a round rate. The Chaplain is back, & is particularly severe on the Colonel who is absent, calling him (as officers report) coward, thief & such like gentlemanly terms. The Chaplain is having charges prefered against him, the Lieut Col & others trying to injure Dr Jas, & various ways, & they in their turn assailed by the Drs friends: they have got the Major Genl Gorman in the affair. I keep dark, & attend only to my duty, a part of which is to do as I would be done by. Jos wife writes to him to come home so he may not become entangled in the mess. It is nothing serious, mere underhanded work which will only work harm to those who are operating to injure others . . .

Now Good night I will take a smoke, & to my cot with a blessing for the little ones, & wife not forgetting Grandma.

Chs

Sunday Eve Decr 28, 9 OClock PM

Once more by my brightly blazing camp fire I resume my pen. Mondzoleski is smoking his pipe, recounting his experience as an Odd Fellow: he was initiated by Father Wildy in 37, ten years before I was initiated . . .

We are having beautiful weather since the rain & thunderstorm of yesterday. I just took a good wash (which I do nearly every day now) over my whole body, & it is not too cold to do so in the open air. I wash oftener in camp than at home. I have a towel for hands, one for feet, & body: water handy, & soap always in its place. So that washing is made easy, & being a luxury I enjoy it frequently, & my hands are as white, & soft as a lady's. There is hardly anything more invigorating than a thorough bathing of the whole body, or more conducive to health, & I wonder that at home I neglect it so much.

I hope you will attend well to the children in this respect: now you have a good girl you can do it with less inconvenience. Be careful not use water too cold for the baby, for it blood warm is best. I hope it has recovered fully from its cold, though its disease was of a dangerous character as either of the Doctors Diagnosed the case.

The boys are all in good spirits at the contemplated payment soon to come off. It will probably be about the first of the month. I am anxious on your acct that it should soon come off. I will then have ten months pay due. If I can pay the Briggs judgment here to Briggs I will do so; thus running no risk of its loss by mail, or express. Boats are so often stopped between this, & Memphis that it is attended with considerable risk to send money, especially as the Express companies will not insure between these two points . . .

I went to the Sutler's this evening to get a few apples, but they had none, so I took some tobacco instead & will solace myself with that prior to retiring, & muse the while of home, sweet home. There is some firing in camp so I will blow my light & close for the present.

Monday 7 AM. I have had a good night's sleep in which I dreamed of home. The morning is beautiful. I never saw so beautiful a sky as we had before sunrise. The sky was filled with detached clouds, each one of which presented most gorgeous colors, beautiful beyond anything I ever saw before. I stood out too long in my slippers, & feel like taking the sick headache, the first I have felt here, but I think a warm breakfast will set all right. The firing last night was from our Pickets, I have not heard the particulars. Kisses for the children. Remember me to Frank, & Anna; and for my dearest Margeret & send the best love of her ever affectionate husband

Chs Brackett

[Monday] Dec 29th 1862

My Dear Charles

[Your] last letter to me was written the 8th of this month but it has seemed a long time since I heard from you. When, When will this war be ended—I do hope I am not losing any of my Patriotism but I do think I can not get along without you many months longer. I feel like "giving up the battle" I am almost discouraged since the last battle at Fredricksburg. That terrible battle has been fought and anxious friends are waiting in painful suspence the "official reports" of the killed and wounded. God grant that my dear one is safe. I was [pleased?] to see you step forward & lend your [endowments?] to the support of that cause upon [which] hung the hopes of the nations of the earth, and I am proud of you today My Charles that you have too much spirit to remain in _____ at home while others do the work of saveing the Government. Yet [I do] want you at home so bad everything has looked so gloomy and lonely since you [were here] the last time . . .

    With a good night kiss and a hope that the "Guardian Angel" will guard, guide, and protect you I am dearest your

Margaret

[continuation of letter from Charles of December 31, 1862]
    Jany 1ˢᵗ 1863. Sunrise. We had an awful time last night with firing through, & in our lines; this with drunkenness among the men worse than you ever dreamed of made an awful time. I was up till after nidnight, & went to bed in my tent beyond the lines, said my prayer, & slept soundly. The Doctor moved his bed to my tent, & with our Revolvers we felt tolerably safe. I feel very well this morn, & will get this letter off before breakfast so that you may get it the sooner. They are fighting at Vicksburgh; The Captain of the Gunboat *Benton* was brot up yesterday dead, his breast perforated by a grape shot the size of an egg, & one arm shot off. The rebels are making a terrible resistance, but the city will fall in our hands if both forces cooperate as they should. They have seventy seige guns mounted on the River to resist the Gunboats, & one hundred thousand men for our land forces. A fleet of Boats is now ready here to take us down to participate in the seige. This is what I have wanted, & I am anxious to go. God grant that the expedition may be successful as I believe it will be.

    The morning is bright, clear, with a slight frost. We have had no cold weather, though plenty of blankets are necessary for comfortable sleeping, & a stove or fire in the tent to keep us warm. There is something about the atmosphere that renders these as necessary as in our colder climate. The long wished for "Year of Jubilee" has now come for the negroes, & their joy is great thereat. Their masters have been very busy for weeks past to induce them to go up to Kentucky, but they wont go north; feeling satisfied that this is the place for them under the circumstances.

    Our soldiers treat them very badly thinking they have done

enough for them to give them a more absolute mastery over them than their masters ever claimed; this of course only from the besotted, ignorant soldiery themselves only a step in advance of the negroes in knowledge, & far behind them in Christianity, & a desire to do as they would be done by. A number of them tried to kill our black Butcher last night with their sabre bayonets, but he was more than a match for them, & drove the whole crew of murderers. Write soon, & often, & a happy new year to you all is the wish of your affectionate husband

ChsBrackett

P.S. I fill the blank side of one sheet with a five dollar bill which the Doctor just handed me. You may need it.

★ ★ ★

SURGEON GENERAL'S OFFICE
Washington, D.C.
Dec 11th 1862

Sir:

You are reported to this Office by the Medical Director, as having failed to forward to him your Report of Sick and Wounded for the month of September 1862.

Should you, after the receipt of this Circular, delay or neglect to forward to the Medical Director the Report above referred to, summary measures will be taken to punish your disobedience of orders.

Very respectfully,
Your obedient servant,
By order of the Surgeon General:
J. J. Woodward
Asst Surgeon, U.S.A.

Charles Brackett
Asst Surg. 9th Ill Cav

Recd Jany 1, 1863 Copy sent. Report was sent at proper time. Orders not disobeyed.

C.B.

★ ★ ★

WHILE DR. BRACKETT REMAINED in camp at Helena, McClernand's expedition was off and running; Fort Hindman dug in. General Holmes told

General Churchill to hold the post at all costs, not knowing the formidable size of the enemy force.

Saty night Jany 4th [3rd] 1863. In
Camp of 9th Ill Cav near Helena Ark.

Dearest Margeret

I am now (9 PM) writing from Major Humphreys tent; he is off on a scout, & wished me to sleep in his tent till his return. It has been raining hard most of the time since yesterday. We have gloomy weather, & gloomy news from all directions, yet I do not believe it all. Not but that I think it might all be true, but that I wish it were not.

I was in town today, & yesterday as a witness before a court of enquiry convened to examine into the case of our Chaplain (Briggs) who was reported "absent without leave". The case is adjourned till Monday. I took dinner on the Steamer "Imperial" said to be the finest boat on the river. We had a good dinner the first I have eaten out of camp since coming down here. The Commissary was with me.

Col Wyman's body was brought up from Vicksburgh day before yesterday. He was killed in an assault on one of their batteries; he had already taken two, & was after the third; his regiment went in seven hundred strong, & came out with one hundred, & forty.

We have awful work in our camp no discipline, & no caution, a perfect set of noisy fellows, more a mob than a Regt of soldiers. The Col is much needed here to restore order, for we have no one here that does it.

Some other Regts do better. The 34 Ind Col Cameron is a model of perfect discipline. I hope ours will get better as I have more fear in our camp of hurt from accidental discharge of fire arms, than I have from secesh guns on a scout, or in a skirmish. Now the men are yelling over the whole camp like devils let loose.

I would give all I have in this world except wife, & children to have peace once again, & I fear that Peace we will not have for some years. We are bound to succeed finally but it will be a long struggle unless our mode of fighting is changed. Our scout is just in with twelve prisoners, & horses caught beyond Lagrange. They had a fine time caught the Rebels at breakfast, drove them & eat their breakfast for them. They caught them about eighteen miles from here, &

after riding all night in the rain. Their Pickets came into our camp thinking we were friends with a "good Evening Gentlemen" & were answered with a "Halt" They looked foolish you may guess. The Prisoners are all fine looking large men, & looked as if they had been well kept. They were well supplied with provisions which our boys got; then burned their nest. The 5th Kansas[40] was with us, & they burn all Guerilla nests, with a good grace.

Well I will close now as the table must be used for supper, & will finish in my own tent.

Kiss the children all for Pa, & accept dearest Margeret the best love of your affectionate husband

Chs Brackett

11 PM—I am now in my own tent sitting on my little camp bed, with my little camp stove right hot, while Mondzoleski, & a young Englishman by name Bowdoin are preparing a hot Punch with Tea, & Whiskey, a regular Russian drink producing most profuse perspiration, & agreeable stimulation. I believe I have made something at home like it from a prescription of Dr Danziger. Dr Jas is asleep in one corner of my tent having had his fill of this drink that Mondzoleski calls "Tchai". He & Bowdoin are quarreling about the orthography of the word, & from that to maccarone; they are fond of many words, & whiskey limbers up their tongues. From this to Italy, & Poland they quarrel like men who have whiskey plenty in them. So with the different European nationalities; their men will quarrel when they get together. Roast Beef always sticks in an Englishman's throat.

Sunday morn Jany 5th [4th] The boys are at breakfast, & I finish this while they are absent. The Doctor has all his traps in my tent; his own not being ready. It makes me uncomfortable to have so many about me. My leisure time that I alone could employ in reading, is lost by the confusion of a crowd in my tent. Good nature makes one many troubles, & continued ones

Sunday Night 11 PM—I had intended to have spent the evening writing you a long letter, but on my return from the 46th Ind where I spent the afternoon I had to visit a patient in quarters, & on my

---

40. Like most members of a medical staff, Dr. Charles saw all of the various units as a hodge-podge of men. They were, to the surgeon, patients needing treatment. For him, and indeed many others in and out of the army, in 1863 it was increasingly difficult to decipher the complex and ever-changing structure of the army in the West.

return stopped with some Officers at the Headquarters, & spent the night so far in talk over our prospects.

Now the night is so far advanced I shall try my lonely cot as soon as my feet get warm. Joseph is quite unwell for a few days, a thing uncommon with him generally so healthy. He (as well as many others of us) is in gloomy spirits at the prospect, & he talks of going home. I hope however that we may soon be doing better. The boys many of them think that we will not be paid off soon, if at all again. You have no idea of the general despondency among the Officers, & men both, but of this the less said the better. I think we will get our pay, at any rate as much as we earn.

Since writing the above I have been to bed, & now about 2 AM I am up again built a good fire, smoked a pipe, & am writing again to my dear one, with whom my thoughts continually associate. Our Officers were telling how much they had done for their wives before leaving home in the way of making wills, Deeds, &c for their benefit. I could think of nothing I had done especially for mine, but consoled myself with the thought that the laws of our good state made that matter as near right as could be. Some had willed property to the wife to be held by her so long as she remained a widow. I would not wish to trammel you with any such restrictions. In case of my death you would receive a certain share of my real estate in fee simple, to do with as you deemed best, whether you should marry again, or remain a widow, & the other share would go to the children. In case of my death in the service you would receive a pension so long only as you remained a widow, & after your marriage the pension would then go to the children until they should arrive at a certain age, sixteen, I think. But I hope we may long live to enjoy our property, & children together of course Yet death may come, & it is well to keep it in mind, not with gloomy feelings, but with a well grounded hope of a better life beyond, where wars, & separations are not known . . .

Monday Jany 5th 1863[41]—The morning is bright, & clear, cool like our October weather after a white frost, just the weather for health. It is operating favorably with the men who all look improved; that is as a general rule; there are always some sick ones, & disabled. My tent door is crowded now, it is after sick call, & the Doctor is not here to prescribe yet; I have to go to town again as a witness, &

---

41. Arkansas Post fell six days later.

will do no prescribing this morning. One poor fellow is just in that I amputated an arm for a few days since; he has been about all the time since, & now wants to know if he can go up the river.

The Rochester boys (in the 46th) are generally well. Dr Grover is hearty as I believe I before wrote . . .

Camp of 9th Ill Cav in woods near Helena
Arkansas Wednesday Jany 7th 1863

Dearest Margeret

It is now three days since I have written to you during which time nothing material has happened with us. No news from Vicksburgh, & nothing from up River, not even a letter from home that I look for most earnestly, & no Paymaster. The same amount of petty skirmishes with daring Guerillas the same work of attending the sick, & wounded; the same making out of returns, Certificates of Disability & Requisition, & the tiresome routine of work daily recurring since we came here.

Truly this is a tedious life, & I am heartily tired of [it] especially when it seems to me we are doing no good, & only eating up the substance of the Government. To be sure we get no pay; yet we all eat, & our horses eat; & harness & Saddles, & other gear spoil for lack of use; rust out; waste more by one month of such disuse than by six months of active service, men languish, & die for lack of exercise to keep them in health, & by free distribution of whiskey which will find its way into camp.

Every day I make my tent a little more comfortable, make my bed in a long box; just big enough to hold me with my blankets; I sleep warm, & the stove makes the tent tolerably comfortable for writing, & reading. I have just finished reading Oliver Twist one of Dickens first novels, which I read twenty years ago. I want you to read it to Louisa. Perhaps I can send it to you; this copy one of the boys (Edward Brackett Bugler to Co H) brought from Mississippi. Edward is a sort of cousin, a son of Brackett of Chicago . . .

We have little reliable news from Vicksburgh for the past four days. Genl Steele is reported badly wounded, & Vicksburgh taken; this however mere flying report; we are all ready for a move, & have been for weeks. An order was issued a few days since for four hours daily drill, this has a good effect. Gen Gorman commands now, &

is brushing up the troops so they may be efficient in case they are needed.

There is already much better order in camp than a week ago; the men are severely punished now for firing in camp except under orders, & since the last scout up the St Frances, & Clarendon roads there is not so much of bold dashing into our lines; they are put more on the defensive; yet they will bear close watching.

I am regaled every night lately with music from the negroes of one of the companies, Co H. They have a violin, Banjo, Bones, & sort of Pipe that makes very pleasing music heard from a distance; they generally keep it up till near midnight. I have never been in their shanty, generally being engaged in matters of more moment. When not busy at work I am either reading, or writing to you. I write few if any letters except to you aside from those on business. I do not feel like writing more. I will answer Sarahs letter one of these days. Her last is the best letter she ever wrote. A boat is now coming up the River; perhaps bringing news from Vicksburgh. You shall hear tomorrow.

Good night, pleasant dreams & kisses for all

Thursday Jany 8th—The morning is cloudy, warm, with Rain making with this aluminous soil decidedly bad walking . . .

I am glad you were able to do so well for the priest, & hope you will not be less able to help those who perchance may be more needy. There is never any loss in giving to the poor. It comes back in many ways to bless the giver. There is not so much good in giving to those not needy, or to the vicious poor—a man like Clouse for instance.

A rumor reaches camp that we have Vicksburgh with two hundred cannon, & a loss on our part of twelve thousand men.[42] The cost is great, but all right I suppose. I believe I could have taken the place with less loss, landing a force west of the River large enough to cut off communication from that quarter; landing east of the River a force to hold the R Road running east, & permitting them to give battle out of their entrenchments, when with the Gunboats I would have engaged their River Batteries. This would have been a slow, but a sure way to get their town. It is a hard job to engage men equal in numbers behind entrenchments. The attacking party

---

42. Dr. Brackett refers here to the Battle of Chickasaw Bluffs, December 27–29, 1862, which was actually a Rebel victory with 208 killed, 1,005 wounded for the Union.

ought to number five to one to make it an equal fight with ordinary defences. Our Proslave generals have a fondness for sending "Abolitionists" into the hell of two hundred cannon there to be mowed down by thousands, & I think an amiable weakness of the powers that be is to blame for the useless loss of life, & instead of conciliating, will bring the angry tide of war where Jeff Davis in his speech, at Jackson Miss on the 11th Feby/61, said it should go to devastate the Proud Cities, & fair farms of the North . . .

I have to leave now to see some sick negroes.[43] They make me nearly as much trouble as our whole Regt, & I get no pay from them, though Dr Jas makes them fork over for all they get from him, & he gets well paid, but I cannot take from the poor wretched beings anything they have though many of them have money, & many fine things stolen mostly from those once their masters, but now fugitives from justice; that which will reach them sooner, or later, for it must come to all, & for all . . .

Charles

[*letter to Dr. James W. Brackett's wife*]

Camp of Ninth Ill. Cav., near
Helena, Jan. 8, '63

Dear Sister Sarah:

Your very good letter of the 28th Dec. came duly to hand and found me well, as also your husband. It found us also staying about that miserable part of the earth in which it has been our lot to remain so long rusting with disuse. The Doctor Jas. has been using all endeavors to get home since my return here last Nov. the 29th but thus far without success. You will probably not see him until the end of the war unless you see him here, or his health fails so that a change of climate may be necessary to save his life.

I am of your opinion as to the necessity of living a holy life, in order to gain happiness here or in the Spirit land to which we are all hastening. Of that I never had any doubt. As to what constitutes that holy life, people differ only in what I consider the nonessentials, as are agreed as to the essential parts of Godliness. Since entering the army, now almost two years, I believe I am a better man than before; this may not be saying much for my Godliness, but it is better than

---

43. Many doctors on both sides would not treat blacks; Dr. Brackett did so.

if I were worse. I have more faith, a greater trust perhaps, and more humility. I am not ashamed to acknowledge my God and my Savior; through whatever difficulties I pass I feel that God is my sure trust, and though I fall by the way He will lift me and save me from all harm. If death takes me I have a firm hope, for I know that my Redeemer liveth and He is my sure guide.

> "The Lord is my Shepherd, no want shall I know;
> I feed in green pastures; safe folded I rest.
> He leadeth my path where the still waters flow
> Restores me when wandering; redeems when opprest."

I learned this, before I can recollect, in the Presbyterian Church, and from the lips of my loved and loving mother, and as the years of my life roll on they increase in beauty, and significance with me. The seed sown, though slow of growth in many instances, will grow, and produce the fruit all in God's good time. His ways are not always understood by us, but they are always right, and man cannot evade the sure laws He has established. I feel every day my duty to Praise God, Oh My Soul! Praise Him for His Great Goodness.

My sister Elizabeth and you are the only ones who ever write to me on this subject, and you have lost nothing in my estimation by it: however much I have appeared to neglect this matter I believe I have always respected the Christian and I know I have respected Christian principles, and it has been a grievous fault with me that I have too often perhaps seemed to slight them.

Remember me kindly to Eliza and Martha, not forgetting Mrs. Corker to whom present my best wishes, and accept for yourself the best wishes of your

Affectionate brother,
Charles Brackett

Jan 10, 1863

[*Clipping attached, printed poem*]

> "Forget me not! forget me not!
> Though years may pass away
> Ere we may meet upon this spot,
> Forget me not, I pray.

Forget me not when shines the star
I've named so oft for thee;
Then let me dwell, though distant far,
Within thy memory.

Forget me not! when joy and love
Are twining round thy heart,
Then let my image with them move,
But not with them depart."

Rochester Saturday eve Jan 10th/63

My Dear One

Amid much noise and confusion I attempt to write you. The Children make a great deal of noise when the weather is bad They are all well as they are today . . .

I do want to tell you about the Baby, Papa, but can not find words to express my thoughts he is *so* pretty & so smart & so good & so cunning I shall leave you to form your own opinion when you see him. Lyman is the best kind of a boy & does his work manfully but sometimes gets lonely and cries to see Papa—Rosa is a very good little girl we call her the little nurse, Willie loves to sit with her & listen to her singing better than with any of the others except Mama I look upon him as a little charge you have left in my care & which seems to make him doubly dear to us all—he is the wonder of wonders, in the house—Minnie is much worried about her Picture, she fears it is lost because you say nothing about it in your letter to Louisa.

Do Charles try to bring the Pony home I should be much pleased with it I know. Send me your Photograph when you can you know the size I want, dont you? I think from the condition of things at Helena that you are in much danger from night attacks. Oh dear it seems sometimes that it is too much to endure but what can I do it only makes it worse to worry about it I had felt that Helena was safe but shall think so no more. My sheet is nearly full so is my heart of sorrow—O Lord let thy arm of compassion be around my precious Charles & shield him from destruction & death—and imprisonment—and all harm—let his life be precious in thy sight, and grant them success. This is my daily prayer and that you will put your trust in God and ask his protection at all times is the humble request of your lonely

Margaret

accept a good night kiss from the lips of you know who

THE NINTH ILLINOIS CAVALRY was part of the expedition that captured Arkansas Post on January 11, 1863. Lincoln gave command to his friend, McClernand, without consulting Army Chief of Staff Halleck in Washington, or departmental commander Grant in Memphis.

From the Journal:

Mond Jany 12ᵗʰ 1863—Warm clear Reached Ark Post road leading to frm White River. Left Helena Sunday 11ᵗʰ—Dreamed yester of taking out one of my own teeth.

Tuesday 13ᵗʰ—Cloudy warm

Wed 14ᵗʰ—Rain, & wind. Reach landing below St Charles at 11 AM. Gunboats here Lost our way up "Indian Bayou" Ark Post taken Monday. Four thousand prisoners 22 cannon

Thursday 15ᵗʰ—Snow, cool write wf.

St Charles Bluff Ark Thursday
Jany 15ᵗʰ 1863

Dearest Margeret

We left Helena Sunday 11ᵗʰ inst with thirty transports came down here, took Ark Post thirty miles below killing & wounding of the enemy fifteen hundred. Took Four thousand prisoners, & Twenty-two cannon with a loss of five hundred killed, & wounded:[44] came directly here took this place without loss, the rebels evacuating leaving one heavy seige gun. They have retreated to

---

44. McClernand reported his casualties in the Official Records as 134 killed, 898 wounded, and 29 missing. An incomplete return of the Confederate losses listed 60 killed and 80 wounded. The number of artillery pieces captured was reported as 17; seven of the cannons had been destroyed in the bombardment.

Duvals Bluff sixty miles above whither we are how following them. There they may fight again. Our boys carried the Post by storm, & not a single rebel escaped.[45] The weather was so warm we wore no coats, to day we have snow, but not cold. I was sick yesterday feel well today. We have escaped many perils by sea, & land, & have more to encounter. All my baggage was left at Helena to follow us. Vicksburgh is given up by us till we clear Arkansas. Part [of] our fleet is up the Arkansas River for Little Rock. The enemy cannot retreat from Duvals Bluff or from Little Rock; they are surrounded, & must fight or surrender. We think there are fifteen thousand of them at both places.[46]

They are badly scared, & I hope will not fight, as they must be whipped unless we have unforeseen bad luck. It is terrible to have so many men slaughtered. The works here were formidable, but in their pains at the loss at the Post they left this taking all their artillery except the one piece furthest from the River; they had no time to take that. Their Breastworks here extended over a mile with rifle pits all around.

Seven companies of our Regt went overland, & we have not since heard from them.

I will write, if all goes well, from Duvalls Bluff as soon as we take it. Our Regt had no fighting at the Post. We were on a back road to cut off their retreat,[47] but they were all taken in their entrenchments. None of the 46th were hurt. The 4th Ind Cavalry is somewhere here. I saw a grave marked "Robbins Co C 4th Ind Cav" at the mouth of White River in Mississippi. We may see them; that is the Regt Chamberlain belongs to.

Vicksburgh will be our destination if we come out well at Duvalls.[48] That will require the united forces to take. It is almost impregnable. With its fall I believe the war will close; unless they escape capture & get north of us. Richmond will be then cut off from supplies from this direction. We have good news from Grant,

---

45. Some Rebels escaped; after-battle rumor has little relationship to the truth.

46. The reality is that there is no longer any effective Confederate army in Arkansas.

47. In following the original plan, Steele's division encountered a swamp and bayou that Sherman determined to be impassable. McClernand confirmed Sherman's estimate and ordered Sherman to countermarch the division. Later, Steele's division was ordered to move to the right of Stuart's division, and was in that position at 5 P.M. on January 11, approximately the time of the surrender. Gorman's Brigade was not present at the battle.

48. Vicksburg would eventually be the arena for the first major fighting for the Ninth Illinois Cavalry.

& Rosecrans. Kiss the children for father, & accept the most fervent love dearest Margeret of your affectionate husband

Chs Brackett

From the Journal:

Frid Jan 16ᵗʰ—cloudy cool. Reached Clarendon at 7 PM yesterday. Our overland troops there before us. Duvalls Bluff evacuated. Steamer "Blue Wing" escaped us narrowly our troops brot troops prisoners some barefooted. Suffer in this snow. The morning is cold very. Our Hospital attendants have no rations, the Doctor failing, so far, to get them. To steal, buy, or beg is all that is left to them unless they do, as they should, go to Genl Gorman, & lay the case before him. Land at Duvalls Bluff (above two miles) at 3 ½ PM. Took 120 pound, & Eighty-four (84) pound guns; 400 new English rifles & steel pointed Balls for seige guns. Write wf

AT THIS POINT there were no longer any Confederate regulars left in Arkansas. The guerrilla war would continue between pro-Union Arkansas state troops and pro-Confederate Arkansas state troops.

On White River near Duvalls Bluff Ark
Friday Jany 16ᵗʰ 1863

Dearest Margeret.

We are now on our way up the River, have passed Clarendon where we learned that secesh had evacuated, & left the Bluff for parts unknown. Our cavalry that went overland from Helena (seven squadrons of our Regt with others numbering together two thousand) joined us at Clarendon. They had a tedious march owing to bad roads, Rain, & snow. Their Pickets were fired on every night, one killed, & two taken prisoner. Our men took eighteen prisoners, part of whom were barefoot. This was hard for a march in snow, & our boys, having lost some horses by drowning while fording the swollen streams, took the secesh horses & compelled them to walk. They went on by land to the Bluff (fifteen miles) while we steam it by the River fortyfive miles; had I been able to ride I would have gone that way, especially as I want to get me a new horse, & it is easier to capture than to buy one. I have some boils on me which render riding painful. After we leave the boats I will be compelled to ride, but I hope to be better before then.

The steamer that took the cannon, & military stores for the Rebels from St Charles is ahead of us, & can only escape capture by hiding in some Bayou or creek. We hope to get her, though I think it probable she will escape us by hiding. This will be an easy matter now as the streams are all up & are numerous. I hope Blunt, & Herron are able to hold their ground above Little Rock, as in that event we will get all the Arkansas troops. The troops we took at Arkansas Post were Texans mostly, & well armed. Those we are after are also Texans, & Arkansans with a few from Missouri, & they are all as they say "mity sick of fitin' ". Well they may be for they cannot stand an open field fight against one half their number of our men, & we outnumber them greatly so that at bushwhacking they are sure to be surrounded, & they find no rest day or night. They are cruel, to an extent you would hardly credit. At the road running to Arkansas Post from White River lives a widow whose husband, & son were both shot in cold blood by these Devils simply because they suspected he gave some information to our troops last summer when Fitch came up with the fleet. These tales of blood our Northern secesh papers (Devilish in nearly all things) never chronicle; while the least robbery of a chicken roost, or petty outrage committed by a soldier of the Union Army is heralded through all their columns with such false additions as will give them a gloss of extreme outrage on the rights of the Robbers, & murderers & traitors who are their fast friends. The man of our command who was killed coming overland was murdered at his post by a band of these sneaks who crept up Indian fashion & shot him. This was done by night, & a perfect act of murder. Yet the prisoners we took though subject to death under the law will be clothed from our stores, shod, well fed & paroled to repeat their crimes better enabled to do so by our kindness . . .

3 ½ PM—We are now at the Bluff; after I have seen it & gone over its defences, I will write you more concerning it. The boat will soon tie up when I will go ashore, though perhaps we may not stay long, as I hear one of the Captains just saying that some of the boats have gone on up the river; if the swiftest would go directly on we would capture their Boats that have gone ahead. They have one of

our boats the "Blue Wing" taken on the Mississippi a few weeks since by some of their men. If they had much Yankee about them they would destroy our boats by means of Fire Ships, or rafts let loose to float among us by night, but they seem to keep going when they once get a scare, & only stop when they know pursuit is stopped. The boats have all gone on except the "Ruth" a new boat which carries the General, & two others. There are no defences in sight, & only a few old houses; on one of these the Stars & Stripes are floating in the Cold Breeze. The people here say they have had no such cold weather for many many years before. It is hard on their shoeless, ragged soldiers; but not uncomfortable to our well clad, & well fed. I do not know how far up we will go; possibly to Jacksonport, & above as far as they have gone with their boats if we can keep their track. It is unfortunate for us that on our Boat the "J B Ford" we have no Pilot, or Boat Officer who has ever been up this River so they know less about [it] than I do. Now I think of it they have a force at Cotton Plant, & possibly they may make a stand there. We can only guess. They might with masked batteries do us some damage anywhere along the river, but so far they only have a desire to get out of our way.

Saty Jany 17th—We are now above Duvalls Bluff where we found an encampment at a R R Station. We took here four hundred new English Enfield Rifles, two heavy Siege guns a sixty-four, & one hundred twenty pounder; the shot for these were long shot steel pointed, superb shot new, & of English make. The troops escaped by Rail toward Little Rock. We caught twentyfour of one hundred that were left; they threw away their guns, & took to the woods, where they are being hunted out by our cavalry. Our boat, with two others, is going down to a plantation for cord wood a few miles below. This morning is very cold; cold even for a northern climate. Water in a Pitcher in my state room froze solid. Snow is six inches deep. I told you, I believe, that my trunk, & blankets were left at Helena, but I borrowed a quilt, & a blanket, & with my heavy overcoat sleep tolerably well; before this cold spell one thin quilt was enough.

Now 11 AM—we learn a boat is going down so I will fill out & send this. Around the table on which I write four others are also writing to wife or sweetheart. So we get but small amount of elbow room.

Joseph, & Jas just recd letters from their wives, but poor me got none. I filled my pipe smoked; & thought that though they had women at home to write, they had no little baby boy to take their time, so I am best off yet though I would like very much to hear how the little fellow was getting along, & how its good Mother was doing, & the other children.

It is better consolation to think that the wife is attending to the welfare of the little ones, though she does not write often; than to think the children are neglected, & the time for them spent in idleness, or writing vain letters of self glorification.

I love my wife more truly as each day passes, & that love is fostered, & increased by her care over her children & increases in ration as the family circle enlarges; there is no doubt of this. Home has additional attractions according as children clean, tidy, & comfortable, & wife attentive, neat, pretty & loving as mine is there to welcome one when he comes. But good bye dearest & keep the last of this letter for yourself

Truly your affectionate husband, Chs Brackett

From the Journal:

Saty Jany 17ᵗʰ—Cold Clear. Snow six inches deep. very cold last night: Sent letter written yester, day before & today to wf. Letter goes by Hospital Boat *Emma* Dropped down two miles for forage & wood Got plenty; Beef, pork, chickens, & venison. Stopped at Duvalls Plantation, returned after dark.

Sund Jany 18ᵗʰ—Cold, clear: cold very severe for this climate Cannon heard in direction of Little Rock yesterday. No other direct news. Lost Port Monnaie with forty dollars, Recpt from Col Brackett for one hundred, & eighty. Clear cool pleasant Major Humphreys, Capt _____ Dr Jas & Jos W B play whist during evening forgetting it was the Sabbath! I have sick headache again. Bar Keeper has Haemoptosis severe. Genl G drove men at Helena at point of sword to load the "Evansville" acted very strangely for a General This was Sunday 11ᵗʰ inst. Our forces took prisoners & treasure, at Des Arc today. Rations getting low on our boat. Horses till today have been entirely without hay; & have no corn, or Oats. A miserably managed expedition from the start we were ordered from our camp at Helena with two hours notice, & to take in

Haversacks "two days cooked Rations" A week yesterday since getting such orders Our Hospital men have been obliged to board at boats table paying fifty Cts pr meal.

Monday Jany 19ᵗʰ—Cloudy warm. Start Down River at daylight At 10 AM strike shore tear off smoke stack, & part Pilot house. Boats too much crowded to appear safe. Severe headache again. Pass Clarendon forty-five miles from Duvalls Bluff at 11 ½ AM. Our stores are here but we pass on with out stopping for them. Stop at sundown at St Charles, one hundred & twenty-five miles from Duvalls. Wood with Fence Rails below Clarendon. Shoot, & get aboard five beeves, & some pork. Hear fleet unable to reach Little Rock, & returned to Mouth of White River. Commenced using Fowls A___ Solut for relief of disease of skin that appears Periodic.

Thursday Jany 22ⁿᵈ—Cloudy, cool Stopped ten miles from Helena at 1 AM, as pilot thinks. Geo Hall Co F drunk & tied to guard for disorderly conduct. Arrive at Helena 3 ½ PM safely. Absent eleven days from this post. Drunkenness the chief cause of discomfort among us. We stayed last night twentyfive miles from Helena; Pilot mistaken in distance. Due Marsh Clark for board sf & Mondzoleski on Steamer *J B Ford*. Captain of Boat J B Kaufman

Helena Saty Jany 22ⁿᵈ 1863

Dearest Margeret

We have just returned from our trip up White River having been absent eleven days. Our mail was sent after us by another boat, but we missed it. The last letter recd from you was of date I believe the 29ᵗʰ Decr. I am writing aboard the boat the "J B Ford". The mail is just in & I will wait till it is distributed before writing more . . .

We disembarked just at sundown, & then re-embarked as I did not feel able to risk another winter night of storm without shelter or bed. At best my bed aboard the boat is poor, but it is dry, though not warm.

I recd a letter from the Col who is yet at St Louis on Curtis Staff. He thinks the long looked [for] Paymaster will be down soon: how much I wish for it on your acct! I have now nearly eleven months pay due, & am wanting money now really for use here as well as to send home.

We met constantly transports laden with troops for Vicksburgh, & our great wonder is why were we sent up instead of down? But it is one of the mysteries of this mysteriously conducted war . . .

Unless I get heartier soon I shall leave this business for those better able to be at it. Had I control of affairs in my Dept wholly I could stand it better, but under the present management it is only an association with Drunkards, & worse, giving me increased physical labor, with almost constant mental disturbance (this is for you alone to read). I do not want to be named grumbler, & am about tired of acting as toady or catspaw for anyone. You would hardly credit what I might write, but miserable inefficiency pervades the whole "Corps & Armie" Best Officers are prevented acting by superiors in rank only- yet all is progressing as well as might be expected, & with perhaps some actual advantage on our side. We penetrate their country at all points but two & one of them will I hope soon be ours though it will be by great loss of life. The first attack was but a "reconnaissance in force" as they call it to feel their strength & position the next will be the storm that will carry all before it. At Arkansas Post where they felt themselves perfectly secure, at St Charles also, & Duvall's Bluff they had guns that they thought would sink the "Lincum Gun Boats" But england must send men as well as ordinance & ammunition, & then they wont succeed.

The Best heavy ordinance, & pointed steel balls carefully turned in the lathe & as finely finished as a knife or spear, yet we took all— I cant write more now will write when I feel better, & to the children good night Dearest & accept the best love of your affectionate husband

Chs

From the Journal:

Friday Jany 23ʳᵈ—cold Drizzling Landed part men last night, & part this morn All suffering throuqh dmnd neglect of superior? Officers. Recd letter from wf of 10ᵗʰ Col, & Geo Price

Saty Jany 24ᵗʰ—Cloudy cool. Sick every way our men suffering, running to me for help that I cant give them; Yesterdays work used me up. While others will lay quiet in quarters

Helena Sunday Jany 25th '63

Since I left the boat (day before yesterday) I have been staying with a Mr Roworth of this town. On Friday we disembarked in a cold rain, which continued all day, & has not yet stopped. I rode the whole day trying to get a place for our sick, & at last thoroughly drenched, & used up I pitched my horse came in here & have remained here since. The Dr is also here; & unwell. Our tents, baggage &c were shipped after us on Barges in tow, & we hear one is lost, with one of our hospital hands in charge. They were lost in White River. My trunk was with them though I hope not among the lost. I did not tell you about loosing my Porte Monnai on the boat, but now as it is found I will tell you. I had forty dollars in it belonging to soldiers, & lost it in the cabin. I missed it directly, but some one had taken it. I then after one day offered a reward of all the money for the return of the Pocket, Papers, &c. but all to no purpose, & my board bill on the boat went unpaid. On the evening after leaving the boat Dr Jas asked me if I did not want some money to get something to eat with; of course I answered yes, & he gave me my purse all right. He says that I asked him for the purse directly after loosing it, but he evaded a direct reply, & I had given it wholly up.

Our men have these three days bivouacked in open air without tents or other shelter, & the worst mud you ever saw. It must kill numbers of them. Two of them told me they had for three days past absolutely nothing to eat, & they were in the fever of the famine, in the midst of plenty. After, & only then, we are rid of imbecile, & treacherous Officers our armies will achieve the victories that will destroy the last hope of Rebels. Think of sober, good men starved by pampered scoundrels . . .

It is just reported that all the cavalry is ordered north of this point, probably to check the Rebel Cavalry who are dashing into unprotected places to destroy military stores, Bridges, &c. Probably if this is true our headquarters will be in Memphis. I am glad to go anywhere (almost) from here; we have been so long here wasting time, health, & life; ordered twice out of good winter barracks, & now in mid winter without tents even to shelter us.

Our Baggage, Frank tells me, is here or at least the remnants of it; my trunk is safe; my tent, & blankets gone; the Doctor also has lost his clothes.

I shall remain here till I am hearty again if possible. Mr Roworth has been in the secesh army - was at the battles of Iuka, & Corinth; has taken the oath & is a loyal citizen. Mrs Roworth is however an out, & out southern woman. Says the south never will submit never! never! They have the house filled with boarders. I sleep on borrowed blankets on the floor, have it as comfortable as possible under such circumstances. Had boiled milk for supper, & breakfast. This well peppered agrees well with me; indeed except for boils, I would feel pretty well.

Dr James throws himself on my pallet every time I leave it, when he knows I cant sit without suffering; he fills his hide with Brandy & sleeps like a log, yet grumbles if one looks at his bed; how easy it is to grumble when one feels like it; write often dearest to your affectionate husband

Chs.

From the Journal:

Tuesd Jany 27th—Clear cold Ordered to attend sick call for 10th Ill Cav, & 6th Missouri. Recd Letter from wf 25th Ansd. one from Mrs. Sarah B. 26th Jos W B, & Jas W B have been sick since we came from White River board with me at Mr. Roworths, west of Fort Curtis.

Wed Jany 28th—Clear, cold Mud frozen so as to bear up a horse. very cold for this region. make special requisit to Post Surgeon for Opii & Dover

February the 9/1863
Helena Ark

Dear Aunt

Margrett—I take this presant time in wrighting to you a few lines as I had promised I would and supposing that you are ancious to hear from the Doctor—Well I will try and tell you how he *is.* Captian Grover and my selfe wear up with him all day yesterday, and in the eavning we returnd to camp and partook of our suppers and then the Captian returnd back to stay with Uncle Charles for the Knight. But has not returnd yett—the Doctor is gaining but very slow he is perfectley helpless he has no use of his left arm and has gott to be very poor in person. and as soon as he is abele to be moved he will be sent home and I think that Captian Grover will accompany him for the Bracketts are trying to gett leafe of abesents for the Captian and I think that they weant faile to gett it—

but I doant think that Uncle Charles will be abble to be moved for some time yett

So no more at present Give my love to all of the folks. Excuse my short letter as I have nothing of interest to wright onley that it is very mudy hear and very disagrable to get a round wright soon

Yours with Respects Your Nephew

C Chamberlain
Sergant of Company K
46th Reg Ind. vol
Helena Ark

P.S. Since wrighting the above the Captian has returnd and reports the Doctor is gaining. Chester

Hospital Department, 9th Regt Illinois Cavalry.
Helena, February 10th 1863

To Brig Genl Willis A. Gorman,
Commanding Army East. Dist Ark.

In my opinion it is essential in order to save the life of Asst Surgeon Charles Brackett, 9th Regt Illinois Cavalry, who lately applied for a Sick Leave on a Surgeon's Certificate (which application has not yet been answered) and who now has resigned his commission for reasons stated in the Surgeon's Certificate hereto appended, that he soon be removed from this locality to a more healthy region, owing to his debilitated condition it is also necessary that he be accompanied by an intelligent person to care for him on his removal. Captain B. A. Grover of Co. K. 46th Regt Indiana Infantry, having expressed a willingness to take charge of him on such journey, and being a Physician by profession, and a fellow Townsman of said Asst Surgeon Charles Brackett, both residents of Rochester, Indiana, we therefore earnestly request, that Captain B. A. Grover be detailed to accompany said Asst Surgeon Charles Brackett from Helena, Ark. to Rochester, Indiana.

Most Respectfully Your Obt Servt

Jas W. Brackett
Surgeon 9th Ill Cavalry

Isaac Casselberry
Surgeon 1ˢᵗ Ind Cav
Med Director 3ʳᵈ Division

Assistant Surgeon, Charles Brackett, of the Ninth Regiment Illinois Cavalry, having applied for a certificate on which to ground his resignation: I do hereby certify, that I have carefully examined this officer, and find that on the 1ˢᵗ Day of February, 1863, he was attacked with Congestive fever, followed by paralisis of the left arm, and is now confined to his bed unable to help himself in the least: and that in consequence thereof, he is unfit for duty, in my opinion, and will not be able to resume duty for a long time if ever.

Dated at Helena, Arkansas February 10ᵗʰ 1863.

Jas W. Brackett
Surgeon 9ᵗʰ Ill Cavalry

Examined and the acceptance of his resignation respectfully recommended. In consequence of bad health this Officer has not been on duty more than two months since July last.

Isaac Casselberry
Med Director 3ʳᵈ Division A of E A
Approved

This officer has been absent sick more than two thirds of his time—his place in the regiment left vacant by him, has been filled from other regiments.

R. B. Jessup
Med Director army D. E. A

Camp of 9ᵗʰ Illinois Cavalry,
Helena, Arkansas, 13ᵗʰ Feb'y 1863

Dear Margaret,

Charley is quite sick, and has been so all of this month. We think him today somewhat easier, but he is very low with a congestive fever.

On the 29ᵗʰ January, myself, Doctors Charles and James were all sick at a boarding house here, by Mr. Rowarth.

On the 1ˢᵗ Feby Charles was prostrated with the fever which has since kept him to his bed. On the last day of January, Doctor

Castlebury [Casselberry], called on the Doctors James, & Charles. Castlebury, being Medical Director of this Division, & Surgeon of the 1st Indiana Regiment, asking one of them as a favor to go & prescribe for the sick of two other Regiments of this Division which had no Surgeon present. Charley said he would go—I told him not to go, saying, "You are too unwell to prescribe for your own Regiment." But Charley went & was gone about eight hours, in the cold damp tents. That night he was prostrated with the fever, as a consequence Doctor Castlebury calls to see him—Doctor Witherwax of Davenport, Iowa, Asst Surgeon in the 24th Iowa Regt Infantry—a former partner of Charles', & an old acquaintance, calls every day to see him. Doctor Grover, Capt in the 46th Indiana, stays with Charley most of the time: and Doctor James stays with him all of the time; having good nurses from the Hospital to wait on him. He has all the attention & care desirable. He has resigned, & asked leave to go home. As soon as he is able to be removed, I think he will start up the river. We are trying to get permission for Doc't Grover to accompany Charles, which Doctor Grover is anxious to do if we can get the orders of the Command'g Gen'l necessary. Also Doct Hampton, of Texas, formerly Asst in our Regt, now a citizen, has volunteered to accompany Charley.

If he should die going home, know that he died doing his duty—even too zealous to do it beyond his strength. He is dearly loved among the Regiments, officers & men.

We hope he may gather strength for the removal and get to you in improving health.

Most Sincerely Yours,

Joseph W. Brackett

Rochester Feby 19th/63

My Dear One

It is Sabbath evening and the Children all in bed. We have just taken our usual evening lunch of Cake, Cheese, boild ham, Bread & Butter, with cold milk. I wish Papa I could tell you how much we miss your dear face at such times and all other times. I often think that I shall be so happy when I can hear your welcome footsteps again on the stair.

What is the matter Charles—Why is it that I have heard nothing from you for two long weeks almost a month since your last letter was written. It seems as if I could not wait till Tuesday morning—is my dear one sick and I denied the privilege of seeing him and administer to his wants is he in the care of strangers—or what has happened. Oh this awful suspense. I have felt more than usually worried about you for a few days past. I dont know why it is unless it is on account of the reported sickness & mortality at Helena & Vicksburg, my bad dreams about you, your ill health at the time your last letter was written, &c.

I hope Charles that if you can when this reaches you, you will resign and come home. What do you say—will you come? You know Pa that I have never asked you to resign and would not now if I did not think it best considering the condition of things here and there. I attended today a Soldiers Funeral Mr Mackey's son. Mr Lakin preached the Sermon a very good one . . .

Margaret

Monday morning—I finished writting to you last night went to bed and had terrible dreams as Grandma says about you. Oh how I do hope there is nothing in dreams I dont believe there is

MB

Hospital 9th Ill Cavalry
Camp near Helena Ark
Feby 24th 1863

Dear Margaret,

You are aware, ere this reaches you of the passing away of your dear husband, and my good brother, to a better and happier land than this world can afford.

Charley was uncommonly well and in good spirits a few days before he was stricken down and attended to the sick of two adjoining Regiments, whose Surgeons had gone from them one by death, and the other on leave of absence I believe. On the night of the first of Feb 1863 he was attacked by a congestive or Typhoid Fever and in the morning of the 1st was insensible in a great measure with paralysis of the left arm and leg, although they were very sensitive to the least impressions. On the Second day in washing him I discovered a large black spot about the size of my hand on the left of the small of the back, that I knew would slough and form a large and dangerous bed sore. On the morning of the third day having regained his sensibilities he directed my attention to the big toe of left leg that was in a black and swollen state and soon formed an abcess that Capt Grover opened and considerable puss passed off. Charley said that was the old erysipalas coming out. The fever in the mean time high and tongue dry and red. He called for sour drinks, and we gave him current wine & water, current jelly and water, raspberries served for drink and cider & water _____ On the ninth or tenth day his fingers became swollen and abcesses formed on them and one on the inside of his right hand, the left being perfectly powerless. On the thirteenth day he could raise his feet in bed so as to bend his knees, never complained except his hand or foot was touched unguardedly, and then he would relapse in deep and natural sleep. I was with him almost constantly for twenty days until his spirit passed to heaven.

I asked him in one of his lucid spells if he wanted any one in particular to look after his business in the event of his death, and he observed that Margaret knew more about his business than any other person. He expressed a strong anxiety to see home. One day after I was satisfied he could not survive his wear and tear of constitution I observed to him that he was going to see his Father & Mother and no physician but the Saviour of the world could minister to his wants. He said I know you have done every thing for me that could be done, and said "Oh if I was at home." Sometimes he would say, "When will the boat start," "Is Capt Grover going home with me."

Joe and I used all our efforts to get a leave of absence for him immediately after he was taken sick, but could not succeed, and then advised a resignation with a view of expediting a leave of absence, but failing in this, until the day after his death.

Every thing that could be done for his comfort and happiness was generously and freely given.

His spirit passed from Earth to heaven like a gentle sleep without a contortion of body or a moan of agony.

Mr Stradly takes his effects. The case of Instruments he recepted to the U S Government for, and should they be charged to him you can have them sent whence ordered. He has not drawn any money from the Government for about a year, and this you will soon receive I trust . . .

Your affectionate brother

Jas W Brackett

OBITUARY.

DIED—At Helena, Ark., on the 20th day of February, 1863, Dr. CHARLES BRACKETT, of Fulton county, Indiana, and at the time of his decease, Surgeon in the 9th Illinois Volunteer Cavalry.

By this event we have lost one of our most estimable and useful citizens—one widely known, respected, and loved, and whose place in society must long remain unfilled. We may well mourn over the loss which we have sustained by his death. Scarcely another man could have been taken from among us, who would be so often and so sadly missed.

He possessed in a large measure the power of doing good, and enjoyed to an enviable degree, the esteem and confidence of all with whom he was acquainted.—Nevertheless, in the midst of his years and his usefulness, he has been removed from earth. He has passed on, and it is natural and fitting that those to whom he was dear while living, should dwell with feelings of melancholy satisfaction upon the events of his life, and the leading traits of his character.

Dr. Brackett was born at Cherry Valley, Otsego county, New York, June 18th, 1825; received a good academic education, studied medicine, and in 1845, at the age of 20 years, entered upon the duties of his profession, in Fulton county, which thenceforward continued to be his home.

In his new residence, his genial temper, unassuming manners, general intelligence, and successful treatment of the sick, soon secured for him an extensive practice, and gave him the reputation throughout the county, of a skillful and trustworthy physician. This reputation he steadily maintained till the end of his life.

But few events worthy of being written down and published, occur to any one in the discharge of professional duties, and the subject of this notice was no exception to this general rule. He quietly passed along, adding to his stores of knowledge, contributing his influence to promote the well being of society, ministering to the wants of the sick, and enjoying the sweets of domestic life, until the present unhappy civil war broke out.

His whole conduct as a citizen had been marked by a liberal public spirit. From

Smooth back the locks from his high, noble
brow,
Take the last look as he lieth there now!
Noble and god-like, true-hearted and brave
He died as a martyr his country to save.
Far from his home and his loved ones he fell
Doing his duty both bravely and well;
Kneeling at night by the sick soldier's bed,
Watching with him till the spirit had fled!
Staunching the life-tide that flowed from the
spot,
Mangled and torn by the death-dealing shot!
Lay his body to rest in its dark narrow bed
Number him too with our patriot dead;
For the hopes that we cherished "grown sud-
denly dim,
Let us weep in our sadness, but weep not
for him!"
Tho' bitter the tears that in anguish we shed,
Let us weep for the living and not for the dead!
For tho' clouded our skies, and our vision be
dim,
Yet bright were the angels that beckoned for
him;
And the spirits that dwell on the bright
"shining shore,"
Where earth's sorrows and sadness can troub-
le no more,
Have welcomed him home to that beautiful
land,
And found him a place in their radiant band
                                    C. E. F.

his first settlement in Rochester, he regarded himself as identified with the people.—He felt that he was one of the community, and that whatever might affect the happiness or interests of those by whom he was surrounded, was of consequence to him.—If any scheme was undertaken for promoting the public good, he was among the foremost to give it his aid and support.

In his mind the truth was well settled, that if any man would be really useful, he must work where his lot is cast, instead of sighing for more favorable circumstances, and more inviting fields of labor. He was interested in whatever affected the condition of his immediate friends and neighbors, but he felt still more deeply concerned in regard to the general prosperity of the country. He believed firmly in man's capacity for self-government, and regarded our attempt to demonstrate the efficiency and safety of republican institutions as of the highest importance, not only to us, but to the world at large. In his judgment, the preservation of the Federal Union, and the maintenance of the Constitution, were paramount duties incumbent upon every American citizen; in the performance of which he should not shrink from any necessary toil or sacrifice or suffering.

Deeply imbued with this feeling, very soon after the assault upon Fort Sumter, he tendered his services to Gov. Morton, offering to serve in the Union army, in whatsoever capacity he could be most useful, and in August, 1861, he was appointed Assistant Surgeon in the 1st Regiment of Indiana Cavalry.

He immediately joined the regiment, then stationed in Missouri, and continued faithfully to discharge his duties, till Oct. 4th, 1861, when he came home for a few weeks, and before returning, received Feb. 4th, 1862, the appointment of Surgeon in the 9th Regiment of Illinois Volunteer Cavalry. Attached to this new command, he continued in the service until the time of his death, Feb. 20th, 1863, having been absent from his post, only a short time in the fall of 1862, when ill health compelled him to seek repose at home.

During his connection with the army, his duties were always responsible, and sometimes severe; but the unanimous testimony of those associated with him, is that they were at all times faithfully, humanely and nobly discharged. He sacrificed his own ease that he might promote the soldier's comfort, and cheerfully overtasked himself for their good. He relieved their sufferings, cheered their drooping spirits, and inspired their patriotism, by his words and his acts. He thus continued till attacked by disease, and fell in the midst of his labors, and at his post of duty.

He is dead! but his example—the good of his life—shall not die! His character was distinguished by many noble traits, which will be held in grateful remembrance by all who were acquainted with him.—Those who knew him in childhood, can bear ample testimony to his upright deportment, his amiable, generous disposition, his frank, manly independence, his love of knowledge, and his inflexible attachment to truth. These qualities only became more fully developed as he advanced in life.

One of his more prominent traits was a noble simplicity and directness of character. He was a severe disciple of Truth, and worshiped reverently at her altar.—Strong in the consciousness of his own integrity, he had no occasion to disguise his motives or conceal his designs. He loved truth for its own sake, and received it with a hearty welcome, even when presented in the least attractive form.

To him the artificial manners and usages of society were of no value, except as they might tend to elevate and purify human character, and augment the sum of human happiness. He regarded all mankind as members of one great family—children of the same Common Parent—and recognized the existence of common obligations by which the whole brotherhood are bound together. In his view, n were everything; the *trappings* with ich they might be invested, nothing. mingled freely with all classes, earnestly king for truth, and regarded the gem of ual value, whether dropping from the hand of the peasant or the prince.

In his pursuit of knowledge, whether pertaining to his profession, or upon other subjects, he was remarkable for readily grasping principles, and obtaining a clear comprehension of the matter before him, rather than for following the rigid rules of any author, or the precise arrangement of any text-book. Hence his knowledge was eminently practical and accurate; it was wrought into the very texture of his mind and could be called into exercise whenever needed. He was, moreover, independent in pursuing his investigations and forming his opinions. He called no man master, but claimed the right of thinking and judging for himself, and fearlessly announced the conclusions to which his reasonings led him, however they might differ from the opinions of those with whom he was associated. Yet, with all this independence of thought, he was singularly moderate and charitable towards those whom he deemed in error. He could stand firmly upon his own position, without seeking to annoy or wound his opponents, treating their arguments, and prejudices even, with respect and tenderness.

Though not a member of any church, Dr. Brackett ever cherished a profound sentiment of reverence towards God, and the Christian Religion, and heartily received the Scriptures as an authentic declaration of the Divine will. No one ever heard him treat sacred things with disrespect or levity, and few men can be found in any community whose dealings with others are more uniformly regulated by the Golden Rule of our Savior, than were his. He was scrupulously honest and honorable in his business transactions, kind and liberal to the poor, tolerant and charitable in judging the acts and opinions of others; mild and forgiving towards those who had injured him.

Such was our lamented fellow-citizen as he appeared in society; but in the "charm-ed circle" of domestic life, his virtues were known and appreciated as they were nowhere else. Like every true man, he strove to make his home the choicest place of earth. He was an attentive, affectionate husband, a faithful and kind parent. In the hearts of his family, his image will be enshrined forever, and when from the mind of the bereaved widow and orphan children, the poignancy of present grief shall have passed away, instances of his care and kindness, treasured like jewels, in the casket of Memory, will furnish to them an unfailing source of gratitude and consolation.   K.

Decease of Surgeon Charles Brackett, of the 9th Illinois Cavalry.

HEADQUARTERS 9TH ILL. CAVALRY,
CAMP AT HELENA, ARK.,
Feb. 22d, 1863.

At a meeting of the Commissioned officers of the 9th Reg. Il. Cavalry, held at the headquarters of the regiment Feb. 22d 1863, the following preamble and resolutions were adopted, expressive of their sorrow at the loss of their late brother officer, Surgeon CHARLES BRACKETT; who died at this place, Feb. 20th, 1863.

WHEREAS, It has pleased an all wise Providence to take from our midst and from the scene of his usefulness and labor, our beloved friend and Surgeon, Dr. CHARLES BRACKETT, of the 9th Regiment Illinois Volunteer Cavalry.

THEREFORE, Be it resolved, That we tender to the family of the deceased our sincere and heartfelt sympathy in their bereavement.

Resolved, That in his death, we have lost not only an accomplished and scientific Surgeon, who labored among us with the most self-sacrificing zeal, but a friend endeared to us all by his pure and blameless life, and that we will cherish the memory of his good deeds, his great heart and his earnest truthfulness.

Resolved, That in his dying words, *I am glad that I always tried to do right,"* a rich legacy to his children, we recognize the true character of the man, who, from the most exalted patriotism, risked his feeble remnant of life in the service of his country, and died a martyr to his profession and his country's cause.

Resolved, That we will wear the usual badge of mourning for thirty days.

Be it further Resolved, That a copy of the above resolutions be forwarded to the bereaved family of the deceased, and, also, to the Chicago *Tribune,* Logansport and Rochester, Indiana, papers for publication.

HENRY B BURGE,
    Major 9th Illinois Cavalry.
IRA R. GIFFORD,
    Major 9th Illinois Cavalry.
MARLAND L. PERKINS,
    Major 9th Illinois Cavalry.
L. COWEN,
    Captain 9th Ill. Cavalry.
A. CLARK,
    Lieut. 9th. Illinois Cavalry.

Resolutions of Respect.

Hall of Rochester Lodge, No. 47,
I. O. O. F., March 7th, 1863.

Your committee appointed to prepare suitable action to be had in the Lodge, on the occasion of the death of Brother Brackett, which occurred at Helena, Ark., Feb. 20th, 1863, would submit the following:

WHEREAS, it has pleased Almighty God to call from our midst our well beloved brother, Dr. Charles Brackett, a worthy member of this Lodge, to the Grand Lodge above, therefore,

Resolved, 1. That by the death of Bro. Brackett this Lodge has sustained an uncommon bereavement—the loss of an old and valued member, and his family a kind husband and parent, stricken down while in the line of his duty, and in the midst of a life of usefulness to his fellow men.

Resolved, 2. That with hearts chastened with sorrow at the loss we have sustained, we would meekly bow to the will of our Heavenly Master, blessed with the assurance that from the cloud that now encircles us may break forth with a radiance whose heavenly light shall more indelibly fasten in our hearts those cherished principles of our Order, so dear to him who has been thus called from among us—FRIENDSHIP, LOVE, and TRUTH.

Resolved, 3. That the family of our deceased brother have our warmest sympathy in this their great bereavement, and that they will find much to console them in the fact that he fell at his post, doing his duty with a firm trust in the mercy of God, through Jesus Christ, and a heart full of devotion to the interests of his fellow men. Also, in the testimonials of affliction and respect which his death has called forth, and to which his valued services through life have so richly entitled him.

Resolved, 4. That as a mark of our respect, this Lodge will wear the usual badge of mourning, and that a copy of these resolutions be forwarded to the family of our deceased brother, with the seal of the Lodge, and that they be recorded on the journals of our proceedings.

J. B. DE MOTTE,
VERNON GOULD, Com.
ISAAC TRUE,

EPILOGUE
1864 and After

★ ★ ★

Rochester, Mon 18th [January 18, 1864]

Dear Jennie

I have just got my Baby to sleep & have concluded to answer your letter which I was very glad to receive not long since

I dont know the date of it as your aunt Anna has it over at her house. I expect your Aunt Anna & Uncle Francis here tonight to eat Oysters—but here they are come & I will finish after a while

Thursday Morning

Oysters eaten & a hope that you could have been here with us expressed. Children gone to school. Louise is teaching her little brothers & sisters & cousins at home this winter as the road is so bad between here and town.

I believe I have not written to you since my Mother's death I do indeed feel very lonely without her but God's will is always right and we must submit. I feel that she was prepared to go and that she is happy now

It dont seem like home here now since my dear Charles left me but I am compelled to remain here for the present but dont think I shall spend the rest of my life here. I expect to buy some property at South Bend about 50 miles north of this place next fall, where I can put my Children in a good school There is an Academy there where I can educate them from a Primary to a Graduating class I expect to put their money where it can not be stolen from them— in their brains.

You ask me "if I am as I was when you heard from me last" I hardly know what you mean but guess that you thought I might be married again, if you did I will simply say I am and always expect to remain so. I think there can be but one true marriage and that is recorded in Heaven & all others are mere bargains for convenience sake or for company. I dont know which & dont like men well enough to inquire if I ever marry again I shall have to change my mind wonderfully I have never said I would not change my name for I have heard that too often from persons who was only wanting for an offer—but enough of this I dont think it is a very interesting subject.

Louise is almost as tall as I am Lyman is a good, fat, large boy. Rosa and Minie are growing nicely Rosa has worn the applation of "the little mathamitition" at school for her readiness with numbers

Little Charley is the pet of the house he has just got his first pair of boots & says he is a "Union boy". I would like to send you some pichirs but they cost money & that is not very plenty here as I have not received my pension yet or the Dr's back pay. I will send some one of these days dont fail to send me some of yours Louise sends you some scraps of her dresses & aprons & wants to see something that you wear. I have some of your Grandma's shrouding & hair if you would like some of it I will send next time. Tell your aunt Catherine when you write to her that you want one of Willies pictures he is the prettiest Soldiers cousin you have got at least one of the best.

Write to your aunt Anna soon but dont fail to write to me and send those pichers

yours
Maggie

Remember me to all your family

THE FOURTH AND LAST of Dr. Charles's pocket diaries is very short, only six small pages written on each side in pencil. The last dated entry, at the bottom of the next-to-last page, is from January 28, 1863, just before he entered upon his fatal illness. On the back page, undated, is a phrase written very faintly in pencil: "oh! what's the use of living when you've nothing to live for" followed by scribbles.

This was certainly written, not by Charles in his fever, but by Margaret after his death.

Dr. Vernon Gould, an old friend of the Bracketts from early days in Rochester, wrote to Margaret on August 24, 1863:

> " . . . I was glad to hear from you but sorry that you feel still so de-
> pressed in spirits as to think you have little to live for . . . you should
> not suffer the remembrance of the past to destroy the pleasures
> which are left you in the performance of those duties which your
> little family claim at your hands. Those little buds of humanity are
> just putting forth under your guidance petals the separate beauties
> of which shall govern the character of the full bloom—the unfold-
> ing of these in their greatest perfection is sufficient to fully occupy
> your time and cannot but afford you the greatest degree of pleasure.
>
> "We cannot say we are prepared to die while these duties are yet
> in our charge. No parent can say this. Past sorrows cannot, however
> great, destroy the parents' hope in the welfare of their children. To
> such objects must our sorrows finally yield . . ."

Although Margaret protested in her subsequent letter to her niece Jennie Burris that she had no intention of marrying again, she did so on November 26, 1869, to Edwin E. Cowgill of Rochester. They had two children, Harry (died aged four) and Edith, who married Frank E. Bryant. Mr. Cowgill, a kind benefactor to the widow and her five children, died on August 1, 1882.

She turned then to her faithful friend, Vernon Gould, and they were married in 1885. When Dr. Gould died in 1908, she followed him about two months afterwards, on June 14, 1908, at the age of seventy-four. She was known to her grandchildren as "GrandMa Gould."

From her obituary notice:

> *Mrs. Gould was one of Rochester's best known citizens, a lady whose*
> *kindness was made manifest to numerous persons who cannot repay their*
> *obligations to her, only as they may be privileged to reflect charity to the*
> *needy they may find along the pathway of life . . .*

Even in her later years, the loveliness of Margaret Wilson Brackett Cowgill Gould was not diminished.

(*below*) The Cowgill home, at the corner of High and Main streets in Rochester, Indiana.

Cherry Valley, New York

James Brackett
  b. 1782 d. 1852
  m. Eliza Maria Bennett Ely
    b. 1791 d. 1853

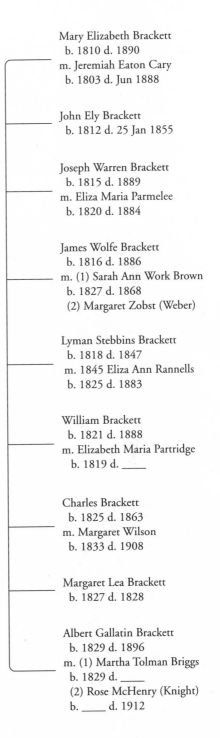

Mary Elizabeth Brackett
  b. 1810 d. 1890
  m. Jeremiah Eaton Cary
    b. 1803 d. Jun 1888

John Ely Brackett
  b. 1812 d. 25 Jan 1855

Joseph Warren Brackett
  b. 1815 d. 1889
  m. Eliza Maria Parmelee
    b. 1820 d. 1884

James Wolfe Brackett
  b. 1816 d. 1886
  m. (1) Sarah Ann Work Brown
    b. 1827 d. 1868
    (2) Margaret Zobst (Weber)

Lyman Stebbins Brackett
  b. 1818 d. 1847
  m. 1845 Eliza Ann Rannells
    b. 1825 d. 1883

William Brackett
  b. 1821 d. 1888
  m. Elizabeth Maria Partridge
    b. 1819 d. _____

Charles Brackett
  b. 1825 d. 1863
  m. Margaret Wilson
    b. 1833 d. 1908

Margaret Lea Brackett
  b. 1827 d. 1828

Albert Gallatin Brackett
  b. 1829 d. 1896
  m. (1) Martha Tolman Briggs
    b. 1829 d. _____
    (2) Rose McHenry (Knight)
    b. _____ d. 1912

Rochester, Indiana

Charles Brackett
  b. 1825 d. 1863
m. Margaret Wilson
  b. 1833 d. 1908

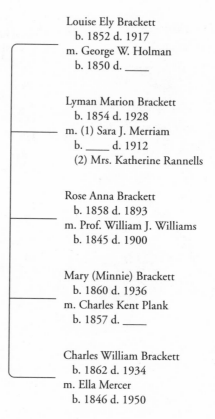

Louise Ely Brackett
  b. 1852 d. 1917
m. George W. Holman
  b. 1850 d. ____

Lyman Marion Brackett
  b. 1854 d. 1928
m. (1) Sara J. Merriam
    b. ____ d. 1912
  (2) Mrs. Katherine Rannells

Rose Anna Brackett
  b. 1858 d. 1893
m. Prof. William J. Williams
  b. 1845 d. 1900

Mary (Minnie) Brackett
  b. 1860 d. 1936
m. Charles Kent Plank
  b. 1857 d. ____

Charles William Brackett
  b. 1862 d. 1934
m. Ella Mercer
  b. 1846 d. 1950

Three of Charles and Margaret's "babies" (*from left*)—Lyman, Rose Anna, and Louise.

Margaret sat for this photo with her children and their spouses around 1892. From left, back row: Lyman Brackett, Charles K. Plank (Mary's husband), George W. Holman, Louise Brackett Holman, and Charles W. Brackett. Second row: Mary "Minnie" Brackett Plank, and Sarah Merriam (Mrs. Lyman) Brackett. Front row: Rose Anna Brackett Williams, Margaret, Edith Cowgill, William J. Williams (Rose's husband), and Ella Mercer (Mrs. Charles) Brackett.

INDEX

NOTE: An asterisk (*) beside a page number indicates a photograph on that page.